D1799880

Civil Liberties in Northern Ireland:

The C.A.J. Handbook

2nd Edition

edited by **Brice Dickson**

Civil Liberties in Northern Ireland

This edition is dedicated to the memory of Madge Davison, who did so much for civil liberties in Northern Ireland before her untimely death in 1991.

Published by the Committee on the Administration of Justice
    45-47 Donegall Street
    Belfast BT1 2FG
    tel: (0232) 232394
    fax: (0232) 333522

British Library Cataloguing in Publication Data
    A catalogue record for this book is available from the British Library

ISBN 1-873285-04-3

    Printed and bound in Belfast
    by Shanway Distributors
    461 Antrim Road
    Belfast BT15 3BJ
    tel: (0232) 777979

Cover designed by Paul Kernan, C.T.R.S. (Community Training and
Research Services)

Contents

The Committee on the Administration of Justice

The Committee on the Administration of Justice (CAJ) is an independent civil liberties organisation formed in 1981 to work for the highest standards in the administration of justice in Northern Ireland. CAJ is affiliated to the Federation Internationale des Droits de l'Homme, an international human rights organisation which has consultative status at the United Nations.

CAJ's membership is drawn from all sections of the community and includes lawyers, students, community workers, trade unionists, unemployed people and academics. The CAJ is opposed to the use of violence to achieve political goals in Northern Ireland.

By carrying out research, holding conferences, lobbying politicians, issuing press statements, publishing pamphlets, circulating a monthly bulletin and alerting the international human rights community, the CAJ hopes to stimulate awareness of justice issues in Northern Ireland and encourage the adoption of safeguards. In the Committee's view, not only are abuses of civil liberties wrong in themselves but, in the Northern Ireland context, they hinder the peaceful resolution of the conflict.

Open meetings for CAJ members and the public are held every two months to discuss a variety of civil liberties issues. Sub-groups work on areas such as policing, a Bill of Rights, emergency laws, international standards, use of lethal force by the security forces, juvenile justice, prisons and racism.

Membership of the Committee

Membership entitles you to receive the CAJ's monthly civil liberties bulletin "Just News", to take part in the work of the sub-groups and to use the CAJ documentation library and clippings service.

If you would like to join CAJ or find out more about its activities, please contact:

CAJ
45/47 Donegall Street
Belfast BT1 2FG
Tel: (0232) 232394
Fax: (0232) 333522

Notes on Contributors

David Bonner is a senior lecturer in law at the University of Leicester.

John Coyle is a barrister in Northern Ireland and a former solicitor employed by the Belfast Law Centre.

Madge Davison was a barrister in Northern Ireland and a former lecturer in law at the Queen's University of Belfast.

Brice Dickson is a professor of law at the University of Ulster at Jordanstown.

Eileen Evason is a senior lecturer in social policy at the University of Ulster at Coleraine.

Ray Geary is a lecturer in law at the Queen's University of Belfast.

Steven Greer is a lecturer in law at the University of Bristol.

Anne Grimes is a solicitor employed by the Belfast Law Centre.

Brigid Hadfield is a reader in law at the Queen's University of Belfast.

Angela Hegarty is a lecturer in law at the University of Ulster at Magee.

John Jackson is a reader in law at the University of Sheffield.

Beverley Jones is a solicitor in Belfast and a former Chief Legal Officer at the Equal Opportunities Commission for Northern Ireland.

Stephen Livingstone is a lecturer in law at the Queen's University of Belfast.

Laura Lundy is a lecturer in law at the Queen's University of Belfast.

Austin Magill is a legal officer with the United Nations' High Commission for Refugees in Vienna.

Steve McBride is a barrister in Northern Ireland and a member of Belfast City Council.

Gerry McCormack is a senior lecturer in law at the University of Essex.

Robert Millar is a barrister in Northern Ireland and a former lecturer in law at the University of Warwick.

Chris Moffat is a researcher and free-lance editor.

Richard Steele is a senior lecturer in law at the Queen's University of Belfast.

Acknowledgements

The contributors to the second edition of this book have once again provided their services free of charge and are to be sincerely thanked for their hard work. Besides the writers, however, many other people assisted in the book's production. Some helped with typing or proof-reading, others with correspondence or liaison; many proffered ideas and lent support in intangible ways. To all of them many thanks. In particular we are especially grateful to Liz Martin, who did virtually all the word-processing, and to Deborah Campbell, Kate Campbell, Patricia Mallon, Martin O'Brien, Mary O'Rawe and Michael Ritchie.

The CAJ must also express its appreciation to the organisations which have helped to fund this book, thereby keeping down the cover price to what we feel is a reasonable sum. Those organisations are the Joseph Rowntree Charitable Trust, the Northern Ireland Voluntary Trust and the Cultural Traditions Group of the Community Relations Council which aims to encourage acceptance and understanding of cultural diversity in Northern Ireland. We are conscious of the confidence which these funders have once more placed in the CAJ and we hope that, in producing a book which should be of interest and value to everyone living in Northern Ireland, we have fulfilled our promises. We are grateful as well to the Rt. Hon. Lord Scarman for contributing a foreword. He had wanted to update his words written for the first edition but unfortunately was not well enough to do so.

We have taken as much care as we could to ensure that the book is accurate as of 1st June 1993. If there are mistakes, please let us know.

FOREWORD

I welcome the publication of this work and congratulate the Committee on its initiative and the authors on their care and restraint. The temptation to produce a campaign document in favour of a Bill of Rights and a more generous statutory provision in the field of social security must have been difficult to resist. But the authors have stuck to their task of setting down in plain English what is the scale of the law in Northern Ireland governing civil rights and liberties and the provision of the essential social services. If they have also let the reader see the gaps and weaknesses in the law's protection of the citizen's rights, so much the better: but they have not allowed campaigning fervour to obscure clear exposition. The law is clearly stated in language which should earn this book a place on every family bookshelf in Northern Ireland.

The non-legal reader may well be surprised at the numerous sources of the modern law. In the old days the laws of Ireland, England, Wales and Scotland were to be found as "common law" in the reported judgments of the judges and as "statute law" in Acts of Parliament. This is still theoretically correct, but the reality is vastly different. The European Convention on Human Rights, which the United Kingdom has ratified and which the European Court of Human Rights interprets, and European Community law, which is to be found in the Treaty of Rome and in the regulations of the European Commission and is interpreted by the European Community's Court of Justice, are important sources of British and Northern Irish law, as the reader of this book will quickly appreciate. And not far below the horizon you will find the United Nations Organisation making its contribution in great instruments such as the Universal Declaration of Human Rights of 1948 and subsequent international covenants. As Lord Denning has said, this incoming tide of law is making its way into our law, even if it has to rely on Parliament allowing it in by passing legislation to open the gates to the flood.

The shape and substance of our law are in a state of transition - Northern Ireland's law, as this book shows, reflects the complexities that face us as we make the necessary adjustments. But the movement is healthy. Let us welcome it. This excellent book will help you to understand what is happening, and to appreciate the value of the developing law to the ordinary man, woman and child.

Lord Scarman

Chapter 1

Introduction

Brice Dickson

In all democracies the law is part and parcel of a wider notion called "the rule of law". By this is meant that no-one, whether an individual or an organ of the government, can be above the law: the law must apply to everyone equally, without any discrimination. Hand in hand with this principle runs the understanding that all individuals have certain basic rights - or fundamental civil liberties - which the state must not take away. It is those rights and liberties which form the subject-matter of this book.

The development of human rights law

After the end of the Second World War, which brought to light horrific violations of human rights in Germany and elsewhere, nations around the world were determined to take steps to guarantee protection to human rights in international and national law. The first concrete manifestation of this was the American Declaration of the Rights and Duties of Man, drawn up by the Organisation of American States in 1948. This was followed just a few months later by the Universal Declaration of Human Rights, produced under the auspices of the newly-created United Nations. In 1950 the member states of the Council of Europe adopted the European Convention for the Protection of Human Rights and Fundamental Freedoms.

Each of these documents concentrated on protecting civil and political rights, such as freedom of expression, freedom of religion and freedom of association. But the American Declaration and the Universal Declaration also embraced social, economic and cultural rights, such as the right to the preservation of health, the right to education and the right to work. The gap in the European framework was filled by the adoption of the European Social Charter in 1961, another document prepared by the Council of Europe. In 1966, in order to supplement the general provisions of the Universal Declaration, the United Nations adopted two further International Covenants, one on civil and political rights, the other on economic, social and cultural rights. The member states of the European Community (the 12 Common Market countries) are in the process of agreeing their own Social Charter, as part of the Maastricht Treaty, notwithstanding some opposition from the current British government.

In national legal systems there has been a comparable growth in human rights law. More than 100 countries now have a written constitution with a Bill of Rights contained in it. The best known system is probably that of the United States of America, where the influence of the first 10 amendments to the Constitution - which are collectively known as the Bill of Rights - has been profound. In more recent years many other former colonies of the British Empire have marked their independence by adopting a constitution which includes guarantees for human rights.

The 1937 Constitution of the Irish Free State (now the Republic of Ireland) places Articles 40-44 under the general title of "Fundamental Rights" and includes such matters as the right to be held equal before the law, the right to one's life, person, good name and property, the right to liberty, freedom of expression, freedom of assembly and association, the right to education for children and the right to freedom from religious discrimination. The 1950 Constitution of India lays down similar legally enforceable fundamental rights. In Canada, a Bill of Rights was enacted in 1960 and was supplemented in 1982 by a more far-reaching Charter of Rights and Freedoms. In Australia - a federal state with a written constitution - and in New Zealand - a unitary state with no written constitution - there are also Bills of Rights. In Hong Kong, which Britain will hand back to China in 1997, there is a Bill of Rights based on the United Nations' Covenants.

Nor is the tendency towards protection of human rights apparent only in countries which have an historical connection with English law. In France, the famous Declaration of the Rights of Man and of the Citizen

(1789) was specifically incorporated into current law by the preamble to the 1958 Constitution of the Fifth French Republic. In Germany, the 1949 Basic Law devotes the first 19 of its 146 Articles to basic rights. Moreover in both these countries the constitutional courts have gone to considerable lengths to develop the substance of these rights.

Enforcement of human rights

It is all very well to have laws on human rights, but if those laws are imperfectly enforced they may as well not exist. International agreements on human rights are especially difficult to enforce because there is, of course, no supreme body to which governments of states can be made answerable; nor, usually, are there any sanctions which can be effectively imposed. The United Nations has tried to get round this problem by asking states to accede to what is called the Optional Protocol to the 1966 International Covenant on Civil and Political Rights. This allows citizens, in effect, to sue their own governments before the United Nations' Human Rights Committee. Likewise, the European Convention can (if a state agrees) be enforced by individuals in the European Commission of Human Rights and then, if the Commission holds in favour of the individual, in the European Court of Human Rights. However, none of these international judgments is backed by a system of penalties if the state concerned chooses not to comply. Enforcement ultimately depends on political pressure, which can often take years to exert.

At the national level, countries differ greatly in the ways in which they permit citizens to claim their rights and liberties. In the USA, any person can challenge the constitutionality of any law in any court. If the Supreme Court confirms that a law made by Congress (the US Parliament) is invalid, then that law can be ignored by everyone in the land. In France, MPs can challenge the constitutionality of a Parliamentary statute before it is officially published but no challenge can be mounted after publication.

In the United Kingdom, Parliament's Acts can be challenged in court only if they run counter to a clear principle of EC law. There can be "judicial review" of lesser forms of legislation, and of administrative and court decisions, but even then the only fundamental rights which can be relied upon by the applicant are the so-called "principles of natural justice" ("no-one should be a judge in his or her own cause" and "everyone has the right to a fair hearing"). There are no written constitutional guarantees in the United Kingdom, no Bill of Rights, no effective way of enforcing the government's obligations under international law in national courts. In Northern Ireland this lack of protection for human rights is particularly noticeable.

The role of non-governmental organisations

In practice, the educational and campaigning activities of non-governmental organisations may be more effective in improving the law on human rights than court actions. A large number of non-governmental organisations now exist, the best known probably being Amnesty International, which has its headquarters in London and national sections throughout the world. Within the United Kingdom the two most prominent organisations are Justice (which is the British branch of the International Commission of Jurists) and Liberty (formerly known as the National Council for Civil Liberties).

In Northern Ireland much valuable work in this area was carried out in the 1960's and early 1970's by the Northern Ireland Civil Rights Association. In subsequent years a number of other organisations have been formed to work on a range of specific civil liberties issues. In 1973 the government itself set up the Standing Advisory Commission on Human Rights to advise it on whether the law in Northern Ireland operates in a discriminatory fashion. In 1976 the Equal Opportunities Commission and the Fair Employment Agency were created by the government to assist alleged victims of discrimination based on sex, marriage, religion or political belief. All of these bodies (including the Fair Employment Commission, which replaced the Agency in 1989) have performed valuable work in their own fields.

In 1981 the Committee on the Administration of Justice (CAJ) was formed as an independent voluntary organisation to carry out more general monitoring of the legal system in Northern Ireland. It has acquired a reputation for accuracy and thoroughness. In publishing the present book, the CAJ is seeking to make its work better known to as wide an audience as possible. It sees its role as being both to provide information and to campaign for change. In the near future the organisation hopes to be in a position to undertake casework on behalf of individual complainants; at the moment it carries out some work on "test" cases and refers complainants to other sources of help.

A Bill of Rights for Northern Ireland?

The CAJ has long been convinced that a Bill of Rights could play an important part in the prevention of injustice in Northern Ireland. The group believes that, unless the rights of all individuals in Northern Ireland are guaranteed equal protection, there is little prospect of a lasting solution being found to the area's problems. A Bill of Rights, in short, is a prerequisite to permanent peace and justice.

One simple method of satisfying the widespread demand for a Bill of Rights would be to incorporate the European Convention on Human Rights into domestic law, as is the situation in many countries on the Continent. But although that Convention is the most successful of all the international human rights documents, it is still far from perfect. It proved of no avail, for instance, to the mother of a boy who, while not himself directly involved in rioting, was killed by a plastic bullet in Belfast in 1976; nor did it assist the workers at Government Communications Headquarters in Cheltenham after the government banned certain trade unions there in 1984. Perhaps most importantly, the European Convention does not grant adequate protection as regards physical or mental disability, education, employment, housing or social security.

The CAJ therefore believes that a more comprehensive Bill of Rights is required for Northern Ireland, one that readily meets the expectations of ordinary citizens. As each of the chapters in this book will show, the law in Northern Ireland rarely confers rights on people but instead controls people's behaviour by placing all sorts of constraints on them: whatever is not affected by these constraints is deemed to be a liberty. The constraints which at present exist are so far-reaching, and the discretion conferred on administrative bodies so all-embracing, that the resulting liberty is at times very narrow in scope. A Bill of Rights could not only increase people's confidence in the administration of justice but also improve the content of the law and make people more physically secure. In May 1993 the CAJ published a draft Bill of Rights which it hopes will be a useful model for further debate.

The content of this book

The chapters in this book are ascribed to particular authors but have been edited so as to make the book more than a disparate collection of essays. The book offers advice and information on a wide variety of common legal problems encountered by people living in Northern Ireland. Needless to say, several of the chapters have had to take account of the "emergency" laws, but much is also said about the "ordinary" laws. We have tried to be comprehensive in our coverage but inevitably there are some omissions. The second edition differs from the first in having chapters on legal remedies and on the rights of the disabled. We have also taken the opportunity to insert a longer section on the position of immigrants. All of the original chapters have been carefully revised and updated. But still we have not been able to say as much as we would have liked about particular topics and we have not included specific information on the rights of consumers, hospital patients or children.

The book begins with a description of court and tribunal structures in Northern Ireland and with an explanation of the European dimension, public law remedies and legal aid. It then moves on to describe police and army powers, where the distinction between emergency and ordinary laws is most apparent. Those powers are very extensive, especially in view of the Emergency Provisions Act 1991, so if they are abused the consequences for individuals can be dire. The next two chapters look more closely at the police's power to question suspects and at the system for handling complaints against the police: the law on the former was significantly altered by the Police and Criminal Evidence (NI) Order 1989, the law on police complaints was radically changed by the Police (NI) Order 1987.

In chapter 7 the position of prisoners is examined, an area which is giving rise to an increasing amount of litigation in Northern Ireland. The impact of the European Convention has often been felt in prisons, but not always to the advantage of prisoners. What amounts to a further variety of imprisonment is described in the chapter on immigration and freedom of movement, where the law relating to exclusion orders issued under the Prevention of Terrorism Act is fully explained. This leads in the next three chapters to an exposition of people's rights to expression and information, whether through demonstrations, meetings, organisations or direct speech.

The two chapters on discrimination, one on religion and the other on gender, illustrate the degree of sophistication which the law must attain if it is to begin to rectify human rights abuses. Northern Ireland is the only part of the United Kingdom or Ireland where discrimination based on religious or political belief is unlawful and the Fair Employment (NI) Act 1989 has considerably bolstered the original 1976 Act. On the other hand there is still no law in Northern Ireland which prohibits discrimination based on race, though the government has declared its intention to rectify this anomaly. The gap is an obvious contravention of international law and certainly works to the disadvantage of the already sizeable Indian, Chinese, Malaysian and Vietnamese communities in Northern Ireland.

Chapter 14 describes the (not so extensive) rights of disabled persons in Northern Ireland, while chapter 15 outlines the law affecting family and sexual life, with particular emphasis on the rights of women. Again, it should be noted that there is not yet any law which prohibits discrimination based on a person's sexual orientation, although the government did change the criminal law on male homosexuality following a decision of the European Court of Human Rights in 1981. The final chapters are devoted entirely to the category known as social and economic rights, which many would argue are even more significant than civil and political rights. The law relating to education has been fundamentally altered by the Education Reform (NI) Order 1989, while the rights of employees have been seriously affected by the Industrial Relations (NI) Order 1992 and the Trade Union Reform and Employment Rights Act 1993. The rights to proper housing and to a decent level of social security are not yet fully recognised in our law, despite the terrible conditions in which thousands of people live.

Each chapter aims primarily to explain the current law and is restrained in offering a critique. But contributors have inevitably found it difficult to conceal their objections to some of the relevant legal provisions and the CAJ would endorse the points they make.

Chapter 2

Remedies

Brigid Hadfield

An important aspect of the law concerns its procedures and remedies. Access to the courts is a central element of justice. A right conferred by law is an empty one without the means of enforcing it. Furthermore, the law should provide procedures which are appropriate for remedying the different types of grievance which may arise. As far as the criminal law is concerned, the law should both ensure a procedure suitable for the gravity of the offence and also avoid undue or oppressive punishment for those who break the law.

This chapter, therefore, sets out the court structure in Northern Ireland, including not only the criminal and civil courts but also tribunals and inquests. The European dimension, as provided by European Community law and the European Convention on Human Rights, is also explained. Particular attention is paid to the remedying of grievances against public bodies, both through judicial review and through a complaint to the Ombudsman. Finally, reference is made to the schemes of legal aid, advice and assistance which provide those in need with financial assistance when dealing with legal problems.

The criminal courts

Criminal offences in Northern Ireland divide into four broad categories: offences which must be tried summarily, those which must be tried on indictment, those which are triable either way - these are called "hybrid" offences - and scheduled offences under the emergency laws.

Summary offences

Offences which must be tried summarily are the least serious offences and are tried in a magistrates' court by a resident magistrate sitting without a jury. Illustrations of summary offences are to be found in the Public Order (NI) Order 1987 (see chapter 9). These include organising or taking part in a public procession in respect of which the required notice has not been given, taking part in a public procession as a member of an un-registered band, trying to break up a lawful public procession or public meeting, riotous or disorderly behaviour in a public place and obstructive sitting in a public place. A person found guilty of such an offence is liable to a sentence of imprisonment (of variable duration but usually not exceeding six months) or to a fine or to both.

Offences triable on indictment

These are serious offences which have to be tried in the Crown Court by a judge and jury. They include murder, manslaughter, rape and robbery. The committal stage for these offences - *i.e.* the preliminary hearing into whether or not the accused person should be "committed" for trial - is heard in a magistrates' court.

Hybrid offences

An offence may be triable either summarily or on indictment in one of three situations. First, the legislation creating the offence may state that it can be tried either way. In this situation, the prosecution will decide how to proceed according to the seriousness of the offence. So, for example, under the Public Order (NI) Order 1987 a person who takes part in a prohibited procession may be tried either way depending on how grave his or her alleged misconduct was. Secondly, some offences normally triable on indictment, for example, theft and indecent assault, may be tried summarily if the resident magistrate who hears the case at the committal stage considers that it is not a serious case and if both prosecution and defence have no objections. Thirdly, a small number of statutory offences normally tried summarily may be tried on indictment if the offence carries a potential sentence of more than six months and if the defendant asks to be tried on indictment.

Scheduled offences

The scheduled offences are those listed in the first schedule at the end of the Northern Ireland (Emergency Provisions) Act 1991 and are those most commonly committed by persons engaged in political violence. The category of scheduled offences cuts across the distinction between summary and indictable offences. Most of the scheduled offences are indictable, in which case they are tried before a "Diplock court", that is, a single judge of the Crown Court, sitting without a jury. Some of the offences are stated by the Act to be a hybrid offence, for example, membership of a proscribed organisation; in this case, it is triable either way. Where it is tried summarily, the Director of Public Prosecutions must consent to the prosecution; the case is heard by a resident magistrate who must, on conviction, give a reasoned judgment for his or her decision.

Some of the scheduled offences may be "descheduled" by the Attorney-General if there is no element of "terrorism" involved in a particular case, but if he or she refuses to do this there is no appeal against the decision.

Inquests

The main legislation on inquests in Northern Ireland is the Coroners Act (NI) 1959 and the statutory rules made under it. There are currently seven coroners and eight deputy coroners in Northern Ireland, all of whom must be solicitors or barristers of at least five years' standing.

The function of a coroner is to investigate unexpected or unexplained deaths, deaths in suspicious circumstances or deaths occurring as a result of violence, misadventure or unfair means. The coroner has a discretion whether or not to order a post mortem; in practice a post mortem will be held in any case where the explanation of a death fails to satisfy the coroner. If the investigation indicates that death was due to unnatural causes then an inquest is likely to be held; this happens in approximately one in five investigations.

The inquest is held in public and is usually held without a jury, but a jury must be summoned where the death occurred in prison, where it was caused by an accident, poison or a notifiable disease, or where it occurred in circumstances which, if they were to continue or recur, would be prejudicial to the health or safety of the public. Unlike England, there is no requirement to summon a jury where a death has occurred in police custody or by the action of the police in pursuance of their duty. A jury has between seven and eleven members, chosen at random from the electoral register.

The purpose of an inquest is to ascertain who the deceased was and how, when and where the deceased came by his or her death. An inquest in Northern Ireland now returns no verdicts as such. Prior to 1981 a coroner or a jury could return a verdict of death by "natural causes", "accident", "misadventure", "his (or her) own act", "execution of sentence of death" or an "open" verdict. Since 1981, however, a verdict must now take the form of "factual findings" only. Neither the coroner nor the jury is permitted to express "any opinion on questions of criminal or civil liability" (rule 16). In practice an inquest is not opened until the coroner has been informed that no criminal proceedings will be brought. Where a person is charged with a criminal offence, the coroner must adjourn the inquest, "in the absence of reason to the contrary", until after the completion of the criminal proceedings, including an appeal. This can lead to delays in the holding of an inquest.

The procedure for the conduct of an inquest is regulated by both statutory rules and the coroner's own discretion, which may be subject to judicial review (see page 14).

The calling of witnesses at an inquest is a matter for the discretion of the coroner, although he or she is prohibited from compelling any person to give evidence "who is suspected of causing the death or has been charged or is likely to be charged with an offence relating to the death" (rule 9(2)). This rule has been upheld as lawful by the House of Lords (*McKerr v Armagh Coroner,* 1990). If such a person volunteers to offer information, it in practice tends to be done in the person's absence by way of the submission of a written statement to the inquest. It is effectively not possible to test or challenge the contents of such a statement other than by direct testimony from other witnesses at the inquest. This practice has been upheld as lawful by the House of Lords (*Devine v Attorney-General for Northern Ireland,* 1992).

Witnesses who do give evidence may be questioned (but not cross-examined) by both the coroner and by other "properly" interested parties to the proceedings, either directly or through a barrister or solicitor. Evidence is given on oath. The questions must be confined to the narrow remit of an inquest. Hearsay evidence is admissible. The relatives of the deceased are not entitled to call witnesses, although they may suggest the names of potential witnesses to the coroner.

Documentary evidence is also placed before the inquest. Relatives of the deceased may be given a copy of the post mortem report before the inquest begins. There is no requirement , however, for other documentary evidence, such as forensic reports, photographs or witness statements, to be given to them before then. They may make a final statement to the jury before the inquest concludes. If the Secretary of State for Northern Ireland believes that a part of the evidence puts national security at risk, he or she can issue a Public Interest Immunity Certificate which may bar the disclosure of all such evidence to the inquest.

At the conclusion of the inquest, the coroner or the jury delivers their findings, which are confined to "a statement of who the deceased was, and how, when and where" he or she died (rule 2(1)). No qualifications or additions are permitted. There is no appeal against the decision of a coroner's inquest, although the proceedings may be subject to judicial review.

Although legal aid for inquests is contemplated by the Legal Aid, Advice and Assistance (NI) Order 1981 for those entitled to be represented at inquests, the relevant provision has never been implemented and legal aid is, therefore, not available for the inquest itself. "Green form" legal aid (see page 21) is available for those who meet the financial eligibility criteria and who want legal advice before the inquest or assistance in preparing for it.

The civil courts

In general terms, the criminal law is primarily concerned with the punishment of those who have broken the law. The civil courts, however, are concerned with compensation and redress, with property matters and with questions of status, such as divorce and adoption. There are three types of court for civil proceedings: they are the magistrates' courts, the county courts and the High Court. Which court a civil matter comes before depends largely on the seriousness of the issue, including the amount of money or the value of the property involved. Civil proceedings are often settled between the parties before the matter reaches the court.

Magistrates' courts

The powers of magistrates in civil matters are less important than their criminal law powers on which they spend the greater amount of time. In civil matters, the procedure used is simple and speedy, and litigants are often represented by a solicitor rather than a barrister. The main civil powers of a magistrates' court relate to some domestic matters, such as financial provision orders, personal protection orders and exclusion orders (see chapter 15 on Family and Sexual Matters). They also deal with small debts, including rent arrears (although there is some overlap with the small claims court), some proceedings brought by landlords (including the Housing Executive and the housing associations) to evict tenants, and licence renewal applications.

County courts

From September 1993 the financial upper limit for most cases coming before the county courts is £15,000 (until then it is £10,000). The county courts can hear claims in tort (for example negligence and personal injury matters), or for breach of contract, some undefended divorce petitions, equality of opportunity and sex discrimination cases, other than in the field of employment (see chapters 12 and 13 on Religious Discrimination and Sex Discrimination) and applications to determine the proper rent for a protected tenancy under the Rent (NI) Order 1978 (see chapter 18 on Housing Rights). The county courts have a special procedure for many claims not exceeding £1,000. This procedure is commonly employed by business and commercial organisations for non-payment of hire-purchase instalments or for money owed for goods which have been delivered or for services rendered, but consumers can also use it when claiming against shops or suppliers. It cannot be used for road accident claims.

The county courts also hear appeals against decisions of the Secretary of State for Northern Ireland on applications for compensation for criminal injuries and criminal damage or for compensation under the emergency powers legislation (see chapter 3 and 4). These are applications by people who have suffered loss because of criminal or terrorist activities.

The High Court

The jurisdiction of the High Court is not limited by the value of the claim. There are three Divisions of the High Court: the Queen's Bench Division, which deals with claims in tort and for breach of contract; the Chancery Division, which deals mainly with property matters; and the Family Division, which deals with petitions for divorce or nullity and matters affecting mental patients. The Queen's Bench Division (Crown Side) deals with applications for judicial review.

Judicial review

Judicial review is the procedure which should be used to challenge the validity of the public decisions of public bodies. Where a contractual or other private relationship exists between the individual and the body, judicial review is not appropriate and other remedies must be sought. Similarly, where an alternative remedy such as an appeal to a tribunal is both available and adequate, that procedure should be followed in preference to judicial review. Public bodies subject to judicial review include the Northern Ireland government departments, government ministers, district councils, the education and library boards, the health and social services boards, the Housing Executive, the lower courts and tribunals, including coroners, and certain decisions of the Royal Ulster Constabulary. Judicial review, therefore, is available against administrative, executive and judicial decision-making. Subordinate legislation, for example, statutory rules and statutory instruments, can also be judicially reviewed. Acts of the Westminster Parliament are subject to judicial review only where it can be argued that there is a conflict with European Community law.

Judicial review is concerned with the procedures employed by a public body in reaching its decision and not with the decision itself, unless the decision is particularly outrageous or absurd. That is, judicial review is not a way of challenging an unwelcome decision, unless it can be argued that an unfair or unlawful procedure has been employed in reaching it. The grounds on which a challenge may be made include these: the body has wrongly interpreted the relevant law, taken into account irrelevant or ignored relevant factors, failed to pursue the policy and objectives of the legislation, unduly restricted its discretionary powers or followed an unfair or biased procedure.

A judicial review may be sought by a person or body with a sufficient interest in the matter, who seeks the leave of the court promptly and in any event within three months of the challenged decision being made. The remedies which the court may grant to a successful applicant for judicial review include *certiorari* (which quashes the public body's decision), *mandamus* (which compels a person or body under a duty to act to do so), *declaration* (which declares what the law is or the rights of the parties are) and *prohibition* (which prevents the public body from proceeding to an unlawful decision).

These remedies lie in the court's discretion and the court may refuse a remedy if it believes that the applicant's conduct merits this or if it is in the public interest to do so.

Appeals

In both criminal and civil matters, an appeal will lie against the decision of the original court. Although some other courts do have an appellate jurisdiction, the main appeal court is the Court of Appeal in Belfast. In criminal matters, an accused person may appeal to the Court of Appeal on a point of law, on a question of fact or against sentence. In some situations the accused person will need the "leave" or permission of the court before he or she can appeal. The prosecution cannot appeal against the acquittal of an accused person, although the Attorney-General may refer a point of law to the Court of Appeal for its opinion. This does not affect the acquittal at all, but the opinion of the Court will guide the prosecution in future trials. The Attorney-General also has the power to refer a case to the Court of Appeal where he or she believes that the sentence imposed by the Crown Court was too lenient. The Secretary of State also has the power to refer a conviction to the Court of Appeal either as an appeal against conviction or for the opinion of the Court on a point of law. This is what occurred in the case of the Armagh Four in 1992.

The Court of Appeal also has jurisdiction in civil matters, particularly on points of law. In both criminal and civil matters an appeal may lie, with leave, to the House of Lords in London. Only a few appeals are taken to the House of Lords each year, and these are cases of major legal importance.

The enforcement of civil judgments

A person who has lost litigation may be ordered by a court to pay money to the winner of the litigation. These people are known respectively as the judgment debtor and the judgment creditor. The judgment debtor is required to pay within a reasonable time. If he or she does not do so, then the judgment creditor may ask the Enforcement of Judgments Office to send the debtor a document called a notice of intent to enforce. This orders the debtor to pay within ten days. If the debtor still does not pay, the creditor may apply to the Office for actual enforcement of the judgment. As this can be an expensive procedure, it should be followed only if the creditor is sure that the debtor has assets with which to pay. If the debtor does not have the means with which to satisfy the order, the creditor must accept that the original judgment in his or her favour may be worth nothing.

The Enforcement of Judgments Office is at:

- Bedford House,
  Bedford Street,
  Belfast BT2 7NR,
  tel: (0232) 245081.

Tribunals

Tribunals are now very much a part of the legal system, dealing with tens of thousands of cases every year. A tribunal is established (by legislation) where the intention is to provide a system of dispute resolution which is both specialised and also speedy, cheap, informal and accessible. A tribunal is often composed of three people, of whom only one, the chairperson, is legally qualified. The best known tribunals are industrial tribunals (which deal with employment rights, including those relating to equality of opportunity), social security appeal tribunals and the Mental Health Review Tribunal.

An appeal often lies on a point of law from a tribunal decision to the Court of Appeal, although there may also be an intermediate appeal before this stage is reached. Where the legislation provides an individual with recourse to a tribunal, he or she should, as a general rule, follow that procedure rather than judicial review. Tribunal decisions are themselves also subject to judicial review, but an applicant will be successful only if one or more of the factors mentioned above is present.

European Community law

The law of the European Community is part of the domestic law of the United Kingdom. Community law covers many areas of economic and social activity, most notably the free movement of goods, the free movement of workers and the common agricultural policy. It also deals with matters designed to protect the enjoyment of these freedoms, for example, the freedom to provide and to receive services, freedom of establishment, social security and sex discrimination (see chapter 13). EC law is to be found in the Treaties of the European Community, including the Treaty of Rome and the Single European Act, in the Community's Regulations and Directives and in the decisions of the European Court of Justice (the ECJ). The ECJ is the Community's main court and sits at Luxembourg.

If a matter comes before a Northern Ireland court or tribunal involving Community law, one of two procedures may be followed. If the Community law is clear, the domestic court must follow and apply it (and if necessary not apply any conflicting domestic laws). If the meaning of the Community law is not clear, the domestic court may make a reference under Article 177 of the Treaty of Rome to the ECJ. While the reference is pending, the domestic proceedings are suspended. The ECJ gives its ruling on the meaning of Community law only (not on the domestic law), leaving the domestic court to apply the ruling on Community law to the facts before it. Lower courts and tribunals have a discretion whether or not to make an Article 177 reference; domestic courts and tribunals against whose decisions there is no judicial remedy under domestic law *must* make a reference on questions concerning the interpretation or application of Community law. The Article 177 procedure cannot be invoked in those areas of domestic law not actually or potentially affected by European Community law.

The European Convention on Human Rights

The European Convention on Human Rights (the ECHR) is an international treaty which has been ratified by the United Kingdom government and which is, therefore, binding upon it in international law. It is not a part of domestic law, which means that its provisions cannot, unlike European Community law, be directly invoked by an individual before the domestic courts. It may, however, be used by the courts to resolve any ambiguities which may exist in domestic law.

The ECHR deals with the protection of rights, for example the right to life, to liberty, to a fair trial and to respect for one's private and family life. It also seeks to protect fundamental freedoms, including freedom from torture or inhuman or degrading treatment or punishment, freedom of thought, conscience and religion, freedom of expression and freedom of peaceful assembly.

Those states which have ratified the ECHR are required to secure to "everyone within their jurisdiction" the rights and freedoms set forth in the Convention (Article 1). These states - known as High Contracting Parties - may be proceeded against for an alleged breach of the Convention either by another High Contracting Party or by an aggrieved individual. This latter right exists only if the state has accepted the right of individual petition, which the United Kingdom government has done since 1966.

The individual lodges his or her complaint with the European Commission of Human Rights at Strasbourg, and the Commission must first decide whether the petition is admissible. It will be inadmissible if all domestic remedies have not been exhausted or if it is out of time, anonymous, substantially the same as a matter already examined by the Commission, manifestly ill-founded or an abuse of the right of petition. The petition must also relate to a matter covered by the Convention, in terms of substance, location and time of the alleged violation. Usually it needs to be lodged within six months of the final decision on the matter in the national courts.

If the petition or complaint is admissible, the Commission will undertake an inquiry and try to secure a friendly settlement, which must be compatible with the terms of the Convention. If it is not possible to secure a friendly settlement, the Commission will draw up a report indicating whether or not there has been a breach of the Convention. The matter may, within three months, be referred to the Court of Human Rights, which also sits at Strasbourg. A case can only be referred to the Court by one of the High Contracting Parties involved (including the state whose national is alleged to be a victim) or by the Commission. The individual complainant does not have the power to refer the matter to the

Court. If the matter is not referred to the Court, it is resolved by the Committee of Ministers of the Council of Europe.

The Court's decision is binding on all the states involved in the case, although in practice most states delay before changing their law or administrative practice to bring it into line with the requirements of the Convention. The Court may also order the High Contracting Party to pay compensation to the successful petitioner.

The Ombudsman

The term "Ombudsman" in Northern Ireland covers two distinct offices, although they are in practice held by the same person. There is first the office of Parliamentary Commissioner for Administration and second that of the Commissioner for Complaints.

The function of the Parliamentary Commissioner is to investigate complaints of maladministration made against the Northern Ireland government departments. The complaint must be made by a person who feels that he or she has suffered injustice as a result of the maladministration and the complaint should be made within 12 months of the action or inaction complained of. "Maladministration" is not defined in the relevant legislation but covers, for example, neglect, inattention, delay, incompetence, unfair discrimination, ineptitude, perversity and arbitrariness.

The complaint should be made to the Ombudsman via a Westminster Member of Parliament, who has a discretion whether or not to refer the complaint to the Ombudsman. He or she may decide to deal with the matter instead. If a person writes directly to the Ombudsman, he or she will, where the complaint merits further investigation, ask the complainant to refer the matter back through an MP.

The Ombudsman is completely independent of the government departments and the service provided is free of charge. He or she has full access to all files and records. The purpose of an investigation is to ascertain whether or not there has been maladministration; the Ombudsman has no jurisdiction to investigate the merits of decisions reached without maladministration. The Ombudsman does not usually investigate complaints where there is an alternative remedy, particularly an appeal to a tribunal or judicial review.

Once an investigation has been completed, the Ombudsman sends a report of the investigation to the complainant, the referring MP and to the relevant government department. If the Ombudsman upholds the complaint, he or she will try to secure appropriate redress for the complainant, such as an apology or the payment of compensation. In some cases, as a result of an Ombudsman investigation the department concerned will change its procedures. The Ombudsman (whose reports are considered by Westminster's Select Committee on the Parliamentary Commissioner) cannot, however, compel the government department to provide any redress to a complainant.

The Ombudsman can also investigate complaints about personnel matters in the Northern Ireland Civil Service. Complaints against Westminster government departments are within the jurisdiction of the United Kingdom Parliamentary Commissioner, whose jurisdiction therefore includes the Northern Ireland Office, the Northern Ireland Court Service, the Inland Revenue and the Ministry of Defence.

The second office held by the Northern Ireland Ombudsman is that of Commissioner for Complaints. In that capacity he or she investigates complaints of maladministration made by an aggrieved individual against local and public bodies in Northern Ireland; these bodies include the district councils, the education and library boards, the health and social services boards, the Housing Executive (although its own internal complaints procedure should be resorted to first), the Labour Relations Agency and the Local Enterprise Development Unit.

There is direct access to the Commissioner for Complaints, whose services are both free and independent, but the complaint usually needs to be made, at the latest, within six months. The Commissioner cannot question the merits of a decision taken without maladministration, nor will he or she usually investigate a complaint which could be the subject of legal proceedings or an alternative investigatory procedure. Certain matters also fall outside his or her jurisdiction, including the commencement or conduct of civil or criminal proceedings and actions taken by doctors or dentists.

If the Commissioner's investigations disclose that there has been maladministration, he or she will try to secure a settlement, for example an apology or the payment of compensation. If this is unsuccessful, the complainant may apply to a county court for compensation. The Attorney-General may also, at the request of the Commissioner, seek an injunction or a declaration from the High Court to restrain a public body from persistent maladministration.

The Northern Ireland Ombudsman is:

- Mrs Jill McIvor
  Progressive House
  33 Wellington Place
  Belfast BT1 6HN
  tel: (0232) 233821

The UK Parliamentary Commissioner is:

- Mr William Kennedy Reid
  Office of the PCA
  Church House
  Great Smith Street
  London SW1P 3BW
  tel: (071) 276 3000

Legal aid, advice and assistance

There are various types of legal aid schemes designed to provide financial assistance in legal matters. The controlling legislation is the Legal Aid, Advice and Assistance (NI) Order 1981 and the regulations made under it. The schemes are strictly "means tested" in terms of both disposable income and disposable capital and from April 1993 the financial limits were altered so as to make help available primarily to people who are on income support.

- The "Green Form" scheme (its popular name) allows a solicitor to offer advice on any area of the law of Northern Ireland. The advice may be written or oral; it includes preparation for but does not extend to representation itself. The assisted person may be required to make a financial contribution which in any event cannot exceed £86.00 in value.

- "ABWOR" - assistance by way of representation - is based on the green form scheme and is available for the Mental Health Review Tribunal and disciplinary hearings before Boards of Visitors in prisons (see chapter 7).

- Civil legal aid covers most civil proceedings in the higher courts (excluding libel actions) but it is not available for either inquests or tribunals. The Department of Health and Social Services assesses financial eligibility for civil legal aid. The Law Society's Legal Aid Department also applies a "merits" test to determine whether or not it is reasonable for the party concerned to take or defend the proceedings in question. An assisted person may be required to make some financial contribution.

- Criminal legal aid relates to the defence of criminal proceedings by a solicitor or barrister. If granted by the court concerned it is entirely free.

Chapter 3

The Powers of the Police

Brice Dickson

This chapter sets out the powers of the Royal Ulster Constabulary which people in Northern Ireland are most likely to encounter in everyday life. Much of the law was altered by the Police and Criminal Evidence (NI) Order 1989 - the PACE Order - which came into force on 1st January 1990. This Order is similar in many respects to the Police and Criminal Evidence Act 1984, which governs the position in England and Wales. Books on that Act are therefore relevant to the law in Northern Ireland as well. The position regarding police powers in relation to "terrorist" offences is governed by the Prevention of Terrorism (Temporary Provisions) Act 1989 (the PTA) and the Northern Ireland (Emergency Provisions) Act 1991 (the EPA).

The power to stop and question

Contrary to popular belief, the police do not have a general power to stop and question people. This is true not only of pedestrians but also of people in cars or any other form of transport. The police can, of course, *attempt* to stop and question people, and many of us may well comply with the police's request and will readily answer questions. But there is no legal obligation to stop when asked to do so or to answer questions put by a police officer. The PACE Order confers powers on the police to stop people for the purpose of searching them, but it does not take away a person's right not to be stopped for questioning.

To stop a person lawfully the police have to carry out an arrest. During the period of detention after an arrest the police can ask questions but the person arrested is still under no legal duty to reply. In fact, when questioned at any time it is very often sensible to remain silent until a solicitor is present. As England's Lord Chief Justice Parker put it in *Rice v Connolly* (1966): "the whole basis of the common law is the right of the individual to refuse to answer questions put to him (*sic*) by a person in authority". However, as explained more fully in chapter 5, one of the consequences of the Criminal Evidence (NI) Order 1988 is that the silence of a detained person may later constitute corroborative evidence of guilt. At present this is not the position in England and Wales, though the Royal Commission on Criminal Justice, due to report in June 1993, may possibly recommend a change in the law.

After the police have collected information from persons whom they have stopped and questioned, they can immediately destroy it or store it, indefinitely if they wish and on computer if necessary. The United Kingdom's Data Protection Act 1984 prevents citizens from gaining access to data which is "required for the purpose of safeguarding national security" or "held for the prevention or detection of crime". The latter phrase would cover most of the information held by the police. The 1984 Act also does not apply to non-computerised records: a card-index system, for instance, is immune from the access provisions (see also chapter 11).

Exceptions to the general rule

There are a number of important exceptions to the general rule that the police cannot arbitrarily stop and question people. These mainly concern road traffic and terrorist incidents. The law on the former is virtually identical to that in England and Wales and will not be examined here. The chief exception in the realm of terrorist incidents is section 23 of the Northern Ireland (Emergency Provisions) Act 1991. According to this, any constable may stop and question any person for as long as is necessary in order to put questions about:

- his or her identity and movements, and
- what he or she knows concerning any recent explosion or any other recent incident endangering life or concerning any person killed or injured in any such explosion or incident.

If a person fails to stop when required to do so under section 23, or fails to answer to the best of his or her ability any question addressed under this section, he or she is liable to be fined up to £2,000.

There is some doubt over the exact scope of section 23. No-one knows for sure, for example, whether in law the identity of a person includes his or her date of birth and address; the answer may depend on whether or not the person has a common name. The section also gives no indication as to how much detail must be provided about your movements, although the duty to answer to the best of your ability probably means that you must be as detailed as the police wish. The locality a person is coming from and going to must be disclosed, but it would be unreasonable to have to give the names of the people just visited or about to be visited. Nor is the meaning of "recent" in section 23 clear. But the questions asked do not have to be related to acts of terrorism, so "any other incident endangering life" might refer to a fire or a car accident. There is no obligation to answer questions relating to one's occupation, family or friends.

The power in section 23 can be used to stop pedestrians but is most frequently used at vehicle check points (VCPs). There is no legal obligation to show a driving licence at a VCP, but it is an easy way of proving your identity. As yet there has been no authoritative ruling as to what exactly constitutes "stopping" within section 23. Knocking on a person's door and putting questions to the person who opens it may not qualify, but temporarily preventing someone from moving from his or her position in a queue or at a counter would probably be enough. Being approached while standing at a street corner would certainly constitute being "stopped" in this context.

The power to arrest

Arrests under the "ordinary" law

The Police and Criminal Evidence (NI) Order 1989 contains provisions governing "arrestable" offences, a category which includes offences carrying a sentence of five years or more as well as some less serious offences for which an Act of Parliament has already provided some kind of arrest power. The full list is in article 26 and Schedule 2 of the Order. It includes the following:

• smuggling offences under the Customs and Excise Acts;

- offences under the Official Secrets Act;
- indecent assault upon a female;
- taking away a motor vehicle;
- "going equipped for stealing";
- loitering and importuning by a prostitute;
- impersonating a voter at a polling station;
- failing to provide a breath test, or being in charge of a motor vehicle while under the influence of drink or drugs;
- public order offences under the Public Order (NI) Order 1987; and
- all other offences for which a person who is 21 or over may be sent to prison for five years.

The Order also provides that the police can arrest without a warrant any person who is reasonably suspected of attempting or conspiring to commit any of the listed offences, or of inciting, aiding, abetting, coun-selling or procuring their commission. Article 27, moreover, makes it clear that the police may arrest someone for a non-arrestable offence if the service of a summons (requiring later attendance at court) is not prac-ticable or appropriate. Service will not be practicable or appropriate if a person's name or address cannot be readily ascertained or is doubtful, if a child or other vulnerable person needs to be protected, or if the person to be arrested would otherwise suffer or cause injury or damage to property, commit an offence against public decency or cause an unlawful obstruction on a road.

There also exists a judge-made power to arrest someone for commit-ting or threatening to commit a breach of the peace and the 1989 Order maintains the rule that the police may arrest any person so long as a warrant for that purpose has been issued to the police by a Justice of the Peace. The JP must be satisfied that the police reasonably suspect the person of a crime and that his or her voluntary co-operation is unlikely. Once a person has been dealt with by a court for the offence alleged in a warrant the warrant ceases to be valid and cannot be used to justify a later arrest (*Toye v Chief Constable of the RUC*, 1991).

In all situations a police officer is entitled to use reasonable force when carrying out an arrest. The 1989 Order says that in exercising any power under the Order, the police "may use reasonable force, if necessary" (article 88). However, the use of unreasonable force, or of reasonable force in circumstances where it is not necessary, will not make the arrest unlawful. It will only make possible a civil claim for assault. Using force to effect what is in any event an unlawful arrest may lead to the police having to pay so-called exemplary damages to the victim, as in *Carroll v Chief Constable of the RUC* (1988).

An arresting officer must also indicate that the arrest is taking place and give a reason for it (unless the reason is very obvious). This was made clear in *Christie v Leachinsky* (1947) and confirmed by article 30 of the PACE Order. If it later turns out that the reason for the arrest was not a good one the person arrested can claim compensation for so-called false imprisonment and malicious prosecution. But if the police show that they had "reasonable and probable cause" for acting as they did, perhaps because the person arrested had confessed to the alleged crime, no compensation will be awarded (*Cooke v Chief Constable of the RUC*, 1989).

It remains the case that an ordinary citizen has the power to make what is popularly known as "a citizen's arrest", though the extent of this power is not as great as in the case of the police. It does not permit a citizen to arrest someone who is about to commit an arrestable offence, and it does not allow an arrest for an arrestable offence which the citizen reasonably believes has been committed but which in fact has not been (*R. v Self*, 1992). Given the difficulty of knowing which offences are arrestable and which are not, it is unwise for ordinary people to try to take the law into their own hands in this way.

In 1990 there were 22,848 arrests under the PACE (NI) Order; in 1991 the figure went up to 25,012.

Arrests under the "emergency" laws

Ever since the creation of Northern Ireland in 1921 there have been special powers conferred on the police. After the Northern Ireland Parliament was abolished in 1972 the Northern Ireland (Emergency Provisions) Act 1973 was passed. In 1974 this Act was supplemented by the Prevention of Terrorism (Temporary Provisions) Act (the PTA), which was enacted for the whole of the United Kingdom but designed to deal only with violence connected with the political affairs of Northern Ireland. The EPA in force today is that enacted in 1991; the current PTA was enacted in 1989 and it applies to "international" terrorism as well.

The main arrest powers conferred on the police are in section 17 of the EPA 1991 and section 14 of the PTA 1989. Section 17 permits a police officer to "arrest without warrant any person who he or she has reasonable grounds to suspect is committing, has committed or is about to commit a scheduled offence or an offence under this Act which is not a scheduled offence". When the list of scheduled offences and other offences created by the EPA is compared with the list of offences for which a person can be arrested without warrant under the PACE (NI) Order 1989, there is almost a complete overlap. There is therefore a good case for allowing section 17 to lapse. It has been used only about 20 times since 1977 because other emergency arrest powers are much more wide-ranging.

The arrest power in section 14 (1) of the PTA 1989 is so important that the exact wording deserves to be set out in full:

> *"Subject to subsection (2) below, a constable may arrest without warrant a person whom he has reasonable grounds for suspecting to be*
> *(a) a person guilty of an offence under section 2, 8, 9, 10 or 11 above;*
> *(b) a person who is or has been concerned in the commission, preparation or instigation of acts of terrorism to which this section applies; or*
> *(c) a person subject to an exclusion order."*

The section applies to all acts of terrorism except those connected solely with a part of the United Kingdom other than Northern Ireland. This means that animal rights protestors in England, or arsonists in Wales, cannot qualify as terrorists whatever their behaviour. The offences referred to in section 14 (1) (a) are membership of or support for a banned organisation, failing to comply with an exclusion order (see chapter 8), contributing to acts of terrorism or to the resources of banned organisations, and assisting in the control of terrorist funds. But it is section 14 (1)(b) which is by far the most all-embracing provision, for it allows arrests for unspecified crimes provided only that the police reasonably suspect involvement in acts of terrorism. "Terrorism" itself is not an offence, but suspected terrorists can be arrested. The government claims that this power is necessary because it helps to prevent terrorism; the arrest powers in the PACE Order, including the one which authorises arrest of any person reasonably suspected of being about to commit an arrestable offence, are deemed inadequate. It is clear, moreover, that, just as in the case of the PACE Order's powers, "reasonable suspicion" for the purposes of section 14 can be constituted by acting on the instructions of a superior police officer (see *Moore v Chief Constable of the RUC*, 1989, and *Brady v Chief Constable of the RUC*, 1991).

If the police arrest a person under the emergency laws, they still have to indicate why the arrest is occurring and under what power. If subsequent questioning - or the lack of it - shows that there were no real grounds for reasonably suspecting a connection with terrorism, an action in the civil courts for false imprisonment may succeed. It is a fact that, during the last five years, three-quarters of the persons arrested in Northern Ireland under section 14 of the PTA have later been released without being charged. This might suggest that the arrest powers are being used not just for the legitimate purpose of rounding up genuine suspects but for the illegitimate purpose of harassing people or fishing for snippets of incriminating evidence about other people. Alternatively, it might mean that people who are arrested supply no evidence which the police can rely upon to found a charge.

The use of arrest powers just for information-gathering is possibly a contravention of Article 5(1)(c) of the European Convention on Human Rights, which says that arrest or detention must be for the purpose of bringing the person "before the competent legal authority on reasonable suspicion of having committed an offence or when it is reasonably considered necessary to prevent his (*sic*) committing an offence". In *Brogan v UK* (1988), however, the European Court of Human Rights held that the PTA's definition of "terrorism" ("The use of violence for political ends, including any use of violence for the purpose of putting the public or any section of the public in fear") was well in keeping with the Convention's notion of an "offence".

What is clear is that, if the police arrest someone under paragraphs (a) or (c) of section 14(1), the precise grounds for the arrest must be notified at the time. This is a rule made by the judges which has not been expressly abolished by the PTA. Unfortunately, there is nothing to stop the police from arresting someone under paragraph (b) even though they may have enough suspicion of more particular offences to arrest under one of the other two paragraphs. But if a person disputes the lawfulness of an arrest under paragraph (b) the police must still supply details ("in general terms") of the matters which constituted reasonable grounds for the arresting constable's suspicion that the person was involved in terrorism (*Clinton v Chief Constable of the RUC*, 1991).

In 1990 there were 1,614 persons arrested under the emergency laws in Northern Ireland, of whom 433 (27%) were charged with some kind of offence; in 1991 the figures were 1,788 arrested and 437 (24%) charged.

The power to stop, search and seize

The police do not possess a general power to stop and search anyone at will. A person may, of course, consent to being stopped and searched, but if consent is withdrawn the search must cease immediately. The consent may also be limited, for instance, to a search of a person's pockets or handbag. In this case any more extensive search will be an assault.

The police do possess limited stop and search powers conferred by legislation, in particular the Police and Criminal Evidence (NI) Order 1989. As a rule, because it can be difficult to know whether the police are acting within their powers when conducting a search, it is better if the person being searched, rather than resisting the search and risking a prosecution for obstructing the police in the execution of their duty, submits to the search while informing the police that he or she is not consenting voluntarily. The police should be asked to name the exact power under which they are acting so that the terms of it can be checked later. If the police act in a high-handed fashion, or in breach of the powers conferred upon them, the person searched should lodge a complaint (see chapter 6) or think about bringing a civil action (see chapter 2).

A person can also be lawfully searched once he or she has been arrested. Any weapon or evidence of a crime discovered can be seized. The person's home can be searched too, or the place where the arrest has occurred, provided that there is some connection between that place and the suspected offence. If the police uncover evidence relating to a crime during the course of an unlawful search, that evidence is still admissible in a court of law but a civil action against the police can be begun.

Searches under the "ordinary" law

The PACE (NI) Order 1989 empowers police officers to stop, detain and search any person if they have reasonable grounds for suspecting that they will find stolen or prohibited articles. An article is prohibited if it is an offensive weapon or something intended for use in a burglary or theft. Any such item may be seized and need not be returned. The power can be exercised only in a public place. People who are in a garden or yard connected with a dwelling cannot be searched unless the police have reasonable grounds for believing that those people do not reside in the dwelling and are not there with permission.

Before a search is begun, the constable must prove that he or she is indeed a police officer (by displaying a card or giving his or her police number and station). The constable must also indicate the object of the proposed search, the grounds for making it and the fact that a written record will be made available to the person if requested within the next year. During the search a person cannot be required to remove any item of clothing in public, except an outer coat, jacket, headgear and gloves. Nor can he or she be detained longer than is reasonably required for the search to be carried out.

The duty to make a written record and the prohibition on requiring clothes to be removed do not apply to searches following an arrest, although an arrested person can be searched only if the custody officer considers it necessary to permit a record of the person's possessions to be taken. The search must be conducted by an officer of the same sex as the person searched and special conditions apply to "intimate" searches (see below). In any event, after a person has been arrested and taken to a police station, the station's custody officer must record everything which a person is carrying. Any of these things may be retained by the custody officer provided reasons are given, though clothes and personal effects may be seized only if the officer believes that the arrested person may use them to inflict injury, damage property, interfere with evidence, assist an escape, or if there are reasonable grounds for believing that the items may be evidence relating to an offence.

In 1992 the RUC searched 982 persons and vehicles under the "ordinary" law, 69% of these being searches for drugs. The number of arrests resulting from these searches was 267 (27%).

Intimate searches

These are defined as "a search which consists of the physical examination of a person's body orifices". They require the written authorisation of an officer of at least the rank of superintendent, who must first have reasonable grounds for believing that an arrested person may have concealed on his or her body a "Class A" drug or anything which could be used to cause injury while in custody. "Class A" drugs include heroin but not amphetamines or cannabis and they can be searched for only by a registered doctor or nurse and not at a police station. Other intimate searches should also be conducted by a doctor or nurse unless a police officer of at least the rank of superintendent considers that this is not practicable, in which case they must be carried out by a constable of the same sex as the person searched; they can be conducted at police stations.

A written record must be kept by the custody officer of the parts of the body that have been searched, and why. Anything found during an intimate search may be retained only in the circumstances outlined above in relation to clothes and personal effects.

In 1992 the RUC conducted one intimate search under these powers.

Searches under the "emergency" laws

By virtue of section 19(6) of the EPA 1991 any police officer may stop any person in any public place and search him or her for explosives, firearms, ammunition or wireless transmitters. This power can also be exercised elsewhere than in a public place if the police officer has reasonable grounds to suspect the presence of these items. A search cannot take place for other items (see *Carlisle v Chief Constable of the RUC*, 1989). Explosives inspectors also have the power to stop a person in a public place and search for explosive substances (section 20(2) of the EPA 1991). Any item found may be seized.

Section 15(3) of the PTA allows a constable to stop and search anyone whom he or she has the power to arrest under section 14 of that Act. The search must be for evidence justifying an arrest, but there must still be independent grounds for the arrest besides whatever is found during the course of a search. People who have already been arrested under section 14 of the PTA may also be searched (section 15(4)). In both instances the search must be carried out by a person of the same sex.

Strip-searching is nowhere specifically prohibited by the law.

Vehicle searches under the "ordinary" law

Curiously, the exact legal position regarding the stopping of vehicles is unclear even though the relevant powers are largely conferred by legislation. In an English court case in 1982 (*Steel v Goacher*) it was held that the police had a power under the common law (*i.e.* not based on any statute) to stop traffic in order to prevent criminal activity. Failing to stop a car when requested to do so by the police is therefore a more risk-laden thing to do than failing to stop walking when approached by the police.

The ordinary law already set out above in relation to searches of persons also applies to searches of vehicles. A car can be stopped, detained and searched if the police have reasonable grounds for suspecting that they will find stolen or prohibited articles. If a vehicle is parked on land connected to a dwelling, it may not be searched unless the police have reasonable grounds for believing that it is there without the permission of a person who resides there. The rules about the police having to identify themselves before making the search also apply, but no police officer can stop a vehicle unless he or she is in uniform.

Whenever the police search an unattended vehicle they have to leave a notice stating that it has been searched, the date of the search and the identity of the searching officer. The notice also has to indicate that a written record of the search can be requested within a year and that an application can be made for compensation for any damage. This duty does not apply to searches of vehicles at an airport, railway, dock or harbour, to searches of air cargo, or to searches conducted under the emergency laws.

The 1989 Order contains a second power relating to vehicle checks (article 6), but this deals with searches for wanted people rather than for stolen goods or weapons. It authorises a police officer to stop and check vehicles to see if they are carrying people who are unlawfully at large or who are intending to commit, have committed, or are witnesses to an offence (except a road traffic offence). The vehicles to be searched can be chosen in accordance with any criterion, *e.g.* the colour or age of the car or the appearance of its occupants. The authorisation for a road check of this nature must come from a senior police officer and can last for no longer than seven days at a time. In 1992 the power was not used.

Vehicle searches under the "emergency" laws

Because the space inside a vehicle constitutes a "place", the emergency laws conferring powers to enter and search premises or other "places" (see page 36) mean that the police have extensive powers to enter and search cars, buses, vans and lorries. Bicycles and motorbikes are clearly vehicles, but because they have no internal space they probably cannot be searched under these particular powers.

By virtue of section 16 of the EPA 1991, a police constable may enter and search any vehicle if he or she has reasonable grounds for suspecting that it contains a person who could be arrested under the PTA because he or she is reasonably suspected of involvement in terrorism. A similar power is conferred by section 17(2), and section 17(3) allows the police to seize anything which they have reasonable grounds to suspect is being, has been or is intended to be used in the commission of an offence created by that Act or listed in Schedule 1. To enable the police to look for people who may have been kidnapped, and whose lives are in danger, section 21 permits the police to enter any place and search for the missing persons.

The main search power under the emergency laws, however, is in section 19 of the EPA 1991, which allows the police to enter and search any vehicle to look for explosives, firearms, ammunition or wireless transmitters. Caravans may be searched only if an officer not below the rank of chief inspector authorises it. As always, items found may be seized.

A police officer may interfere with the use of a highway, any right of way or the use of a waterway. Anyone who meddles with materials used in the exercise of this power is guilty of an offence carrying a maximum penalty of six months' imprisonment or a fine up to £2,000 (section 24 of the EPA 1991).

The power to enter, search and seize

The police have no general power to enter and search private premises in order to investigate criminal acts. Only in relation to some road traffic offences may they do so. Otherwise they may enter and search only if they have the permission of the occupier, if a breach of the peace is involved or if the requirements of the PACE Order are satisfied.

The relevant provisions of the PACE (NI) Order 1989 are articles 10-25. They deal only with searches of "premises", but this term is defined so as to include any place. It therefore covers outdoor as well as indoor premises, movable or stationary premises and public or private places. The power to search carries with it the power to enter in order to conduct the search.

Entry with a warrant

The police will normally have to obtain a search warrant from a Justice of the Peace in order to enter and search premises. The JP can grant the warrant only if he or she is satisfied that a serious arrestable offence has been committed and that there is material on the premises which is likely to be relevant to its investigation. The JP must also be satisfied that it is not practicable for the police to obtain permission to enter the place, or that a search may be frustrated unless a police officer is allowed to enter immediately.

Applications for warrants must specify the reasons for the proposed search, the premises to be searched and the articles to be looked for. The warrants themselves must be just as specific. They can authorise entry on one occasion only, which must occur within a month and be at a reasonable hour unless this would frustrate the search.

If the police wish to search for personal medical records, documents dealing with counselling or with assistance given by a voluntary organisation, journalistic material or confidential business information, they must obtain either a production order or a warrant, not from a JP but from a county court judge. Before issuing an order or a warrant the judge must normally be satisfied that access to the material is in the public interest. Otherwise similar preconditions apply to the issue of a warrant as in the case of applications to a JP. The only material which is totally exempt from forced disclosure is that which is subject to legal privilege; in the main these are communications with a solicitor (article 12).

Entry without a warrant

Under articles 19 and 20 of the PACE (NI) Order, the only situations where a police officer is able to enter and search premises without a warrant are the following:

- where the officer wishes lawfully to arrest a person whom he or she reasonably suspects is present on the premises;
- where the police wish to search premises occupied or controlled by a person who has been arrested for an arrestable offence because they have reasonable grounds for suspecting that the premises contain evidence relating to that or some other connected arrestable offence;
- where entry is necessary in order to prevent serious personal injury or serious property damage;
- where entry is necessary in order to deal with or prevent a breach of the peace;

- where any statutory provision so permits, *e.g.* the Food and Drugs Act (NI) 1958, section 41.

Seizure

The police can seize and retain anything they are looking for during a lawful search. In addition, by virtue of article 21 of the PACE Order, an officer who is lawfully on any premises may seize anything found there if he or she has reasonable grounds for believing that it has been obtained as a result of an offence, or that it is evidence in relation to any offence, and that seizure is necessary in order to prevent it being concealed, lost, damaged, altered or destroyed. Even information accessible through a computer can be seized under this power, but legally privileged material is exempt (article 12).

Whenever anything has been seized, a written record must be provided, if requested, to a person who was the occupier of the premises or who had custody or control of the thing immediately prior to the seizure. Access to items seized, even if only in order to photograph or copy them, must be permitted by the officer in charge of the investigation unless he or she has reasonable grounds for believing that this would prejudice criminal proceedings. Otherwise items seized may be retained by the police for as long as is necessary. Under section 1 of the Police (Property) Act 1897 a person can apply to a magistrates' court for an order for the return of property or for a statement from the police as to why they think retention is still justified.

Anything seized during an unlawful search may nevertheless be used in court as evidence of an offence. Judges have a discretion to exclude the evidence because of the adverse effect on the fairness of the proceedings (article 76 of the PACE Order), but the person searched can seek compensation only by taking action in the civil courts (see chapter 2). He or she can also lodge a complaint against the police (see chapter 6).

Searches under the "emergency" laws

Under the EPA 1991, searches of any place can be made by the police as follows:

- to arrest a suspected terrorist (section 16);
- to arrest a person suspected of offences listed in the 1991 Act (section 17 (2));

- to look for explosives, firearms, ammunition or transmitter (section 19);
- to look for persons who have been kidnapped (section 21).

If the place to be searched is a dwelling-house then, as far as the section 19 and section 21 powers are concerned, authority to conduct the search must be granted by a police officer not below the rank of chief inspector, and, in the case of section 19 searches, only if the police have reasonable grounds for suspecting the presence of what is being sought. In the four years 1988-91 there were 13,692 recorded searches by the RUC but there are no published figures on the quantities of weapons, ammunition or transmitters revealed by searches of homes. It has recently been held by the European Commission of Human Rights that searches under the section 19 power are not a breach of the European Convention on Human Rights (*Murray v UK*, 1993).

Under section 19(4) and (5) of the EPA 1991, the police may require any person who is in the place being searched to remain in a part of it for up to four hours, though a police officer of the rank of superintendent or above may extend that period by a further four hours if he or she reasonably believes that it is necessary to do so. The police can use reasonable force to ensure that the requirement is complied with and anyone wilfully failing to comply is liable to two years' imprisonment and an unlimited fine. The police can arrest anyone reasonably suspected of committing this offence, which is triable without a jury; it seems, however, that no charges have yet been brought. Recently a challenge to the legality of detention during a house search was unsuccessful before the European Commission of Human Rights (*O'Neill and Kelly v UK*, 1992).

Although section 19 of the EPA 1991 authorises the police to search only for explosives, firearms, ammunition and transmitters, if they find other incriminating items during the course of any search the person in possession of these items can be arrested and charged. Under section 30 of the EPA it is an offence to have in your possession *any article:*

"in circumstances giving rise to a reasonable suspicion that the item is in [your] possession for a purpose connected with the commission, preparation or instigation of acts of terrorism connected with the affairs of Northern Ireland".

The items most likely to be involved in this offence are everyday things which can be used in the making of a bomb, *e.g.* rubber gloves, adhesive tape, bell-pushes, coffee-grinders and kitchen scales. It should also be noted that under section 31 of the EPA it is an offence to have in your possession, unless you have a lawful excuse, any information which is likely to be useful to terrorists in planning any act of violence. The maximum penalty for the offences in sections 30 and 31 is 10 years' imprisonment.

When the police are searching premises they can be assisted by specially appointed civilians such as forensic scientists and police photographers. Unless it is not practicable to do so a written record has to be made of the search specifying the name or description of the apparent occupier of the place searched and of the place itself, the date and time of the search, any damage caused and things seized during the search and the service number of the searching officer. The apparent occupier must be supplied at once or as soon as is practicable with a copy of any such record (section 19(8)-(11) of the EPA 1991).

If, in the exercise of their powers under the EPA 1991, the police take or damage any property (*e.g.* during a house search), the Secretary of State must pay compensation provided a claim is submitted no later than 4 (or exceptionally 12) months after the incident (section 63 of the EPA 1991). Special rules have been issued governing the procedures to be followed when making a claim (see the Emergency Provisions (Compensation) (NI) Rules 1982 and 1988) and the right to compensation under section 63 replaces any other legal right to claim (see *Deehan v Chief Constable of the RUC*, 1990).

The power to detain under the "ordinary" law

The PACE (NI) Order 1989 made radical changes to the law on detention. By article 32 an arrested person has to be taken to a *designated* police station if it may be necessary to keep him or her in detention for longer than six hours. In Northern Ireland the 19 designated stations are in Antrim, Armagh, Ballymena, Banbridge, Belfast (Antrim Road, Grosvenor Road, Musgrave Street, Strandtown), Coleraine, Cookstown, Derry (Strand Road), Downpatrick, Dungannon, Enniskillen, Larne, Limavady, Lurgan, Newtownards and Omagh. Any other station may be used if detention is to be for less than six hours, or if otherwise there might be an injury caused to any person. Article 32(13), however, makes it plain that the duty to take an arrested person to a police station as soon as practicable after the arrest does not apply if the presence of the person is necessary elsewhere in order to carry out immediate and reasonable investigations.

Having been arrested and taken to a police station, a person can be arrested there for a further offence (article 33) but, if a person voluntarily attends a police station "to help with police inquiries", he or she must be allowed to leave whenever wanting to - unless first placed under arrest (article 31). An arrested person can be detained for questioning or released on bail. If the arrest took place under a warrant, the warrant itself may have been endorsed with a note authorising bail. Otherwise the police officer in charge of the station concerned may release the person on bail if satisfied that this would not lead to an injustice.

The maximum period of ordinary detention without charge is 24 hours (article 42(1)). Detention beyond 24 hours is possible only for "serious arrestable offences", a category defined in article 87. It comprises:

- offences which are always serious arrestable offences, such as manslaughter, kidnapping, most sexual offences, firearms offences and causing death by reckless driving (see Schedule 5 of the Order);
- offences for which a person can be arrested under the PTA 1989;
- arrestable offences which lead to, or are intended or likely to lead to, any of these consequences: serious harm to the security of the state or to public order; serious interference with the administration of justice or with the investigation of an offence; the death of any person; serious injury to any person; substantial financial gain to any person; serious financial loss to any person;
- arrestable offences consisting of making a threat which, if carried out, would be likely to lead to any of the above consequences (*e.g.* blackmail or intimidation).

In the case of these offences, a police officer of at least the rank of superintendent and who is responsible for the police station concerned may authorise detention for a further 12 hours, provided there are reasonable grounds for believing that this detention is necessary to secure evidence and that the investigation is being conducted diligently and expeditiously (article 43(1)). In relation to serious arrestable offences the police are therefore able to detain a person without charge for up to 36 hours. In 1992 only 7 persons were kept in police detention for more than

24 hours and then released without being charged. The average detention period for all persons arrested was about seven hours.

Detention beyond 36 hours is allowed only if authorised by a magistrates' court. In 1992 there were 12 applications for extensions of detention, all but one of which were granted; of the detainees involved one was later released without charge. The court can initially require further detention for up to 36 hours. A second court order can be applied for, but the total period of detention since the time of the arrest must not exceed 96 hours (articles 44 and 45). Before the 1989 Order came into force the maximum detention period was 48 hours.

Throughout the period of detention the position of the arrested person must be reviewed. The first review must be carried out six hours after the detention begins and later reviews must be conducted at least once every nine hours. The review officer must be a police officer of at least the rank of inspector who has not been directly involved in the investigation up to that point. As soon as the grounds for detention cease to exist, the arrested person must be released or charged. Once charged, he or she must be released on police bail or brought before a magistrates' court on that day or on the following day. Until his or her release the arrested person is the responsibility of the station's "custody officer", who must have at least the rank of sergeant. It is this officer who must authorise the initial detention and any release.

The power to detain under "emergency" laws

The PACE (NI) Order did not alter the law concerning detentions under section 14 of the PTA 1989. This section allows detention without charge for up to 48 hours, but the period can be extended for up to five days by order of the Secretary of State.

Detentions under the PTA do have to be supervised in accordance with Schedule 3, which requires a review officer to review the detention as soon as practicable after it has begun and thereafter at intervals of not more than 12 hours. The detention cannot continue unless authorised and unless the person detained or his or her solicitor has been given the opportunity to make representations about the detention. But two vital factors make this review process a very different thing from that which is required by Article 5(1)(c) of the European Convention on Human Rights. In the first place, it is conducted by a police officer; although this must be an officer who has not been directly involved in the matter to date, this does not constitute a "competent legal authority" for the purposes of Article 5(1)(c). Secondly, no review needs to be conducted if an application has been made to the Secretary of State for an extension to the 48 hour period (although in practice such reviews do occur). Schedule 3 is therefore not a satisfactory response to the decision of the European Court of Human Rights in *Brogan v UK (*1988*),* where unreviewed detentions for longer than four days and six hours were held to contravene the European Convention. It is still necessary for the government to rely on the notice of derogation which it issued under Article 15 of the Convention which excuses the United Kingdom's continuing breach of the Convention. The validity of the derogation notice was upheld by the European Court of Human Rights in *Brannigan and McBride v. UK* (1993).

Detention for a period longer than that permitted by the law will leave the police open to a civil action for false imprisonment (see chapter 2). In one case, where a woman was detained from 9.30 pm to 10.05 pm simply so that she could then be medically examined (having been at the police station all day), compensation of £300 was awarded (*Petticrew v Chief Constable of the RUC*, 1988). In *Moore v Chief Constable of the RUC* (1989), where Mr Moore was arrested early one morning and held for most of the rest of the day while being interviewed several times, the judge held that it was reasonable for the police to hold him from 6.30 am to 8.00 pm in order to dispel or confirm the arresting officer's reasonable suspicion that he was guilty of the attempted hijacking of a vehicle, but there were one or two hours' detention which the police had failed to justify and damages of £150 were awarded. The Court of Appeal has recently said that the sum to be awarded for unlawful detention should be £600 per hour for up to the first 12 hours; thereafter a lesser hourly sum should be awarded if it appears that the distress caused has lessened (*Oscar v Chief Constable of the RUC*, 1992).

Taking photographs and fingerprints

As a person has no right to his or her own image, the police can photograph people as much as they want. This does not breach the European Convention on Human Rights (*Murray v UK*, 1993). Until recently, fingerprinting someone without his or her consent constituted an assault and could be resisted with reasonable force. But in order to increase the chances of detecting criminals, the PACE (NI) Order 1989 conferred greater powers in this regard.

Article 61 provides that fingerprints (and palm prints) may be taken without a person's consent if a police officer of at least the rank of superintendent authorises them to be taken or if the person has been charged with, or is to be reported for, an offence. In both of these situations the person must already have been detained at a police station. There is no power to fingerprint someone who has not been arrested and if an arrested person has not yet been charged or told that he or she is to be reported there must be reasonable grounds for suspecting that the person is involved in an offence and that the fingerprints will tend to confirm or disprove this involvement. In the absence of consent, the police may use reasonable force to take fingerprints, but a written record must be kept of the reason for taking the prints.

If, after fingerprints have been taken, the person is no longer suspected of having committed an offence, the prints taken, and any copies, must be destroyed as soon as practicable, in the presence of the person involved if requested. The person can even apply for a certificate to show that access to computer data relating to the fingerprints has been made impossible.

Under the anti-terrorism laws - in Great Britain as well as in Northern Ireland - a police or prison officer, or an immigration officer, "may take all such steps as may be reasonably necessary for photographing, measuring or otherwise identifying" a person arrested under the PTA (section 15 (9)). However section 46 of the EPA 1991 confirms that in Northern Ireland fingerprints can be taken without consent only if a police officer of the rank of superintendent or above is satisfied that this is necessary to help determine whether the suspect is involved in terrorism or is subject to an exclusion order (see chapter 8). But any prints taken in these cases do not have to be destroyed later.

A person has no right to know what photographs and other information the police possess. In *Re Gillen* (1990) the applicant was told that his photograph had gone missing from a police station. He sought further details about the loss but the court held that he had to be satisfied with the police's offer of advice on personal safety.

Taking samples

Under the ordinary common law the police have no power to take samples from a person's body. To do so without the person's consent would be an assault. An important statutory exception is the Road Traffic (NI) Order 1981, under which it is an offence to refuse to supply a sample of breath, blood or urine in cases of alleged driving while under the influence of alcohol or drugs. The PACE (NI) Order creates further important exceptions in articles 62 and 63. The Order distinguishes between intimate samples, which can be taken only with the person's consent, and non-intimate samples, which can be forcibly taken.

- "Intimate samples" are samples of blood, semen or any other tissue fluid, urine or pubic hair, or a swab taken from any of a person's body orifices except his or her mouth.

- "Non-intimate samples" are hair other than pubic hair, material taken from a nail or from under a nail, saliva, a mouth swab or any other body swab, a footprint or any other impression of a part of a person's body other than the hand. Peculiarly, mouth swabs are classified as non-intimate samples in Northern Ireland, but as intimate samples in England and Wales.

All samples require the written authorisation of a police officer of at least the rank of superintendent, who must have reasonable grounds for suspecting the involvement of the person in a serious arrestable offence and for believing that the sample will tend to confirm or disprove this involvement. A written record must be kept of the sampling. Intimate samples must be consented to in writing and (except for urine samples) be taken by a doctor. If a person refuses to consent to the taking of an intimate sample, then in any proceedings against that person the magistrate, judge or jury may "draw such inferences as appear proper" (article 62(10)).

The power to use force

Whenever they are carrying out their "ordinary" function of preserving the peace, the RUC are not entitled to use force. They must act with restraint, resisting pressure rather than applying it. Even when controlling crowds or patrolling a procession they must not apply force in an active manner. If they do so, they can be sued for assault.

However, if the police are preventing crime or effecting a lawful arrest, they can use "such force as is reasonable in the circumstances" (section 3(1) of the Criminal Law Act (NI) 1967). The burden of proving that the force used was reasonable lies on the police. For example, in *Wasson v Chief Constable of the RUC* (1987), since the RUC could not prove that their version of how Mr Wasson came to be injured by a plastic bullet was more likely to be true than Mr Wasson's version, they were held liable to pay compensation. But it seems that, even in the absence of any proof that the police knew that the person they fired at was committing an offence (such as driving a stolen car), a judge may still regard the use of real bullets as reasonable force whenever someone drives through a vehicle checkpoint. In *Magill v Ministry of Defence* (1988) it was held that a soldier's act in firing at a 15-year-old driver was reasonable use of force in the prevention of crime. A police officer would probably enjoy a similar immunity in such circumstances, though much would depend on the particular features of each case.

In relation to police powers expressly conferred by the PACE (NI) Order 1989, article 88 says that the police "may use reasonable force, if necessary, in the exercise of the power". The term "reasonable" suggests that the force used must be proportional to the gain the police hope to achieve through exercising the power. The term "necessary" implies that other means of exercising the power must be attempted first. This would seem to impose a stricter test than that contained in the 1967 Act, but as yet no court has ruled on how the two provisions inter-relate.

The power to interfere with property

Section 24(2) of the EPA 1991 is the provision which legalises the actions taken by the security forces whenever private property rights are interfered with in order to counter terrorism. It permits any police officer, if authorised by the Secretary of State, to take possession of any property, to place any structure in a state of defence, to detain, destroy, or move any property, and to do any other act interfering with any public right or with any private rights of property. It is therefore perfectly lawful for the police to take over, say, a house for the purpose of keeping an eye on a nearby building. Land, too, can be requisitioned so that look-out posts or fences can be constructed.

Furthermore, under section 24(3) of the EPA 1991, any police officer may wholly or partly close a highway if he or she considers this immediately necessary for the preservation of the peace or the maintenance of order. To permit more permanent measures to be taken, section 25 empowers the Secretary of State to order the closure of any highway.

Interference with any of this work is a crime, punishable by up to six months in prison and a fine of up to £2,000.

Codes of Practice

Article 65 of the PACE (NI) Order 1989 obliges the Secretary of State to issue codes of practice to cover (a) searches of persons or vehicles without first making an arrest, (b) the detention, treatment, questioning and identification of persons, (c) searches of premises and (d) the seizure of property found on persons or premises. The codes which have been issued in Northern Ireland are almost identical to those in England and Wales. Under article 60 a code must also be issued on the tape-recording of interviews at police stations. This has not yet been published.

For the most part the codes simply repeat in clearer language the provisions of the main legislation, but occasionally they are fuller. For instance, the code on searches of premises says that:

"Searches must be conducted with due consideration for the property and privacy of the occupier of the premises searched, and with no more disturbance than necessary" (para 5.9).

A breach of the codes will not automatically render the police liable to criminal or civil proceedings (article 66). The only available penalty will be disciplinary proceedings. A court, however, can "take account" of a code's provisions when hearing any criminal or civil case, so it might refuse to admit a piece of evidence if it considers that it was obtained in breach of a code.

A very important difference between the codes in England and those in Northern Ireland is that the former (apart from the code on tape-recording) apply also to persons and incidents being dealt with under the PTA 1989. In Northern Ireland such persons and incidents are excluded from the scope of the codes (see article 66(12) of the Order). Instead they are to be governed by a code yet to be issued under section 61 of the EPA 1991. In draft form this code covers only the detention, treatment, questioning and identification of persons detained under the PTA and it contains fewer safeguards for detainees than the equivalent PACE code. PTA detainees do not have the right, for instance, to know the identity of their interrogators, nor can they obtain a copy of their custody record. As yet the Secretary of State has not issued codes dealing with the exercise of other police powers conferred by the EPA, despite the power to do so under section 61.

Chapter 4

The Powers of the Army

Steven Greer

The current legal powers of the army in Northern Ireland are to be found almost exclusively in the Northern Ireland (Emergency Provisions) Act 1991 (the EPA). Law enforcement powers had been conferred upon the army by the Stormont Parliament in the Civil Authorities (Special Powers) Act 1992.

But in 1971 the legality of these powers was successfully challenged in the High Court by two Stormont MPs, on the grounds that the Government of Ireland Act 1920 reserved the making of laws concerning the armed forces in Northern Ireland to the Westminister Parliament (*R. (Hume and Others) v Londonderry Justices*, 1972). Almost immediately the Westminster Parliament passed the Northern Ireland Act 1972, which bestowed new powers on Stormont to make laws concerning the armed forces, provided they were necessary for the maintenance of peace and order in Northern Ireland. The legislation also conferred retrospective validity on any actions taken before its enactment which would otherwise have been invalid because of the High Court's decision. The statutory framework was changed again by the passing of the Northern Ireland (Emergency Provisions) Act 1973. This has since been modified and supplemented on several occasions, notably in 1975, 1978, 1986, 1987 and 1991. All subsequent references are to the 1991 Act.

Although the policy of successive British governments in recent years has been to promote "police primacy", limiting the army to a supportive role, the Royal Irish Regiment (formerly the UDR) maintains a pervasive presence throughout Northern Ireland, with other army units being the principal law enforcement agency in parts of West Belfast, parts of Derry City and in certain border areas. All members of Her Majesty's forces on plainclothes duty are required to produce documentary evidence that they are soldiers if requested to do so when exercising any power conferred by the EPA (section 26(11)). The powers of the military police (the "red caps") used to be the same as those of constables. But since the 1991 Act came into effect they have been the same as those of other members of the army.

The legal powers of the army in Northern Ireland will be considered here under the following heads:

- stop and question;
- personal searches;
- searches of private and other premises;
- examination and seizure of documents;
- arrest;
- detention;
- miscellaneous powers; and
- the use of force.

It should be noted that the search powers are combined with powers to seize munitions, transmitters and scanning receivers. Some suggestions are offered by way of conclusion as to how complaints against the army may be proved and legal rights enforced.

Stop and question

In Northern Ireland, soldiers on duty have the power under section 23 of the EPA to stop people at any time, including when they are travelling in a vehicle, and to question them for the purpose of ascertaining:

- their identity;
- their movements;
- what they know concerning any recent explosion or other recent incident endangering life or concerning any person killed or injured in such an explosion or incident.

It is a criminal offence to fail to stop when required to do so or to refuse to answer such questions to the best of one's knowledge and ability. A person can be arrested on the spot by a soldier for this offence and tried later by a magistrates' court. The maximum penalty is a fine of £2,000. Elsewhere in the United Kingdom the army has no power whatsoever to stop and question anyone.

It is important to realise that under section 23 the power to stop and question can be legally exercised only for one or more of the purposes listed. There is, however, some uncertainty about precisely what sort of questions a person is obliged to answer. For example, the term "identity" is not legally defined and may include not only name but also address and perhaps even age, since two members of the same family may have the same name and address. It is not clear how detailed the answers to questions concerning movements must be. Strictly speaking a general answer should be sufficient since the purpose of this particular aspect of the provision is to oblige people to explain why they happen to be at the specific place at which they were stopped and questioned, and not precisely where they have been or are going. There is therefore probably no legal requirement to give the exact address one is coming from or going to.

Having legally been stopped and asked about identity, movements etc, people may be asked questions by the army about any other matter, but there is no legal obligation to reply. Refusing to answer, however, though entirely legal, may result in suspicions being aroused, will probably prolong the encounter and, in certain circumstances, may also result in an increase in stopping and questioning on other occasions. Harassment of this kind is not legally prohibited: the army can stop and question anyone under section 23 as often as they like.

People are not legally required by section 23 to fill in forms of any kind nor to be photographed. If asked to do so, a person may lawfully refuse. However, if a photograph is taken against a person's will, there is nothing in law that can be done about it.

Personal searches

A soldier's legal power to conduct a personal search varies according to whether the person searched is in a public place or in a private home or other premises. A public place is defined by the EPA as "a place to which for the time being members of the public have or are permitted to have access, whether on payment or otherwise" (section 66). This includes such obvious public places as the street, a shop, a pub or a cinema but it also includes centres to which suspects arrested by the army are brought, as well as hotels, guest houses and hostels.

In public places

Any soldier on duty may stop and search anyone in any public place at any time in order to ascertain whether or not he or she possesses any munitions, a transmitter or scanning receiver (section 19(6)(a)). This power permits entirely random, and legally unchallengeable, searches: the soldier involved need not entertain any particular suspicions about the person searched. There is no legal reason why women cannot be frisked by male soldiers, or men by women soldiers, although there is no evidence that this often happens.

In non-public places

In order to conduct a legal personal search somewhere other than in a public place the army must first lawfully gain entry to the premises. The legal requirements are discussed in the next section. If admittance to any premises including private dwellings has been lawfully obtained, soldiers on duty may legally search anyone found there if they have reasonable grounds to suspect that they may possess a transmitter or scanning receiver, or be in unlawful possession of munitions (section 19(6)(b)). Anyone entering or found in a dwelling-house may also be searched in the absence of such suspicions although entry to dwelling-houses is more tightly controlled than entry to other premises.

Seizure of munitions, transmitters and scanning receivers

During the course of personal searches either in public or non-public places munitions, transmitters and records may be found. "Munitions" are defined as anything capable of being used in the manufacture of explosives, firearms or ammunition, and could include apparently innocuous items such as sugar or wire (section 19(14)). Munitions unlawfully held may be seized and destroyed (section 19(7)(a)) while transmitters and scanning receivers may be seized but not destroyed (section 19(7)(b)). Documents or records discovered may be examined or retained for further examination but not destroyed (see page 52).

Searches of private and other premises

The 1991 Act requires details of searches carried out in both private dwelling-houses and other places to be recorded in writing unless it is impracticable to do so (section 19 (8)-(10)). The occupier (or presumed occupier) is entitled to a copy of this document "at once" or "as soon as is practicable" (section 19(11)). It is an offence punishable by a sentence of two years' imprisonment and/or a fine wilfully to seek to frustrate the object of a search (section 19(12)).

In order to conduct a legal search of premises lawful entry must first be obtained. Different rules govern the legality of entry depending upon the purpose of the search and whether or not a dwelling-house is involved.

The general power of entry

Under section 24 (1) any soldier on duty has the power to enter any premises if he or she considers it necessary to do so in the course of operations for the preservation of the peace or the maintenance of order, or if authorised to do so by the Secretary of State. Anything found as a result may be seized and detained for up to four hours if there are reasonable grounds for suspecting that it is being, has been, or is intended to be used in the commission of an offence (section 18(4)).

Entry and search to effect an arrest

The power to enter and search in order to make a legal arrest, using reasonable force if necessary, is confined to two circumstances:

- The army may enter and search any premises, including private homes, provided that a person suspected of any offence (not necessarily a "terrorist" offence) is actually to be found there (section 18(3)(a)).
- The army may enter any premises to search for persons reasonably suspected of being "terrorists" or of having committed offences involving the use or possession of explosives or firearms. There must, however, be reasonable grounds to suspect that such persons are to be found there even though they are in fact elsewhere (section 18(3)(b)).

In both cases the army also possesses the ancillary powers to deal with resistance from on-lookers and to search the premises, following an arrest, to confirm or dispel suspicions which prompted the arrest (*Murray v Ministry of Defence*, 1988).

Entry to search for munitions etc other than in dwelling houses

Any soldier on duty may enter and search any premises, other than a dwelling-house, in order to discover whether they unlawfully contain munitions or transmitters (section 19(1)). These items, if found, may be seized (section 19(7)). This search power amounts to a power to search at will, although the restraints described at page 49 apply here too.

Entry of dwelling-houses to search for munitions etc

In order to enter a dwelling-house to carry out a search, a soldier on duty must obtain authorisation from a commissioned officer. This must be refused unless there are reasonable grounds to suspect that munitions are unlawfully on the premises in question or that a transmitter or scanning receiver is being kept there (section 19(2)). Any of these items found in such a search may be seized (section 19(7)). Systematic house searches in given areas are unlawful unless the requisite suspicion exists in relation to each house.

Details of the army's formal procedures for house searches under the predecessor to section 19(2) of the EPA 1991 were revealed in the case of *Kirkpatrick v Chief Constable of the RUC and Ministry of Defence*, 1988. Army search teams consist of a leader, a number of search units (in the *Kirkpatrick* case one unit of two soldiers for upstairs and another of two soldiers for downstairs), plus a "scribe" whose function is to keep a log. On gaining entry a cursory search of the entire house is made, the doors are locked, the curtains are drawn and the occupants are assembled in one room usually under "house arrest" (see page 53). Then, in the presence of the occupants, the team leader searches the search units and he himself is searched by the scribe. The occupants are then formally asked if they possess munitions, transmitters or scanning receivers. Next the team leader invites the head of the household to make a tour of inspection so that any pre-existing damage can be recorded. Only then does the search proper commence, with the occupants confined in one room.

Entry to search for persons unlawfully detained

Any soldier on duty may at any time enter and search any place, other than a dwelling-house, in order to discover whether anyone whose life may be in danger is unlawfully detained there. Searches of dwelling-houses for this purpose require the authorisation of a commissioned officer (section 21). This power is intended to be used in cases where someone has been kidnapped or taken hostage.

Examination and seizure of documents

When conducting any lawful search of persons or premises any documents or records, except those protected by legal privilege, may legally be examined if reasonably necessary to ascertain whether they contain information, including details about certain public officials, likely to be useful to terrorists when planning or carrying out acts of violence (section 22(1)). They may also be removed for examination for periods of up to 48 hours, extendable on the authority of an officer of the RUC not below the rank of chief inspector to a total of 96 hours, but may not be photographed or copied (section 22(2),(4),(9) & (10)). A written record of the examination must be kept, a copy of which must be supplied to the person in whose possession, or on whose premises, the document was found (section 28(8)). Wilful obstruction of the exercise of these powers is an offence punishable by imprisonment for up to two years and/or a fine (section 22(11)).

Arrest

Any soldier on duty can arrest anyone at any time, using reasonable force if necessary, provided that he or she has reasonable cause to suspect that that person "is committing, has committed or is about to commit any offence" (section 18). To the extent that an arrest may be made for any offence (not necessarily a "terrorist" offence), soldiers serving in Northern Ireland have more extensive powers than the police possess under both ordinary and emergency laws.

No warrant is required for an arrest by the army, but two basic conditions must be fulfilled:

• If called upon after the event to justify the arrest (for instance in a claim for compensation for unlawful arrest) it is not sufficient for the soldier in question to have genuinely believed that the person arrested was committing, had committed, or was about to commit, an offence. The court must be persuaded that there were *reasonable* grounds for believing that the person arrested was, for example, acting in a suspicious manner. The order of a superior officer would probably constitute reasonable grounds for the purpose of an arrest.

- The soldier carrying out the arrest must usually state that he or she is making the arrest "as a member of Her Majesty's forces" (section 18(2)). Unlike in the case of arrests by the police, the offence in question need not be disclosed at the time of the arrest nor during the subsequent period of detention in army custody. This appears to be a breach of Article 6 (3)(a) of the European Convention on Human Rights.

Many of the arrests currently carried out by the army may be abuses of the section 18 power since their purpose, it seems, is to gather information rather than to detain someone genuinely suspected of an offence.

Detention

The army in Northern Ireland possesses two separate detention powers:
- detention during the course of a search and
- detention following an arrest.

Detention during the course of a search

The army has the power to hold under "house arrest" people found in or entering both private dwellings and other places while searches are being conducted for munitions, radio transmitters and scanning receivers (section 19(4)). Such detentions are lawful provided those carrying out the search reasonably believe that they are necessary for the purposes of the search. The initial period of detention can last for up to four hours, but it can be extended for a further four hours if a police officer of at least the rank of superintendent reasonably believes this is necessary. Any person who is not resident in the place being searched can be stopped from entering it. Reasonable force can be used to enforce these requirements and wilful failure to comply with them is an offence triable without a jury and punishable with up to two years' imprisonment and/or a fine (section 19(12)).

Detention following an arrest

Under section 18 of the EPA the army has the power to detain people whom it arrests for up to four hours. During this period the person arrested has no legal right of access to a solicitor or to have a friend or relative notified about the arrest. At the end of the four hours detainees must either be released or handed over to the police for re-arrest.

There is still some doubt about precisely what powers the army possesses over persons it has lawfully arrested and detained (see generally *Murray v Ministry of Defence*, 1987). It is of course illegal for detainees to be assaulted, tortured or subjected to inhuman or degrading treatment. But minor indignities, such as being made to sit facing the wall of a small cubicle while the detention is processed, have been tolerated by the courts. Detainees may legally be frisked upon arrival at detention centres, but not as a matter of routine. Such searches have been held to be unlawful when the detainee was asleep in bed before arrest and was watched getting dressed by a member of the arrest squad.

It is lawful for detainees to be questioned about the offence(s) which motivated the arrest, but the person arrested has an obligation to answer only those questions concerning identity and movements, recent explosions and any other recent incident which endangered life. It is not an offence to refuse to reply to other questions nor, strictly speaking, should a refusal to reply be to the disadvantage of an accused at a subsequent trial. The provisions of the Criminal Evidence (NI) Order 1988, which effectively abolish the right to silence (see chapter 5), apply only to silence in the face of police not army, questioning.

It is not clear if the power to inspect documents discussed on page 52 applies to civilians under military arrest, although it is available prior to arrest. Photographing those arrested and detained by the army is not legally prohibited.

Miscellaneous powers

Under section 24 the army has a number of miscellaneous powers most of which require the authorisation of the Secretary of State, or someone to whom he or she has delegated the decision. Those which do not are the powers wholly or partly to close a road or divert traffic and to prohibit or restrict the use of any waterway if it is considered immediately necessary for the preservation of the peace or the maintenance of order. Those which require the Secretary of State's approval are the powers under section 24 (2) to:

- take possession of any land or other property;
- take steps to place buildings or other structures in a state of defence;
- detain any property or cause it to be destroyed or moved;
- interfere with any public or private rights, including carrying out work on any land which has been seized under the Act.

Anything found as a result of the exercise of these powers may be seized and detained for up to four hours if there are reasonable grounds for suspecting that it is being, has been, or is intended to be used in the commission of an offence (section 18(4)). Impeding the exercise of these powers is an offence triable by a magistrates' court and punishable by a maximum sentence of six months' imprisonment and a £400 fine.

The use of force

Any person in Northern Ireland is legally entitled to use:

"such force as is reasonable in the circumstances in the prevention of crime, or in effecting or assisting in the lawful arrest of offenders or of persons unlawfully at large" (Criminal Law Act (NI) 1967, section 3(1)).

By and large this includes the right to defend oneself, since lawful self-defence is also crime prevention. The army possesses an extra power under the EPA to use force if it is needed to gain lawful entry (section 28(4)). If the necessity for the use of force is in dispute, a court's view of whether it was necessary must prevail, not that of the army. But in practice these are unlikely to diverge.

"Reasonable in the circumstances"

Controversy has raged over how the courts and the prosecuting authorities in Northern Ireland have interpreted this key phrase particularly when the lethal use of firearms by the security forces has been at issue. In theory, the unreasonable use of force for the purpose of law enforcement exposes the soldiers concerned to a criminal prosecution, and their "employers", the Ministry of Defence, to a civil suit for compensation. However, in practice, there is often an official reluctance to drag army personnel through the criminal courts. Even where prosecutions are brought for the lethal use of firearms, the trial is conducted by a "Diplock" court, where the reasonableness of the force is decided by a judge sitting alone, without a jury.

Diplock judges have considered a wide range of factors relevant to such decisions. The result has been, in almost all cases, that particular uses of force have been characterised as "reasonable" and, therefore, legal. These factors have included: the "general wartime situation" in Northern Ireland, the character of the area in question and the problems it poses for the security forces, whether the accused honestly and reasonably believed it was his duty to open fire because he believed his target was a member of a terrorist organisation, and whether the accused honestly and reasonably believed he, or other colleagues, were about to come under fire even though the suspects in question may not have been armed (see *R v MacNaughton*, 1975; *Attorney-General for Northern Ireland's Reference*, 1976; *Farrell v Secretary of State for Defence*, 1980).

In civil cases, where damages are sought, settlements are often reached out of court, without admission of liability, so it is not possible to say that the army has accepted the legal blame. But where such cases do reach court the crucial issue, as in a criminal trial, is whether the force used was "reasonable in the circumstances". Civil courts, however, accept a lower standard of proof than criminal courts because the consequences for the defendant are less serious. Until recently, the reasonableness issue could have been decided by a civil jury if either party chose this mode of trial. But in 1987 the civil jury was largely abolished in Northern Ireland for the trial of personal injury and fatal accident cases.

Pursuing complaints and enforcing rights

It can be seen, therefore, that in relation to all the powers available to the army the law imposes certain limits. Breaches of these limits, if proven, can have significant legal consequences. The action which may be taken by a party aggrieved by an alleged violation of the army's legal powers will depend upon whether the complaint concerns damage to property or some other alleged wrong, such as injury to the person or illegal arrest and detention.

Damage to property

Persons whose property is taken through the operation of the EPA have a statutory right to compensation, provided that they were not committing an offence on the relevant occasion. Section 63 sets out the procedure for making a claim. Applications should be made to the Secretary of State, usually within four months of the incident in question, but up to a year can be allowed in special circumstances. Appeals against the Secretary of State's decision can be lodged at a county court.

Other wrongs

Other wrongs may amount to criminal offences and create other non-statutory rights to compensation. It is virtually impossible to pursue a private prosecution against the army (*i.e.*, without the assistance of the police or the Director of Public Prosecutions), since there will be enormous problems in obtaining adequate evidence. In any event, the DPP and the Attorney-General, who is a member of the government, can interfere in any private prosecution and terminate it. Public prosecutions of military personnel will involve the DPP for Northern Ireland and, therefore, may be subject to political considerations. Taking a civil claim for compensation against the army is easier and in many cases, including those involving the use of firearms, the Ministry of Defence has settled out of court, generally without an admission of liability. There is some chance of success even in those cases which do go to court.

Certain basic guidelines are worth following when seeking redress for alleged wrongs committed by the army:

- The more that is known of the real extent of the army's legal powers the better, because this heightens awareness of possible violations as they occur. This, in itself, may be sufficient to vindicate rights. For instance, if a soldier attempts to destroy documents during a street search, a question concerning his or her legal authority to do so may be enough to prevent it from happening.

- If a breach of the law is suspected, notwithstanding attempts to prevent it, the victim should try to take note of what is happening and write down the details as soon as this becomes possible (times, exact locations, who was involved, etc). He or she should also ask for the names, numbers and units of the soldiers in question. Every army patrol is now required to carry cards identifying their regiment number with a phone number where complaints may be lodged. Soldiers are under orders to distribute the cards to anyone seeking to make a complaint against them.

- Legal and political representatives should be contacted and a complaint lodged with the local army commander. The address of the army's headquarters is Thiepval, Lisburn, Co. Antrim. The Northern Ireland (Emergency Provisions) Act 1991 establishes an Independent Assessor for Military Complaints to review the manner in which the army deals with complaints but not to investigate complaints independently. The Independent Assessor should be contacted if a complaint against the army itself is not dealt with satisfactorily. The police should be involved if the complainant suspects that what has occurred amounts to a criminal offence, such as an assault.

Pursuing legal actions against the army is not easy, even when the complainant is obviously in the right, but it is not impossible. A few people have done so with success. The army's own recent figures show that nearly 10% of all complaints of non-criminal behaviour are substantiated. In 1992 the army's own Central Complaints Office investigated 282 non-criminal complaints; in addition there were 427 criminal complaints against the army investigated by the RUC.

Chapter 5

Questioning Suspects

John Jackson

The investigation of crimes was originally the responsibility of jurors, then of magistrates. During the nineteenth century the task was given to the police. As explained in chapter 3, the police do not have a general power to stop a person for questioning unless he or she is placed under arrest. Nor do they have a general power to detain someone for the purpose of getting "help with police inquiries". There is no half-way house between voluntary co-operation with the police and arrest for a specific offence.

The absence of any duty to reply to police questions is usually referred to as "the right of silence". It also protects defendants (*i.e.*persons accused of crimes) from having to give evidence at their trial. We shall see, however, that this right has been limited by the Criminal Evidence (NI) Order 1988. A person other than a defendant is protected by the right of silence at a trial only to the extent that he or she can claim the privilege to decline to answer a question which may incriminate him or her in a criminal offence (see page 75).

The "voluntariness" principle

The police must conduct their questioning of suspects within the law and it is always open to a person who has been assaulted in the course of police questioning, perhaps for the purpose of extracting a confession, to bring a civil action against the police officers involved. In a case involving a man whose ear-drum was perforated, the High Court of Northern Ireland held that if a person is lawfully arrested for the purpose of questioning but is subsequently assaulted during questioning, the detention becomes unlawful and the person is entitled to a writ of *habeas corpus* to secure release (*Ex parte Gillen*, 1988).

Until recently, the most significant restriction on the power of the police to question suspects was the rule that a statement could be used as evidence only if it had been made voluntarily. This meant that, when an accused person challenged the validity of a confession which he or she had allegedly made, the prosecution had to prove beyond a reasonable doubt that the statement had not been obtained "by fear of prejudice or hope of advantage held out by a person in authority". This test was later extended to require the prosecution to show that the statement was not obtained by "oppression". "Oppressive questioning" was defined by one judge as:

> *"questioning which by its nature and duration or other attendant circumstances (including the fact of custody) excites hopes such as the hope of release or fears, or so affects the mind of the subject that his (sic) will crumbles and he speaks when otherwise he would have stayed silent".*

Whether there was oppression in an individual case depended on many elements, including the length of time intervening between periods of questioning, the length of any specific period of questioning, whether the accused had been given proper refreshment and the characteristics of the person who made the statement.

Article 74 of the PACE Order

In a major modification of the voluntariness principle under article 74 of the Police and Criminal Evidence (NI) Order 1989, the prosecutor now has to prove that the statement was not obtained by oppression of the person who made it or in consequence of anything said or done which was likely to render it unreliable. The voluntariness principle, therefore, no longer applies. Yet another test applies where the accused is charged with a serious scheduled offence under the Northern Ireland (Emergency Provisions) Act 1991 (see page 65).

The "admissibility" of a confession (*i.e.* whether it can be accepted as proper evidence in a court of law) is frequently tested at what is known as a "*voir dire*" or a "trial within a trial". This is when the judge asks the jury to withdraw so that it cannot be influenced by hearing evidence which the judge might rule to be inadmissible. If an alleged confession is ruled inadmissible by the judge, the prosecution may not adduce evidence of what was said by the accused at the *voir dire* at a later stage of the trial, provided the evidence was relevant to the issue at the *voir dire*. If what the accused says at the *voir dire* were to be admissible at the trial, it might significantly impair his or her right of silence at the trial.

For the purposes of article 74 of the PACE Order, "oppression" is defined to include torture, inhuman or degrading treatment and the use or threat of violence, whether or not amounting to torture (article 74(8)). This seems a narrower definition than at common law, but the word "includes" in article 74(8) entitles the courts to extend the categories of oppression to the kinds of conduct and circumstances considered oppressive at common law. In their interpretation of the equivalent English provision, however, the English courts have restricted oppression to the exercise of authority or power in a burdensome, harsh or wrongful manner, unjust or cruel treatment, and to the imposition of unreasonable or unjust burdens in circumstances which would almost always entail some impropriety on the part of the interrogator (*R. v Fulling*, 1987).

The other kind of evidence which is wholly excluded under article 74 is a confession made in consequence of conduct likely to render it unreliable. This extends the categories of behaviour which may exclude a confession beyond threats and inducements, but makes it clear that a confession will be excluded only where the conduct was *likely* to render unreliable any confession which the accused might have made as a result. Much will depend on what is considered by judges to make a confession unreliable.

Rules on police questioning

The conduct of police questioning used to be governed by what were known as the Judges' Rules, so called because they had their origin in a set of rules formulated and approved by the judges of the English King's Bench Division in 1912 and 1918. A second version of them was approved in 1964 and these were adopted in Northern Ireland in 1976. Appended to them was a set of Administrative Directions, which were concerned with affording persons questioned with reasonably comfortable conditions and adequate breaks and refreshment, and with creating special procedures for persons unfamiliar with the English language or of immature age or feeble understanding. It is important to realise, however, that neither the Judges' Rules nor the Administrative Directions had the force of law; they were merely statements of good practice which judges were entitled to take into account when deciding whether a police officer had acted lawfully or not.

New guidance and Code

In December 1988, as a consequence of the Criminal Evidence (NI) Order 1988, the Northern Ireland Lord Chief Justice, on behalf of all the judges in Northern Ireland, issued a Practice Note cancelling the Judges' Rules and announced that to replace them the Secretary of State had issued written guidance to the Chief Constable of the RUC. The guidance requires a constable who is questioning a person in order to discover whether or by whom an offence has been committed to caution that person in the following terms:

> *"You do not have to say anything unless you wish to do so but I must warn you that if you fail to mention any fact which you rely on in your defence in court, your failure to take this opportunity to mention it may be treated in court as supporting any relevant evidence against you. If you do wish to say anything, what you say may be given in evidence."*

The new guidance also requires that suspects in custody be given a written notice setting out the terms of the Order so as to ensure that they are fully aware of the consequences of their action. The guidance has been incorporated in a Code of Practice for the Detention, Treatment and Questioning of Persons by Police Officers, issued under article 65 of the PACE Order and is to be incorporated in a new Code of Practice governing the questioning of persons arrested and detained under the Prevention of Terrorism (Temporary Provisions) Act 1989 (the PTA). The Code of Practice issued under PACE applies to all suspects except those arrested under the PTA. Under the Code the new caution has to be given to all arrested persons. It requires that an accurate record be made of each interview with a person suspected of an offence and that the record be signed by the suspect as correct. Interviews in police stations cannot be conducted without the consent of the custody officer, who is an officer not involved in the investigation of the offence but who has the responsibility for the treatment of detained persons.

In any detention period of 24 hours, a suspect must be allowed a continuous period of at least eight hours for rest. When an interviewing officer considers that there is sufficient evidence to prosecute a suspect and that the suspect has said all that he or she wishes to say about the offence, the officer must bring him or her before the custody officer, who is then responsible for considering whether he or she should be charged. On being charged the suspect should again be cautioned and given a written notice showing particulars of the offence and stating the terms of the caution. Questions relating to the offence should not be put to him or her after charge unless they are necessary to prevent harm to some other person or to clear up an ambiguity in a previous answer. Another Code is to be issued under article 60 of the PACE Order to cover the tape-recording of interviews at police stations.

Young and mentally handicapped persons

The Code of Practice for Detention etc. requires that a person under the age of 17, or a person who is mentally handicapped, must not be interviewed or asked to provide a written statement in the absence of an "appropriate adult", unless an officer of the rank of superintendent or above considers that delay would involve an immediate risk of harm to persons or a serious loss of property. An "appropriate adult" means, in the case of a juvenile, the juvenile's parent or guardian, a social worker or a responsible adult over 18 who is not a police officer.

Article 58 of the PACE Order creates a new section 52(2) of the Children and Young Persons Act (NI) 1968, so that there is now a duty where a juvenile is in police detention to take such steps as are practicable to ascertain the identity of a person responsible for his or her welfare and to inform that person, unless it is not practicable to do so, why and where the juvenile is being detained.

Enforcement of the rules on questioning

Judges have discretion under the common law (*i.e.* non-statutory law) to exclude from proceedings any statement which has been obtained unfairly. It is their duty to see that the accused has a fair trial according to law (*R. v Sang*, 1979). In one Northern Irish case other matters which were considered relevant to the judge's discretion included the reason that led the accused to say what he or she did, whether the police had acted improperly in order to get him or her to crack under the strain, and the unlawfulness of the police conduct, but it was stressed that the "paramount criterion" was the fairness of the accused's trial (*R. v McBrien and Harman*, 1984).

Article 76 of the Order states that in any criminal proceedings the court may refuse to admit evidence on which the prosecution proposes to rely if it appears that, having regard to all the circumstances, including the circumstances in which the evidence was obtained, the admission of evidence would have such an adverse effect on the fairness of the proceedings that the court ought not to admit it. The effect of this is that, just as the courts have a broad common law discretion to exclude statements obtained unfairly, the courts now have a broad statutory discretion to exclude statements obtained in breach of a Code issued under the Order. It is worth noting that the courts in England have been much more prepared to use their power to exclude statements under the statutory discretion (which has been in force there since 1986) than they have ever been prepared to do under their common law discretion.

The Codes of Practice issued under the PACE Order, like the Judges' Rules, do not have the full force of law. Article 66(7) merely states that a police officer shall be liable to disciplinary proceedings for a failure to comply with any provision in a code. As regards whether a statement obtained in breach of a code can be used as evidence, article 66(10) states in effect that in all criminal and civil proceedings the courts may take such account of any breach as they think fit. In some cases this will mean excluding the statement.

Questioning under emergency legislation

A number of emergency powers were enacted for Northern Ireland in 1973 on the recommendation of the Diplock Commission. These powers are now enshrined in the Northern Ireland (Emergency Provisions) Act 1991(the EPA). The Diplock Commission believed that, as regards police questioning, the voluntariness principle was, with its technical rules, hampering the course of justice. In particular, the decision in *R. v Flynn and Leonard* (1972) had excluded statements obtained as a result of questioning which was designed to build up an atmosphere in which the initial desire to remain silent was replaced by an urge to confide in the questioner. The Commission considered that, if human lives were to be saved and destruction of property prevented in Northern Ireland, the security authorities must have the power to build up an atmosphere of this kind. To this end it proposed that the admissibility of confessions should depend on the much lower standard of the absence of torture or inhuman or degrading treatment, a standard derived from the European Convention on Human Rights.

The current rules

The position today is that if a person being tried on indictment (*i.e.* in the Crown Court) for a scheduled offence (*i.e.* one listed in Schedule 1 of the EPA) wishes to challenge the admissibility of a statement allegedly made by him or her, he or she must adduce evidence which on the face of it shows that he or she was subjected to torture or to inhuman or degrading treatment or to any violence or threat of violence in order to induce the making of the statement. The prosecution must then satisfy the court that the statement was not obtained in this manner (section 11 of the 1991 Act).

The insertion of the words "violence or threat of violence" clarifies one of the difficulties with the European Convention's standard, which was whether it precluded the use of violence altogether. Another difficulty is what degree of psychological pressure is permitted within the standard. It seems that statements made by a suspected member of a terrorist organisation after periods of searching questioning *are* to be admitted notwithstanding that at the outset the suspect did not wish to confess and that the interrogation caused him or her to speak when otherwise he or she would have stayed silent (*R. v Dillon and Gorman,* 1984). Whilst such questioning would have constituted oppression at common law, it is not in itself considered "degrading" within the European Convention standard.

Judges' discretion and other rules

Shortly after the enactment of the emergency legislation in 1973, the Lord Chief Justice explained that:

"there is always a discretion, unless it is expressly removed, to exclude any admissible evidence on the ground that (by reason of any given circumstance) its prejudicial effect outweighs its probative value and that to admit the evidence would not be in the interests of justice" (R. v Corey, 1973).

This discretion has since been written into section 11 of the EPA Act, which states that the court has discretion to exclude a statement if it appears that it is appropriate to do so in order to avoid unfairness to the accused or otherwise in the interests of justice.

An early case under the emergency legislation suggested that the involuntariness of the confession at common law was a ground for the exercise of the discretion to exclude the confession, although it was emphasised that the mere fact that a confession had been obtained involuntarily did not necessarily mean that it would have to be excluded (*R. v Tohill*, 1974). More recently, the courts have been cautious to ensure that the discretion is not exercised so as to defeat the will of Parliament, which was to admit statements made after periods of searching questioning by persons suspected of "terrorist" involvement (e.g. *R. v Cowan*, 1987).

Reforming interrogation procedures

Concern about the treatment of suspects held under emergency legislation by the security forces led to an inquiry in 1978 by Amnesty International. Furthermore, in 1979 a Committee of Inquiry into Police Interrogation Procedures in Northern Ireland, chaired by Judge Bennett, made a number of recommendations on interrogation procedures. One of these was that there should be a Code of Conduct applying specifically to interviewing officers. The Code should prohibit certain kinds of conduct and regulate the length and time of interviews. In June 1979 the Secretary of State announced that the Chief Constable had with his approval issued "Instructions" to implement the recommendations of the Bennett Committee. The Code of Practice issued under the PACE Order for the Detention, Treatment and Questioning of Persons does not apply to persons arrested under section 14 of the PTA, but section 61 of the EPA requires the Secretary of State to issue statutory codes of practice on the detention, treatment, questioning and identification of such persons and a draft version of these Codes was circulated in late 1992.

Like the Codes of practice issued under the PACE Order, the new Codes will lack the full force of law, but failure by police officers to comply with them may make them liable to disciplinary proceedings (unless criminal proceedings are pending against them) and the provisions of the Codes may be taken into account by the courts in deciding whether to admit confessions. In view of the courts' discretion to exclude statements which are otherwise admissible under section 8 of the 1978 Act, it would also seem that the courts may exercise their discretion to exclude statements obtained as a result of a breach of the Codes.

The new draft Codes will not apply to arrests made by the army. The Code on Detention, Treatment and Questioning will offer levels of protection which are similar to but not as extensive as the Codes of Practice issued under the PACE Order. Unlike the PACE Codes, persons arrested under the PTA are not to be permitted to talk on the telephone with anyone, have writing materials or receive visits, although there are restricted rights of access to a lawyer (see page 68). The new Code makes provision for the possibility of examination by a medical practitioner of the detained person's choice, but unlike the PACE Code this can only take place in the presence of the Medical Officer called by the police.

Despite these proposed changes, there continues to be international criticism of the treatment of PTA suspects in the interrogation centres to which they are taken. The government has refused to extend its plans to tape-record interviews of suspects arrested under the PACE Order to these suspects. It has also refused to extend the lay visiting scheme introduced in 1991 to monitor the treatment of PACE suspects to suspects detained under the PTA. Instead it announced the appointment in 1992 of an "independent commissioner" who is able to pay random visits to the interrogation centres and oversee the conditions under which detainees are held.

The right of access to a lawyer

Under article 59 of the PACE Order, a person arrested and held in custody is entitled to consult a solicitor privately at any time if he or she so requests. The police may delay in complying with the request only if the person is in detention for a serious arrestable offence and if an officer of at least the rank of superintendent authorises the delay. In any event, delay is permitted only for up to 36 hours from the beginning of the person's detention. The allowable reasons for delay are:

- that there are reasonable grounds for believing that the exercise of the right will lead to interference with evidence or witnesses, or to the alerting of other suspects; or
- that it will hinder the recovery of property or the proceeds of a crime.

Article 57 also entitles a detained person to have someone informed that he or she has been arrested, subject to the same grounds of delay as in article 59. Arrested persons have no absolute right to be told of their entitlements under articles 57 and 59, but the Code of Practice says that they should be told. Articles 57 and 59 specifically exclude from their scope persons arrested or detained under section 14 of the PTA.

A person detained under section 14 has a right under section 45 of the 1991 EPA to consult a solicitor privately if he or she so requests and section 44 of the same Act enables a detained person to have someone informed of the fact that he or she has been arrested. The detainee must be informed of these rights as soon as practicable after being arrested. The police may delay in complying with any request under sections 44 and 45 only if such delay is authorised by an officer of at least the rank of superintendent and the delay must not extend beyond 48 hours from the beginning of the detention. The grounds of delay are broader than those allowed under article 59 of the PACE Order, extending to interference with the gathering of information about the commission of acts of terrorism and to alerting any person so that it will be more difficult to prevent an act of terrorism or to apprehend a person in connection with an act of terrorism. The Northern Ireland Court of Appeal has held that it is sufficient that the police reasonably believe that there is a real risk of a legal adviser being used as an unwilling agent to convey information of use to terrorists (R. v Harper, 1990). The police do not need to cease questioning until the lawyer arrives. Moreover, the access permitted need not be unrestricted, provided consultations are allowed at intervals of 48 hours.

The right of access to a lawyer has been described in one English decision as "one of the most important and fundamental rights of a citizen" (R. v Samuel, 1988). But the English courts appear to require some causal correction between any breach of the right and any resulting confession before they are inclined to exclude confessions on the grounds of denial of the right of access to a lawyer and the Northern Ireland Court of Appeal has recently approved of this approach (*R. v Harper*). The Northern Ireland courts have, however, recognised that the decision of a police superintendent to delay access to legal advice or to delay a suspect's right to have someone informed of detention is clearly one of an official affecting public rights and is therefore liable to judicial review (*In Re Duffy's Application*, 1992; *In Re McKenna's Application*, 1992).

The right of silence before trial

Research indicates that only a minority of subjects in fact exercise their right to say nothing when questioned by the police, which suggests that the right may not be the valuable safeguard it is often claimed to be. The provisions of the Criminal Evidence (NI) Order 1988, however, which allow adverse inferences to be drawn from a person's silence in a number of circumstances, make it even less likely in the future that silence will be maintained in the face of police questioning.

A number of laws impose a duty to answer questions or provide information:

- Section 26 of the Official Secrets Act 1939 provides that a policeman of at least the rank of inspector may be authorised to require a person to furnish information regarding an offence under section 1 of the Act.
- Under road traffic legislation, the police have a right to require the driver of a car to present his or her driving licence, and, if the driver is alleged to be guilty of an offence under the legislation, to give his or her correct name and address and those of the owner of the car (Road Traffic (NI) Order 1981, articles 177 and 180).
- As regards emergency legislation, section 23 of the 1991 EPA has already been dealt with in chapters 3 and 4. Another emergency exception to the right of silence is section 18 of the Prevention of Terrorism (Temporary Provisions) Act 1989, which makes it an offence for a person who has information about an act of terrorism or about people involved in terrorism to fail to disclose it without reasonable excuse.

Even when there is no statutory duty to answer questions, there is nothing to stop the police asking them and, if at any stage a person indicates that he or she wishes to remain silent, there is no obligation on the police to stop asking questions, although the Codes of Practice for Detention etc. requires police officers not to ask questions after a suspect has been charged, unless the circumstances are exceptional.

Enforcement of the right of silence

The citizen's right of silence in the face of police questioning has traditionally been enforced by two general rules. One was laid down in *Rice v Connolly* (1966), where the court held that silence cannot lead to a charge of obstructing the police in the execution of their duty. The second general rule states that, at a trial, the prosecution and the trial judge should not suggest to the jury that an adverse inference may be drawn from an accused person's silence when questioned by the police. Until recently the only exception to this rule was where two persons are speaking on even terms and one charges the other with something which the other says nothing to repel. In this instance the judge may make some comment, but even here he or she must be careful, for it has been held that to ask the jury to consider whether the person's silence in these circumstances indicates guilt or innocence is to short-circuit the intellectual process that has to be followed. Where the accuser is a police officer, the parties cannot normally be said to be on even terms, although everything depends on the circumstances.

Recent restrictions on the right of silence

The most serious dent in the general rule that adverse inferences should not be drawn from silence is created by the Criminal Evidence (NI) Order 1988, which defines three situations when adverse inferences may be drawn in court from an accused's silence *before* trial. Article 3 provides that, when an accused relies in his or her defence on some fact which he or she failed to mention when questioned or charged by the police, then if the fact is one which the accused could reasonably have been expected to mention, the court or jury may draw such inferences from the failure as appear proper and may treat it as corroboration of other relevant evidence against the accused.

The other two situations when adverse inferences may be drawn are more limited. Article 5 provides that a court or jury may draw such inferences as appear proper where, after being arrested, a person fails to account to the police for the presence of an object, substance or mark on his or her person or in a place where he or she was arrested if the object, substance or mark is reasonably believed by the police to be attributable to the person's participation in an offence. Article 6 permits inferences to be drawn from a refusal by a person when arrested to account for his or her presence at a particular place at the time the offence was committed.

As already noted, the Codes of Practice issued under the PACE Order and to be issued under the EPA require that persons who are questioned by the police be warned about the effect of article 3 (see page 62). In addition, the guidance and the Code require that before a constable questions a person about the matters in articles 5 and 6, he or she must inform the person that there is reason to believe that what has been found is attributable to the person's participation in an offence or that the person's presence at the time of the alleged offence is attributable to his or her participation in it. The person must then be asked to account for what has been found or for his or her presence and warned that a failure to do so may result in a court deriving such inferences from the failure as appear proper.

The courts have now in a number of decisions drawn adverse inferences against accused persons for their failure to respond to police questioning. In one case Article 3 was invoked against the National Director of Publicity for Sinn Fein when he refused to reply to police questions after being arrested with seven others for unlawfully detaining a man suspected of being a police informant. The accused denied the charge and explained his silence on the ground that as a Sinn Fein spokesperson he had advised other people to remain silent and had to maintain this stance himself. But the Lord Chief Justice held that the failure to speak gave rise to very strong inferences against him that the innocent explanation which he offered in court was false (*R. v Martin and Others*, 1991).

Questioning at the trial

The general rule, subject to an important exception in the case of an accused person, is that if a person is a "competent" witness, *i.e.* if his or her evidence may lawfully be admitted by the court, then that person may be lawfully *compelled* by the court to give evidence or to suffer the penalty for contempt of court. This means that he or she will be required to answer any questions put in court, unless some objection is taken by a party that the question cannot be answered on the ground that it would infringe the rules of evidence such as the hearsay rule, or the rule prohibiting opinion evidence, or the rules on character evidence.

Privileged communications

The witness can also object to answering a question if able to claim a "privilege". There are privileges connected with self-incrimination (see page 75), professional legal communications, and "without prejudice" negotiations.

Professional legal privilege extends to all communications passing between a client and his or her legal adviser in the course of seeking or giving legal advice. Also covered are communications between a party or his or her legal adviser and a third party which are made for the purpose of pending litigation. In addition, all good faith offers of compromise between parties are privileged where litigation is pending or contemplated. Until recently a husband or wife could also refuse to disclose any communication made to his or her spouse during the marriage, but this privilege ceased to have effect when article 79(8) of the PACE Order 1989 came into force.

One issue which the Northern Irish courts have not yet had to face is whether communications between priests and penitents are privileged. The courts in England do not seem to recognise such a privilege but the Supreme Court in the Irish Republic has held that communications made in confidence to a parish priest by his parishioners are privileged.

Communications between doctors and their patients and between journalists and their informants are not privileged. Section 10 of the Contempt of Court Act 1981, however, states that no court may require a person to disclose the source of information contained in a publication for which he or she is responsible unless that disclosure is necessary in the interests of justice, or national security, or for the prevention of disorder or crime.

Evidence through TV links

Article 81 of the PACE Order allows three categories of person, with the court's permission, to give live evidence through television links in the Crown Court. The three categories are witnesses outside Northern Ireland, witnesses aged less than 14, and witnesses who will not give evidence in open court through fear. The second category is restricted to cases involving certain offences of a sexual nature, cruelty and offences of assault or causing or threatening injury. The comparable English provision (section 32 of the Criminal Justice Act 1988) does not cover persons in the third category.

Children as witnesses

Since the general rule is that no testimony can be admitted as evidence unless it is given under oath, no child may give sworn testimony unless he or she appreciates the solemnity of taking an oath and understands that taking an oath involves an obligation to tell the truth over and above the ordinary duty of doing so. However, by section 57 of the Children and Young Persons Act (NI) 1968, the court may accept the written testimony of a child "of tender years" provided the child is possessed of sufficient intelligence and understands the duty of speaking the truth. In practice, children under 14 are normally questioned by the judge about their understanding of telling the truth.

Accused persons and their spouses as witnesses

Accused persons have been competent to give evidence on their own behalf in Northern Ireland only since 1923, but an accused person is not a competent witness for the prosecution in any criminal case. If the Crown wishes to rely on the evidence of an accused person who is prepared to give evidence against a co-accused, it has four options available to it. Firstly, it can file a *nolle prosequi* with reference to his or her case, *i.e.* discontinue the prosecution. Secondly, it can state that no evidence will appear against the accused, in which case an acquittal will follow. Thirdly, it can obtain an order for separate trials and, fourthly, it can get the accused to plead guilty, in which case it is desirable that he or she be sentenced before being called on behalf of the prosecution.

Article 79 of the PACE Order has changed the law by making each spouse competent to give evidence against the other in all cases. The spouse can testify on behalf of a co-accused spouse where the offence charged involves an assault on the spouse or on a person under 17.

Informers as witnesses

Informers are perfectly competent to give evidence against accused persons, but there is a rule that an accomplice (*i e.* an actual participant in the crime that the accused is alleged to have committed) must not be called on behalf of the prosecution unless the accomplice has already been prosecuted or it is made clear that a current prosecution will be discontinued. Without this rule a person against whom proceedings were pending would have every inducement to make his or her story sound as convincing as possible when giving evidence against co-participants. In fact, of course, even when an accomplice has been prosecuted, there may still be a considerable inducement to make his or her story sound convincing, such as when he or she has made a deal with the authorities ensuring an early release from prison, police protection on release or a financial reward. The trial judge has a discretion, which is rarely exercised, to exclude the evidence of an accomplice who is operating under "powerful inducements".

In recent years a number of terrorist trials in Northern Ireland have proceeded on the basis of accomplice evidence. The accomplices involved have been called "supergrasses" in view of the large number of defendants implicated on their evidence. These trials caused a number of concerns, notably that many of the supergrasses were granted complete or partial immunity from prosecution or were given promises of having to serve only short sentences, and that their testimony was in a number of cases uncorroborated. There is no rule of law that the testimony of suspects needs to be corroborated in this manner, and a number of defendants were convicted on the uncorroborated evidence of supergrasses. But these convictions were almost all overturned on appeal and there have been no major supergrass trials since 1983.

The accused's right of silence at the trial

Article 4 of the Criminal Evidence (NI) Order 1988 provides that, if at the trial of the accused the court considers that there is a case for him or her to answer, the court shall call on him or her to give evidence and if he or she refuses without good cause to answer any question, the court or jury may draw such inferences from the refusal as appear proper. Such evidence may also be treated as corroboration of any evidence given against the accused. The effect of this is to make it less attractive for accused persons to exercise their right of silence at the trial and to limit the right of an accused person to force the prosecution to prove the offence charged.

The courts have drawn adverse inferences against accused persons who have not testified in a number of cases. In *R. v Murray* (1992) the

House of Lords upheld the view of the Court of Appeal that the 1988 Order changed the common law regarding the comments and inferences which could be drawn from an accused's silence at trial. The House of Lords held that once the prosecution has made out a *prima facie* case and the defendant refuses to testify, a judge or jury may draw such inferences from his or her silence as are dictated by common sense and may in a proper case draw the inference that he or she is guilty of the offence charged.

Article 78 of the PACE Order 1989 abolished the right of an accused person to make a statement from the dock without swearing an oath. The advantage to an accused of making an unsworn statement was that it permitted him or her to put a defence to the jury without having to submit to questions in cross-examination. The disadvantage was that the judge and jury were unlikely to be impressed by a defendant who did not submit to questioning.

The privilege against self-incrimination

One important occasion when a witness who is compelled to give evidence may refuse to answer a question is when there is, in the opinion of the court, a danger that the answer would expose the witness to prosecution for a crime. This privilege, known as the privilege against self-incrimination, extends to answers which would incriminate the witness's spouse. No adverse inference should be drawn by the judge or jury from the fact that the privilege is claimed.

A significant restriction on the privilege is contained in section 1(e) of the Criminal Evidence Act (NI) 1923, which provides that any accused person who elects to give evidence may be asked any question in cross-examination notwithstanding that it could tend to make him or her appear guilty of the offence charged. Section 1(f)(ii) and (iii), however, prevent the defendant being asked about his or her previous misdeeds if the intention is to damage his or her credibility, unless the defendant gives evidence of his or her good character, or casts imputations on the prosecutor or witnesses for the prosecution, or gives evidence against any other person charged in the same proceedings.

Chapter 6

Complaints Against the Police

Brice Dickson and Robert Millar

The law on the handling of complaints against members of the Royal Ulster Constabulary was changed quite significantly by the Police (NI) Order 1987, the RUC (Complaints) Regulations 1988 and the RUC (Discipline and Disciplinary Appeals) Regulations 1988. The 1987 Order created a new monitoring body called the Independent Commission for Police Complaints (referred to here as the ICPC or as the Commission). This replaced the Police Complaints Board, which operated between 1977 and 1988. Other relevant legal provisions are contained in the Police Act (NI) 1970 and in the Police and Criminal Evidence (NI) Order 1989.

The complaints system deals only with the alleged misconduct of individual members of the RUC and applies if, for instance, a person has been assaulted, treated uncivilly or placed under arrest without good reason. The system differs if the complaint is against an officer above the rank of chief superintendent or if the grievance is of a more general nature (see pages 86-89). It should be noted that the Home Office has proposed radical changes to the system for dealing with complaints against the police in England and Wales and that these are likely to be adopted in Northern Ireland too within the next two or three years.

How to make a complaint

As a guide to the operation of the complaints system, the ICPC has issued a leaflet entitled "Complaints Against the Police", copies of which are available from the Commission itself, police stations, public libraries and Citizens' Advice Bureaux. A complaint may be lodged in any of the following ways:

- writing to the Chief Constable at RUC Headquarters, Brooklyn, Knock Road, Belfast BT5 6LE;
- calling at any police station;
- writing to or calling at the ICPC at 22 Great Victoria Street, Belfast BT2 7LP (tel: 244821);
- going to a local advice centre or to a solicitor, from where the complaint can be forwarded to the Chief Constable or to the ICPC; depending on the complainant's means, legal aid may be available to help pay for advice from a solicitor;
- asking a friend to do any of the above on the complainant's behalf.

Complaints cannot be officially lodged with bodies such as the General Consumer Council, a local district council, or the Ombudsman. It is important when making a complaint not to exaggerate, to be sure of all the facts and, if possible, to have at least one reliable witness. A complaint is unlikely to succeed if the only evidence is the complainant's word against that of a police officer. The complainant should always keep a copy of any letter he or she has written setting out the details of the complaint.

In practice, complaints about incidents which occurred more than 12 months prior to the lodging of the complaint will not be investigated unless there is a good reason for doing so.

What happens to a complaint

As soon as the Chief Constable receives a complaint, he (or his deputy) must take steps to preserve evidence relating to the conduct complained of. If the complaint relates to a senior officer he must refer the matter to the Police Authority and explain this to the complainant (see page 86). If the complaint relates to any other officer the Chief Constable must record it and decide whether it is suitable for informal resolution. He may appoint another member of the RUC to help him make this decision.

The sorts of cases which are appropriate for informal resolution are those where a preliminary investigation shows that the conduct complained of was lawful and reasonable and simply requires explanation. But the legislation makes it clear that a complaint is not suitable for informal resolution unless the complainant gives his or her consent and the Chief Constable is satisfied that the conduct complained of, even if proved, would not justify a criminal or disciplinary charge.

If the complaint is suitable for informal resolution the Chief Constable must try to resolve it informally and again may appoint another police officer to do this on his behalf. In practice this means that a meeting will take place between this supervisory police officer (of at least the rank of inspector) and the complainant, at which an attempt will be made to resolve the matter to each side's satisfaction. If the complaint is not suitable for informal resolution or if informal resolution of the complaint is unsuccessful the Chief Constable must appoint a police officer to investigate it formally and must refer the complaint within 48 hours to the ICPC. As soon as it appears that a police officer may have committed a disciplinary or criminal offence, the Chief Constable may suspend him or her from duty until the matter has been fully dealt with.

Who investigates complaints?

The power to investigate complaints is given only to the police themselves. The investigating officer (the IO) will usually be from the RUC's Complaints and Discipline Branch, which currently employs about 70 officers. He or she will be of at least the rank of inspector and will normally be two ranks above that of the police officer who is being investigated. The Chief Constable, the Deputy Chief Constable, and any member serving in the same sub-division or branch as the officer being investigated cannot be appointed as the IO. If he wants to, the Chief Constable may appoint an IO from another police force in the United Kingdom, but this discretion is rarely exercised.

The IO will contact the complainant (usually within one week of the complaint being made) and ask to interview him or her. If the complainant feels unhappy about going to a police station, he or she should ask that the interview take place, preferably in the presence of a witness, at his or her own home or somewhere else, such as a local advice centre or a solicitor's office. The police will usually agree to any reasonable arrangement which is suggested. When a complainant makes a statement to the IO, he or she should ensure that the final version sets out accurately what was said and should request a copy. If the complainant is not satisfied with the statement, he or she should ask for it to be changed before signing it .

If there are witnesses who saw the incident being complained about, their names and addresses should be given to the IO so that they too can be interviewed. These witnesses should again make sure that they get a copy of any statement they make to the police.

If a complainant refuses to co-operate with the investigation of his or her complaint, the Chief Constable may ask the ICPC to dispense with the need to take any further action. Should this happen the complainant will receive a letter from the Commission informing him or her of the fact. If the complainant feels that he or she *has* co-operated or that there has been a misunderstanding, contact should be made with the Commission immediately. Some complainants are reluctant to co-operate with investigations because they fear that the statements they make may later be used against them by the police in related civil or criminal proceedings. But in a recent case in England the judge held that the complainant's statement should not be used by the police in this way (*Ex parte Wiley*, 1992). However, as a general rule complainants have no right of access to other statements or documents collected during the course of the investigation into their complaint. They have this right only if they can show that access to the written information is "necessary for disposing fairly" of their civil claim for damages (*Lanigan, McCotter and Tumelty* v *Chief Constable of the RUC*, 1991)

The Commission for Police Complaints

The main function of the Commission is to supervise the investigation of complaints. It does not itself do the investigating. The Commission presently consists of a chairperson, two deputy chairpersons and five other members, all appointed by the Secretary of State. They serve for up to three years at a time, all but one on a part-time basis. As they must not be current or former members of any police force in Britain or Ireland, they are meant to serve as independent monitors of the way in which complaints against the police are handled.

There are some investigations which the Commission *must* supervise; all others it *may* supervise if it wishes to. Those which it must supervise are complaints alleging that the conduct of a police officer resulted in death or serious injury (*i.e.* a fracture, damage to an internal organ, impairment of bodily function, a deep cut or a deep laceration).

Where an investigation is to be supervised by the Commission, the person appointed to conduct the investigation must be approved by the Commission. The Commission can then impose requirements as to how the investigation is to be conducted. For instance, it can insist that the investigation be provided with additional staff and resources, that particular persons be interviewed or that certain forensic evidence be sought. The supervising Commission member does not, however, become directly involved in the process of investigation itself. He or she does not usually attend interviews with the accused police officer or witnesses.

Once the supervised investigation is complete, the investigating officer must submit a report to the ICPC and send a copy to the Chief Constable. The ICPC then considers the report and submits to the Chief Constable a statement as to whether the investigation has or has not been conducted to the Commission's satisfaction. The Commission should send copies of this statement to both the complainant and the police officer whose conduct has been investigated.

As a general rule no disciplinary or criminal charges can be brought against a police officer who is the subject of a supervised investigation until the ICPC has issued a statement on the investigator's report. The only exception to this is where the Director of Public Prosecutions (the DPP) thinks that there are exceptional circumstances which make it undesirable to wait before bringing criminal charges against the officer concerned. If an investigation of a complaint is not supervised by the ICPC, the IO will send his or her report directly to the Chief Constable.

Criminal charges

When the Chief Constable receives a report (whether or not the investigation has been supervised) he must decide whether it indicates that a criminal offence may have been committed by a police officer; if it does, the Chief Constable must send a copy of the investigator's report to the DPP, who will then decide whether to prosecute the officer in the criminal courts.

If the officer is charged

If the DPP decides to prosecute, the disciplinary aspects of the case will be delayed until the criminal proceedings are completed. The trial will be conducted in the same way as other cases. If it is a summary (*i.e.* fairly minor) offence it will be dealt with entirely at a magistrates' court, with a right of appeal to a county court (and if necessary to the Court of Appeal). If the offence is an indictable one (*i.e.* a major offence), it will be dealt with initially at a magistrates' court, but the magistrate will simply decide, in so-called "committal proceedings", whether there is a *prima facie* case against the police officer. If there is, the officer will be committed for trial at the Crown Court. In cases related to "terrorist" incidents, this trial may be before a judge sitting without a jury (a "Diplock" court). There is no right of appeal against a magistrate's decision in committal proceedings, but after the Crown Court trial the accused has a right of appeal to the Court of Appeal.

In criminal proceedings the person who lodged the complaint against the accused police officer may well be called as a prosecution witness, but otherwise he or she will probably not be involved in the trial.

If the officer is not charged

If the report of the investigator is not sent to the DPP, or if the DPP directs that no prosecution should take place, there is little that the complainant can do to initiate criminal proceedings. He or she can send letters and evidence to the DPP with a request that further consideration be given to the laying of criminal charges, but because the DPP is under no legal obligation to give reasons for his decisions - and in practice rarely if ever does so - it is virtually impossible to mount a legal challenge against them, even by way of judicial review. The complainant would need to be able to show that there was very convincing evidence of a criminal offence having been committed before a judge would be prepared to overrule the DPP's exercise of discretion. The complainant can also contemplate bringing a private prosecution, but this will be expensive (no legal aid being available) and the DPP still has the power to take over private prosecutions and then to terminate them (*Ex parte South Coast Shipping Co. Ltd,* 1992).

If criminal charges are not laid against the police officer, or are laid and then withdrawn, the Chief Constable must consider whether to bring disciplinary charges against the officer under the RUC's Discipline Code. This Code is set out as Schedule 1 of the RUC (Discipline and Disciplinary Appeals) Regulations 1988.

Until quite recently, the practice, in accordance with the Home Secretary's Guidance to Chief Constables, had been to apply the so-called "rule against double jeopardy" to cases which the DPP had decided not to prosecute. According to this rule, if a person has been tried in a court of law and acquitted, he or she must not be tried at a later date for the same offence. The Home Secretary was of the opinion that this meant that even though a police officer had not been placed on trial, he or she could not be charged with a disciplinary offence which was in substance the same as the criminal offence which the DPP had decided not to prosecute!

The legality of this practice was successfully challenged in England in *Ex parte Madden and Rhone* (1982) and it is now clear that in deciding whether to press disciplinary charges the Chief Constable must consider afresh the merits of each case. In doing so he will still take the views of the DPP into account, especially if the Director has decided that there is insufficient evidence to warrant a criminal prosecution, as this may suggest that the evidence would also be insufficient for disciplinary proceedings. On the other hand, there may be cases where the alleged misconduct is fairly trivial when viewed as a criminal offence but is much more serious when viewed as an offence against police discipline.

Disciplinary charges

The RUC's Discipline Code lists and describes 18 disciplinary offences with which a police officer may be charged. The names of the offences are:

- discreditable conduct (*e.g.* acting in a disorderly manner)
- misconduct towards another police officer
- disobedience to orders
- neglect of duty
- wilful or careless falsehood
- improper disclosure of information
- corrupt practice (*e.g.* accepting a bribe)
- improper practice (*e.g.* writing a job reference for someone without the Chief Constable's consent)

- abuse of authority (*e.g.* using unnecessary violence)
- discriminatory behaviour
- neglect of own health
- improper dress or untidiness
- damage to police property
- drunkenness or drug taking (if it renders the officer unfit for duty)
- drinking on duty or soliciting drink
- entering licensed premises while on duty
- criminal conduct (if an officer has been found guilty by a court of law)
- being an accessory to a disciplinary offence.

If the officer is charged

In accordance with the principle against double jeopardy, described above, a police officer will not be charged with a disciplinary offence which is in substance the same as a criminal offence for which the officer has already been tried in the courts. This means, for instance, that if the DPP decides that the complaint amounts to an allegation of assault and he or she prosecutes for the crime of assault, then whatever the outcome of the court case the officer cannot subsequently be charged with the disciplinary offence of "abuse of authority by using unnecessary violence", since this is in substance the same as the criminal offence of assault. An officer who has been convicted of any criminal offence may, however, be charged with the disciplinary offence of "criminal conduct".

In complaint cases (unless the accused officer has already admitted guilt) the Chief Constable must send to the ICPC a memorandum indicating whether he is preferring disciplinary charges, and if so which ones. After receiving the memorandum, the Commission must itself decide whether the investigator's report indicates that a criminal offence may have been committed and whether an officer ought to be charged with that offence. If it decides that an officer should be so charged it must tell the Chief Constable to send the investigator's report to the DPP, together with a copy of the original complaint. But the ICPC cannot itself direct that criminal charges should be laid against a police officer. If the ICPC disagrees with the Chief Constable's decision not to prefer disciplinary charges, it may recommend that charges should be brought, and which ones. If the Chief Constable is still unwilling to act against an officer, the Commission *can* direct that disciplinary charges be brought.

The disciplinary hearing

The procedures for dealing with disciplinary offences are laid down in the 1988 Discipline Regulations. They apply in all disciplinary cases, not just those where breaches of discipline allegedly arise out of complaints from members of the public. The disciplinary charges will be formulated by the Chief Constable and all relevant documents must be supplied to the police officer. The House of Lords recently decided that officers under investigation cannot sue the Chief Constable for negligence if the investigation has not been properly conducted (*Calveley v Chief Constable of Merseyside,* 1989).

At the disciplinary hearing the officer can be represented by another police officer or, in specified cases, by a solicitor or barrister. The specified cases are those where the officer who has formulated the charges against the accused is of the opinion that the charges, if proved, could lead to the accused being dismissed from the force, required to resign or demoted. The hearing will usually be conducted either by an internal disciplinary board (consisting of two members of a rank not lower than assistant chief constable) or by a single officer of the RUC appointed by the Chief Constable. Some cases, such as those connected with the Stalker-Sampson inquiry of 1986-87, may be remitted instead for consideration by the Chief Constable of a police force in Great Britain. If the case is one where the ICPC has directed the bringing of disciplinary charges, or which the Commission sees as exceptional, it will be heard by a disciplinary tribunal consisting (usually) of the RUC Chief Constable as chairperson and two members of the ICPC.

Disciplinary hearings are held in private and a word-for-word record of what is said is kept. A complainant can attend and can be accompanied, if the officer-in-charge considers it appropriate, by a friend or relative who is not to be called as a witness. But, unlike in criminal trials, if the complainant is to be called as a witness, he or she cannot attend at any time before being called, and the officer-in-charge may always tell the complainant and his or her companion to withdraw if sensitive information might be about to be disclosed. The complainant is also allowed to put relevant questions to the accused officer and powers exist to compel the attendance of witnesses.

All disciplinary charges must be proved beyond reasonable doubt (the same standard of proof as in a criminal trial). It is the officer in charge of the hearing who decides what punishment to impose, though in a disciplinary tribunal the views of the two members of the ICPC must be taken into account. If the hearing has been chaired by a Chief Constable from a force in Great Britain, the power to punish still lies with the RUC Chief Constable. The punishments available are dismissal, a requirement to resign, reduction in rank, reduction in salary (for up to 12 months), a fine, reprimand and a caution.

Disciplinary appeals

An officer can appeal to the Chief Constable within 14 days of being notified of the punishment imposed by a disciplinary board. There is a further right of appeal to the Secretary of State, who, unless he is satisfied that there are sufficient grounds for allowing the appeal without an inquiry, may appoint three persons to hold an inquiry and report to him. An inquiry must be held if an officer who has been punished by dismissal, a requirement to resign or demotion, so requests. The persons appointed to conduct an inquiry will be (a) a barrister or solicitor (to act as chairperson), (b) a serving or retired inspector of constabulary or a retired chief officer, and (c) a retired RUC officer of a rank similar to that of the accused officer.

In most cases the appeal tribunal will hold a hearing to take evidence. The complainant (if the case involves a complaint) will be given at least 28 days' notice of the hearing and the rules governing participation in the proceedings are essentially the same as those outlined above in connection with disciplinary hearings, though any evidence given will be taken on oath. The appeal tribunal reports to the Secretary of State, who may allow the appeal, dismiss it, or substitute a less severe punishment. This decision is final, unless, for instance, the accused officer can prove a breach of natural justice, in which case he or she could bring an application for judicial review in the High Court (see chapter 2).

If the officer is not charged

Even if the Chief Constable accepts that a complaint has been substantiated by the IO's report, and that there is sufficient evidence to support disciplinary proceedings, he may decide it is inappropriate to press disciplinary charges, and the ICPC may confirm this. In cases such as these the complainant will receive a letter from the ICPC offering an explanation. If the letter states that the complaint has not been substantiated, this may be because the complainant's account of the incident has not been accepted or because the evidence available to support the complaint is felt to be insufficient to meet the standard of proof.

If the ICPC's letter indicates that the complainant's account of the incident has been substantiated but that no officer has been charged with a disciplinary offence, this may be because it proved impossible to identify the officer involved or because the offence was very minor. The letter may convey the Deputy Chief Constable's apologies or indicate that, although no formal disciplinary action has been taken, the officer concerned will be spoken to by his or her divisional commander; this is known as "action short of the Code". If the case is covered by the rule against double jeopardy (see page 82), this will be mentioned.

If the complainant is not satisfied with the explanation offered as to why no disciplinary charges have been laid against the officer concerned, he or she should contact the ICPC, who may then offer to send a member of staff to the complainant's home to help clarify why the complaint has not resulted in disciplinary action.

Complaints against senior officers

If a complaint is made against one of the 14 officers in the RUC above the rank of chief superintendent it should still be lodged in one of the ways mentioned on page 77. But the procedures to be followed thereafter differ from those already outlined for junior officers. It remains the duty of the Chief Constable to obtain and preserve evidence relating to the conduct complained of, but he sends particulars of the complaint to the Police Authority, the body given the general duty by the Police Act (NI) 1970 to maintain an adequate and efficient police force in Northern Ireland. It consists of a chairperson, a vice-chairperson and between 14 and 20 other persons, all appointed by the Secretary of State. As well as its particular role in relation to complaints against senior officers, the Authority has a statutory duty to keep itself informed (which it does through its Complaints and Public Relations Committee) as to the manner in which complaints from members of the public are dealt with by the Chief Constable.

Once the Police Authority has received a complaint against a senior officer it must record it. If it is satisfied that the conduct complained of, even if proved, would not justify a criminal or disciplinary charge, the Authority may deal with the complaint according to its discretion. In any other case it must appoint another member of the RUC or of another United Kingdom police force to investigate the complaint. The Investigating Officer cannot be the Chief Constable or any police officer serving in the same sub-division or branch as the senior officer under investigation. The Authority must also refer the complaint to the Independent Commission, which has the same duties and powers concerning supervision of investigations as it has in relation to complaints against junior officers.

The IO submits his or her report to the Police Authority and (if it has been a supervised investigation) to the Commission. The Commission (if involved) must in turn submit a statement to the Authority indicating whether it is satisfied with the conduct of the investigation. The Authority must then send a copy of the investigator's report to the DPP unless it is satisfied that no criminal offence has been committed. When the question of criminal proceedings is out of the way the Authority will consider whether disciplinary proceedings need to be taken. The senior officer may be suspended from duty as soon as it appears to the Chief Constable that a criminal or disciplinary offence may have been committed.

If the senior officer admits a disciplinary offence, the Police Authority may impose a punishment immediately. Otherwise the Authority will instruct a solicitor to draw up the particulars of the alleged offence. The charge will be heard by a tribunal consisting of a single person appointed by the Police Authority with the approval of the Secretary of State. To assist the tribunal the Authority must also appoint one or more assessors, approved by the tribunal, who must not be the Chief Constable, a civil servant, an inspector of constabulary or someone working for the Police Authority. After the hearing, the tribunal submits both to the Police Authority and to the accused a report with its findings and any recommendations for punishment. It is the Authority which finally decides what action to take. The punishments available are dismissal, requirement to resign or reprimand. As in the case of junior officers, a senior officer can appeal to the Secretary of State, who may appoint one or more persons to hold an inquiry and to report to him.

We are not aware of any complaint ever having been made against a senior officer in the RUC, so the system just described has not so far been activated.

General complaints against the RUC

It must be noted that the criminal and disciplinary procedures outlined in this chapter, whether for junior or senior officers, are applicable not just in cases arising out of complaints lodged by members of the public. They also apply (with the exception of the involvement of the ICPC) where suspicion of the commission of offences derives from other sources, *e.g.* from reports submitted by fellow police officers, media allegations or information submitted by politicians. In such cases investigations and hearings may be conducted even though there is no specific complainant involved. Nevertheless, the ICPC may still have a role to play.

For a start, the Commission *must* supervise the investigation of any matter which, in the opinion of the Secretary of State or Police Authority, indicates that a police officer may have committed a criminal or discipli-nary offence and which ought in the public interest to be investigated under the Commission's supervision. The Commission *may* also supervise the investigation of a matter indicating the commission of an offence which has been referred to it by the Chief Constable or the Police Authority and which, in the opinion of all three bodies, should in the public interest be subjected to a supervised investigation. All of these supervised investiga-tions will proceed in the manner already indicated in relation to com-plaints. Only in the past couple of years have matters been referred to the ICPC under the latter headings mentioned in this paragraph. These have been cases involving death or injury caused by the use of police firearms and have been referred to the ICPC by the Chief Constable. As far as we are aware, no matter has yet been referred by the Secretary of State or Police Authority.

The ICPC must make a report every year, and a more general one every three years, to the Secretary of State. It must also, at his request, report on such matters relating generally to its functions as he may specify. In addition, the Commission may issue a report to the Secretary of State on any matters coming to its notice to which it considers that his attention should be drawn because of their gravity or other exceptional circumstan-ces. Copies of such a report must be sent to the Police Authority and to the Chief Constable. As yet, however, no reports other than annual and triennial reports have been deemed necessary. As part of its 1988-91 Triennial Review Report the ICPC did make nine recommendations for improving the complaints system, but the government has accepted only six of these. In particular the government has refused to give the ICPC a power to supervise in the public interest any matter considered by the ICPC to be of a grave or exceptional nature.

Compensation

Even if a complainant succeeds in having his or her complaint upheld as a result of an investigation, this does not mean that he or she is entitled to any compenstion for losses or injuries sustained. If the police officer concerned is found guilty of a disciplinary charge or a criminal offence, as a general rule the complainant will obtain compensation only if he or she brings separate proceedings in a county court or the High Court. In such court actions the complainant need only prove his or her case on a balance of probabilities, not beyond all reasonable doubt. However in practice it can be difficult to persuade a judge that one has been mistreated by the police. Although several people have succeeded in obtaining compensation for police misconduct (it is the Police Authority which pays the money), usualy the claims are settled out of court. Compensation for false imprisonment or assault will often be relatively high.

Statistics

Compared with its counterpart in England and Wales (the Police Complaints Authority), the ICPC is kept busy. The number of cases referred to the ICPC in 1992 for possible supervision was 2,548; the number referred to the PCA was 4,476. The ICPC undertook supervision in 396 cases while the PCA did the same in 757. As regards the outcome of cases, in Northern Ireland just 39 formal disciplinary charges were laid against police officers in 1992, a ratio of one charge for every 65 cases referred; in England and Wales 252 formal disciplinary charges were laid, a ratio of one charge for every 18 cases referred . In a further 49 cases 62 "informal disciplinary actions" were taken in Northern Ireland; the figure for England and Wales was 899 such actions. In Northern Ireland the DPP directed just 8 criminal charges, one for every 319 cases referred; in England and Wales, where 100 criminal charges were directed in 1992, the ratio was 1:45. On these figures the substantiation rate for complaints in Northern Ireland was therefore 4.3%; in England and Wales it was 27.9%.

Of all the cases considered by the ICPC during 1989-92, 16.9% (1,554 out of 9,145) resulted from complaints made by people arrested under the Emergency Provisions Act or Prevention of Terrorism Act. Of the allegations made in these complaints (a total of 1,991), 1,126 (56.5%) were of assault during an interview with the police. A further 106 (5.3%) alleged assault prior to arrival at the police station. It is a fact difficult to believe, but nonetheless true, that the ICPC has not been able to substantiate a single one of these allegations; the reason repeatedly given, apart from the complainant's refusal to co-operate with the investigation, is "insufficient evidence."

Chapter 7

Prisoners' Rights

Stephen Livingstone

Northern Ireland currently has five prison establishments. These are at Belfast (Crumlin Road), Maze, Maghaberry, Magilligan and Hydebank Young Offenders' Centre. On 31st March 1992, the last time for which official figures are available, there were 1,758 men and 38 women in these prisons. Of these:

- 349 were on remand,
- 213 were young offenders,
- most of the remand prisoners were held at Belfast prison,
- all women prisoners were held at Maghaberry,
- over 50% of the convicted prisoners were serving long term sentences - four years or more,
- 337 prisoners were serving life sentences or sentences of detention at the Secretary of State's pleasure, which amounts to over 24% of the convicted population; the equivalent figure for jails in England and Wales is just 6%.

Prisons in Northern Ireland are under the authority of the Secretary of State, who appoints the governors, medical officers and all other officers. These officers must report to the Secretary of State, who in turn makes an annual report to Parliament on the working of the prison service.

For each prison the Secretary of State must also appoint a Board of Visitors from members of the public. These Boards have three functions:
- to inspect the prison regularly and make an annual report to the Secretary of State;
- to hear prisoners' complaints;
- to adjudicate upon the most serious disciplinary charges.

Legal rights of prisoners

In 1982, in the House of Lords case of *Raymond v Honey*, Lord Wilberforce said:

> *"Under English law a convicted prisoner, in spite of his (sic) imprisonment, retains all civil rights which are not taken away expressly or by necessary implication."*

This was certainly a great advance on earlier pronouncements, some of which had stated that the courts would not hear the claims of "disgruntled prisoners". But it still left prison law in a state of uncertainty because in the absence of a Bill of Rights or written constitution it is not clear what "civil rights" *any* of us have. It is also unclear what rights are removed by "necessary implication".

Perhaps the first place to look for an indication of what rights and duties prisoners have is the Prison Rules (NI) 1982. These relate to a wide range of matters such as letters, visits, medical treatment, food, religion and discipline. Prisoners should be shown a copy of these rules on request (rule 16 (3)), while families can obtain a copy of them from HMSO at £2.95. The rules, however, are very vague on many points and are normally amplified by Standing Orders issued by the Northern Ireland Office. Most of these are unpublished but two can now be obtained from HMSO. These are:
- Standing Order 4 (on prisoners' privileges, including access to books, newspapers, the prison library and personal possessions) (£1.60)
- Standing Order 5 (on visits and correspondence) (£1.50)

The vagueness of the rules, and the secrecy which surrounds Standing Orders, obviously limit their usefulness as a source of prisoners' rights. Another limitation is the fact that courts have held on a number of occasions that a breach of the rules by the authorities does not of itself give a prisoner a right to sue. Small wonder that advocates of prisoners' rights have consistently criticised this position and called for a legally enforceable code of rights.

Courts have nevertheless held that they will look at the Prison Rules when deciding whether a right asserted by a prisoner, such as to a fair hearing in a disciplinary procedure, or to privacy as regards correspondence, has been breached. Therefore a prisoner who feels that the authorities have done something that they have no right to do, or have prevented the prisoner from doing something that he or she has a right to do, might look at the Prison Rules when framing a legal claim. That claim might take one of a number of forms, *e.g.*:

- that the rules have nothing to say on the issue, *e.g.* where a prisoner is injured by another prisoner and claims compensation from the prison authorities;
- that the rules do cover the issue but are being interpreted wrongly, *e.g.* where the authorities claim that the rule entitling a prisoner to a fair disciplinary hearing does not entitle him or her to call a witness;
- that the rules are themselves invalid because they contravene the Prison Act (NI) 1953 or the European Convention on Human Rights, *e.g.* where the authorities claim that they can intercept all correspondence with lawyers.

Asserting prisoners' legal rights is not therefore a simple business, as it may require reference to private law, public law or European law. In addition, nearly all cases will involve claims by the authorities that the right asserted must be denied on security grounds. Prisoners who feel that their rights have been infringed are thus well advised to seek legal advice, a topic discussed later in this chapter.

Rights automatically lost on conviction

Things have changed from the days when conviction for a felony automatically led to a prisoner forfeiting all his or her property. By section 9(1) of the Criminal Justice Act (NI) 1953, legal restrictions on the property of convicted prisoners were abolished. Currently the most important rights lost by convicted prisoners are public rights:

- they are disqualified from voting in Westminster elections during the period of their imprisonment;
- they are disqualified from becoming members of the House of Commons if they are serving a sentence of a year or more in prison; this does not of course apply to prisoners on remand, who remain entitled to vote or stand for election at all times;
- there appear to be no express disqualifications from either voting or standing at local elections, but electoral law relating to proxy and postal voting disables prisoners from casting votes they may be entitled to;
- any person sentenced to five years or more or to detention at the Secretary of State's pleasure is permanently disqualified from jury service;
- any person who serves a sentence of three months or more is thereafter disqualified from jury service for 10 years.

Internal grievance procedures

For a variety of reasons a prisoner may wish to complain about prison conditions or prison authorities' actions without resorting to legal proceedings. If so, he or she may wish to use the internal complaints procedure. This is an alternative procedure: there is no requirement to pursue a grievance internally before taking legal action.

Any prisoner with a grievance can request to see the governor, a member of the Board of Visitors or an officer of the Secretary of State. This request must be noted and reported to the governor as soon as possible (rule 41). The governor must see prisoners who have made such requests at a convenient hour every day, except at the weekends and on public holidays. When a member of the Board of Visitors or officer of the Secretary of State visits the prison, they must be told of any requests to see them and Board members must see any prisoner who has made such a request. However, there is no clear indication in rules or standing orders as to whether and how quickly a reply must be given to a prisoner's complaint.

A prisoner may also wish to write to an MP, an MEP or the United Kingdom Ombudsman (the Northern Ireland Ombudsman's jurisdiction does not include prisons). However, if the complaint relates to a particular case and especially if it alleges misconduct by a member of prison staff, the correspondence is likely to be stopped or censored by the governor unless the matter has first been raised through the appropriate channels. These are:

- for adjudications or misconduct by staff, a petition to the Secretary of State;
- for all other matters, an application to the Board or a visiting officer of the Secretary of State.

In England and Wales the Secretary of State must appoint an Inspector of Prisons to investigate conditions and report to the Secretary of State. The Inspector's remit also extends to Northern Ireland.

Security classifications

Unlike the rest of the United Kingdom, all Northern Ireland's prisons (with the exception of Hydebank Young Offenders' Centre) are classified as high security prisons but power exists for the Secretary of State to classify individual prisoners within a prison into higher and lower security classifications. As a result of recommendations by the Hennessey Committee report on the escape of 38 paramilitary prisoners from Maze prison in 1983, a further informal classification was established. This is usually known as being on the "Red Book". Such prisoners are moved within Maze prison every two to three weeks. While such classifications are not formally authorised by legislation, courts have generally been willing to uphold the authorities' discretion in this area.

Access to legal advice

The European Court of Human Rights has recognised that a prisoner's access to justice under Article 6 of the European Convention on Human Rights includes access to lawyers. A prisoner may therefore write to a legal adviser with a view to taking legal proceedings over any matter. Where this concerns an allegation of ill-treatment against a prison officer or the prison authorities, such a letter cannot be stopped on the grounds that the complaint has not been raised through normal channels. A prisoner may also write directly to the courts about a complaint and such a letter cannot be stopped.

When a prisoner has become a party to legal proceedings (*i.e.*when a writ has been issued) letters between the prisoner and the legal adviser may not be read or stopped unless the governor has reason to believe they contain material which is not relevant to the legal proceedings (rule 62(3)). The European Court of Human Rights has indicated in the 1992 case of *Campbell v UK* that reading of *any* correspondence with lawyers is a violation of the Convention, unless the authorities have good reason to believe that the correspondence threatens security or prisoner safety. This ruling is not yet reflected in the Prison Rules. Prison authorities are also required to provide reasonable facilities for lawyers to discuss pending proceedings with prisoners. A prisoner need give only 24 hours' notice that he or she wishes to discuss proceedings with a legal adviser and need only disclose that such a meeting relates to such proceedings. Standing Orders indicate that all legal visits should be in the sight but not the hearing of a prison officer and rule 62 (1) requires this where the prisoner is a party to legal proceedings. Prisoners who are party to proceedings may also be examined by a doctor of their own choice in the sight but out of the hearing of a prison officer (rule 62 (6)).

The right to correspond and to read

Prisoners have a right to correspond with:

- their close relatives
- their MP and MEP
- the Ombudsman
- the European Commission of Human Rights.

A prisoner can write to any other person or organisation but the governor may stop any letter where he or she thinks that such correspondence would constitute a genuine and serious threat to the security or good order of the prison.

A prisoner on remand has the right to send and receive as many letters as he or she wishes. Convicted prisoners may send and receive one letter after entering prison and thereafter one "statutory" letter a week. Postage on this letter will be paid for out of public funds and statutory letters cannot be withdrawn or withheld as a punishment. A prisoner can also send one extra letter a week on which the postage is paid at public expense. Subject to the discretion of the governor, a prisoner can write additional extra letters. Postage on these will normally be at the prisoner's expense but in a case of need a prisoner can apply to the governor to have these paid for out of public funds. The number of letters allowed varies from prison to prison.

All letters to and from a prisoner (except those relating to legal proceedings) can be read by the prison authorities and may be stopped if their content is found to be "objectionable" (rule 58 (4)). A guide to the meaning of "objectionable" can be found in Standing Order 5B 29. The main grounds are that the letter contains:

- material relating to an escape
- threats of violence to someone inside or outside the jail
- coded messages
- specific allegations of ill-treatment not previously raised with the governor, Board of Visitors or the Secretary of State (though complaints or comments about prison conditions should not be stopped)
- material intended for publication for payment.

Where a letter is stopped, a prisoner should be told and given an opportunity to re-write it. In some prisons in England and Scotland prisoners may purchase phonecards and make telepone calls subject to the same type of restrictions that apply to letters. This facility is not yet available in Northern Ireland but is under consideration by the Northern Ireland Office.

Books, newspapers and periodicals are all regarded as privileges. However, it is clearly arguable that denying a prisoner access to a particular document violates his or her right to receive information, as guaranteed by Article 10 of the European Convention on Human Rights, unless justified under the qualifications in Article 10(2). According to Standing Order 4, prisoners can receive newspapers or periodicals from visitors or can order them by subscription directly from a newsagent or publisher. Subscriptions must cover a period of not less than two weeks for newspapers and not less than three months for periodicals. As the entitlement to newspapers and periodicals is regarded as a privilege, Standing Order 4 indicates that they may be removed as a punishment or if the governor feels that the content of the newspaper or periodical could prejudice the security, good order or discipline of the prison, could put at risk the lives of prison staff, is wholly or mostly in a language other than English or Irish (except where the prisoner is wholly unfamiliar with

English) or in the medical officer's opinion could have an adverse affect on the prisoner from a medical or psychological point of view. A prisoner will normally be allowed to keep a "reasonable" number of books and periodicals in the cell.

A prisoner may obtain soft-backed books either from a friend or relative or directly from a newsagent or publisher, but he or she will not normally be allowed to retain more than six books in a cell in addition to a Bible, library books, a dictionary and approved texts issued by the prison education officer. Books are regarded as privileges and Standing Order 4 indicates that they may be removed on the same conditions as newspapers and periodicals.

Visits

Convicted prisoners are entitled to one statutory and three "privilege" visits per week. Remand prisoners are entitled to as many visits as they wish; in practice they are normally allowed three per week. Visits usually last for 30 minutes. Where a prisoner is sentenced to solitary confinement as a punishment, the statutory visit should still be allowed unless the governor feels that the prisoner's behaviour and attitude are such that removal from solitary confinement would be undesirable or impracticable. If this does happen the statutory visit should be postponed and a prisoner should receive all the missed statutory visits at the end of the period of solitary confinement.

Prisoners may receive visits from close relatives and any other person, subject to the Secretary of State's and governor's discretion. In *McCartney v Secretary of State for Northern Ireland* (1983), the courts upheld the Secretary of State's decision to prevent a Sinn Fein councillor from visiting a friend in prison on the basis of evidence of Sinn Fein's support for violence. A prisoner must give the name and address of each adult person whom he or she wishes to have as a visitor and must be informed if any application for a visiting permit is refused. Visits between close relatives where both are in prison will be permitted provided this does not pose a threat to the security or good order of the prison.

Up to three people will normally be allowed to visit a prisoner at each visit. Visits should take place with visitors seated at a table and will be in the sight of a prison officer, but for domestic visits they should be outside the hearing of a prison officer. Visits can be stopped if a visitor attempts to pass any unauthorised article to a prisoner and visitors cannot carry recording equipment, cameras or videos; they can make notes during a visit but these can be taken out of the prison only with the permission of the governor or of the prison officer instructed by the governor to decide upon such matters.

Clothes and food

Both remand and convicted prisoners are entitled to wear their own clothes. The governor may, however, prohibit the wearing of certain clothing if this is judged to be prejudicial to the good order or security of the prison. Limits on the amount of clothing a prisoner can possess are set by each prison, but generally prisoners are allowed up to three of each item of clothing. Clothes can be left for a prisoner as part of a parcel. Convicted prisoners are generally allowed one parcel per week while remand prisoners can receive a parcel each day (except Sunday). These parcels may also contain food, confectionery, tobacco and toiletries. Special parcels are allowed at Christmas, Easter and Hallowe'en.

Prisoners on remand can be supplied with food at their own, or friends' or relatives', expense. All prisoners should be provided with prison food which is wholesome, nutritious and well prepared (rule 66(1)). prisoners with special dietary requirements should inform the prison medical officer, who is required to inspect prison food regularly. Standing Order 14 instructs governors properly to observe the relevant provisions of food and drugs laws.

Education

Educational classes have to be established at every prison and the prison authorities are required to encourage every prisoner able to profit from educational activities to do so. The prison authorities are also required to provide facilities for private study of correspondence courses, though the Secretary of State has power to determine what books and papers may be received from outside.

Religion

Where a prisoner belongs to a denomination for which no chaplain has been appointed to that prison, the governor is required to do what is reasonable, if requested by the prisoner, to arrange for visits by a minister or priest of that denomination.

A prisoner may also be allowed an occasional visit by a family priest or minister, or by the priest or minister of the area where he or she last resided. Such visits do not require a permit and should take place either in the sight but out of the hearing of a prison officer or in the presence of a prison chaplain.

Medical treatment and hygiene

A prisoner who feels unwell should be allowed to see the prison medical officer. Where the medical officer feels a prisoner's health is endangered by imprisonment, he or she should inform the governor and Chief Medical Officer. A prisoner can refuse any medical treatment unless it is an emergency and must give written consent before any major form of treatment is begun. Time spent in hospital counts as part of a prisoner's sentence.

The Prison Rules also contain a number of provisions relating to general hygiene, *e.g.* requiring every prisoner to have a hot bath or shower once a week and placing a duty on the prison authorities to provide prisoners with toilet articles necessary for health and cleanliness. Standing Orders instruct governors to observe the provisions of the Health and Safety at Work (NI) Order 1978 with regard to washing and bathing facilities.

Prisoners are entitled to one hour's outdoor exercise a day (weather permitting; if the weather is bad the exercise can be taken indoors). prisoners segregated for punishment retain normal exercise privileges.

In law the Northern Ireland Office owes a "duty of care" to protect prisoners from injury. Therefore, if a prisoner is injured, *e.g.*while working, or as the result of an assault by another prisoner or a prison officer, he or she may be able to claim against the prison authorities.

Searches

Prisoners and their visitors can be searched by the prison authorities. Searches may be carried out at such times as the governor orders but must take place according to the directions of the Secretary of State (rule 9 (3)). The courts have ruled that there is no requirement to give reasons for a search.They can be conducted only by and in the presence of officers of the same sex as the prisoner and must be conducted in as seemly a manner as is consistent with anything being discovered. For instance, prisoners must not be stripped and searched in the sight of another prisoner. Searches should be conducted only on arrival, final departure or after the prisoner has left the prison and returned for whatever reason (such as to make a court appearance, go to hospital or visit a prisoner in another jail), though the governor has power to order a search on other occasions. Searches carried out in a way which violates these guidelines could constitute an assault.

Segregation

The governor may segregate a prisoner from other prisoners where he or she feels it is in the prisoner's own interests or where it is desirable to maintain good order and discipline in the prison. Cases have suggested that failure to segregate some prisoners, such as known sex offenders, may breach the authorities' duty of care if they have no other policy for reducing risk to the prisoner and that prisoner is subsequently assaulted. However, a governor may not segregate a prisoner for more than 24 hours without the authority of a member of the Board of Visitors or the Secretary of State (rule 25 (2)). If such authority is given, the position must be reviewed every month. Prisoners in segregation must be visited every day by the medical officer and if he or she so advises the governor must return a prisoner to association.

This type of individual segregation for security reasons is different from a policy of segregating prisoners from different religions or factions. Such a policy seems neither to be prohibited nor required by law.

Women prisoners

Because the number of women prisoners in Northern Ireland's jails is declining (down from 75 in 1977 to 44 in 1992) and makes up a small proportion of the total prison population (only about 2% of the total prison population), women prisoners here are often ignored. Such small numbers may have a detrimental effect on women prisoners' access to work and education programmes. Failure to accord equal work and education facilities to those given to men may amount to unlawful sex discrimination. Women prisoners became a focus of attention during an increase in strip-searching in Armagh prison (where all women were then kept) in 1983-4.

In general, Prison Rules and circular instructions apply equally to women as to men. There are some differences. Rule 65 (3), for instance, states that male prisoners may have their hair cut as directed, while rule 65 (4) says that in respect of female prisoners this may not be done without the prisoner's consent unless the medical officer considers it necessary on health grounds.

The most significant difference relates to pregnancy and young children. Under rule 45(1), prisoners expected to give birth before the end of their sentence should be removed from the prison to a suitable hospital for whatever period the medical officer considers necessary. A mother and baby unit exists at Maghaberry prison and prisoners may keep their babies with them in the unit until the baby is nine months old. But the courts have upheld a governor's discretion to remove a baby from the mother's custody, without giving her a hearing, where he or she considers it necessary for the welfare of the child or the good order of the prison.

Discipline

Prisoners may be subject to disciplinary punishment only for a limited and specific number of offences. These offences have a definable content and convictions on disciplinary charges may be challenged if a governor or Board of Visitors has misinterpreted the rule setting out an offence.

A prisoner should be given notice of charges as soon as possible. The governor must normally inquire into the charge laid on the next day and at that inquiry give the prisoner a fuller account of what is alleged (rules 29(5) and 30(2)). A prisoner must be given sufficient time to prepare a defence; if he or she feels that the time allowed was insufficient, an adjournment should be asked for at any subsequent hearing.

If the charge is regarded as a minor one it will be heard by a prison governor or assistant governor, who, if he or she finds the prisoner guilty, may impose a range of punishments including loss of up to 28 days' remission, loss of privileges for up to 28 days or solitary confinement for up to three days (rule 32(1)). Where the charge is regarded as more serious (in practice this normally means any assaults on prison officers or repeated offences), the governor may refer the case to the Secretary of State, who always delegates it to the Board of Visitors. The Board may impose more severe punishments, including loss of up to 180 days' remission and solitary confinement for up to 56 days (rule 33(2)).

Whether a case comes before a governor or a Board, a prisoner is entitled to a fair hearing and to put his or her own case fully (rule 30(2)). He or she should be allowed to see all the statements made in the case, to call witnesses (except where these are called only to disrupt the proceedings), and to cross-examine witnesses who have given evidence (especially where hearsay evidence has been given, or there are inconsistencies in the evidence).

A prisoner can also ask for legal representation. This is very unlikely to be granted before a governor and there is no right to legal representation before a Board. However the governor or Board must consider carefully a number of factors (in particular the seriousness of the offence, whether any difficult points of law are involved, and the prisoner's capacity to conduct his or her own defence) before deciding whether or not the prisoner should be legally represented. Court decisions have indicated that, if a governor or Board unreasonably refuses representation, this may be a reason for overturning a disciplinary conviction. If representation is granted, a prisoner will be entitled to legal advice and assistance to meet the costs.

In deciding whether a prisoner is guilty, a governor or Board must seek proof "beyond all reasonable doubt". A number of cases have come before the Northern Irish courts on the application of this standard to cases where an offence has been committed but is denied by two prisoners who share a cell. The courts appear to have ruled that the governor or Board can convict both prisoners if there is evidence of collusion, such as an organised protest campaign, but may not do so where no such evidence exists. If a governor or Board finds the standard of proof is not satisfied on a serious charge it may not substitute a conviction on a less serious one. Also, any punishment given must be clearly set out in the decision of the Board or governor; it cannot be added to by a subsequent action of the governor. In a recent case, for instance, it was held that a governor could not remove a prisoner's bedding while the prisoner was serving a disciplinary punishment in solitary confinement: removal of bedding was in effect an extra punishment which had not been awarded by the Board.

If a prisoner feels that any of the above requirements have not been met and that he or she has been denied a fair hearing, he or she may seek to have the conviction quashed, though failure to comply with a procedural requirement does not automatically ensure that a conviction *will* be quashed. Courts have generally been fairly strict about quashing decisions where there have been procedural errors by Boards of Visitors but have refused to quash decisions by governors despite procedural errors where they feel the same result would have been arrived at even if the right procedure had been followed.

There is no system of appeal against disciplinary penalties. The Secretary of State may, though, reduce any punishment, as may the governor or Board (rule 37). At the moment this power appears to be purely at the discretion of the relevant authority.

Life sentence prisoners

Given the high proportion of Northern Ireland's prisoners serving life sentences, the release procedures for such prisoners are of particular importance. Although there is provision for judges to recommend that prisoners should remain in jail for the rest of their lives, this power is very rarely used and nearly all prisoners sentenced to life are released after a number of years.

Life is the mandatory sentence for an offence of murder, and is the maximum sentence available for a range of other crimes including attempted murder, manslaughter, causing an explosion and the most serious firearms and sexual offences. Those convicted of murder who were under 18 at the date of the commission of the crime can be sentenced to detention at the Secretary of State's pleasure (and are commonly known as "SOSP" or "pleasure" prisoners).

The decision as to when to release such prisoners is that of the Secretary of State. However, to advise the Secretary on such matters the Life Sentence Review Board (LSRB) has been created. This body is composed of Northern Ireland Office officials, a senior DHSS medical officer, a psychiatrist and the Chief Probation Officer. The LSRB normally first reviews a case after 10 years, though it may consider it earlier, and decides whether to recommend that the prisoner should be released or that the case should be reviewed later (usually after a period of between one and five years). Though the grounds on which this decision is based have not been expressly stated in law, officials have frequently referred to two criteria:

• the seriousness of the offence

- the likelihood that, if released, the prisoner will commit another violent offence.

In reaching its decision the LSRB considers material such as:
- information about the prisoner's offence
- any comments by the trial judge in passing sentence
- the prisoner's age and background (including any previous offences)
- reports made by the prison staff
- relevant medical or psychiatric reports
- written submissions by the prisoner or comments made during a pre-hearing interview with a governor.

Neither the prisoner nor any representative is allowed to attend the LSRB hearing. If the Board refuses to recommend release, the prisoner will not be given any reasons but will simply be told that his or her case will be reviewed again in a specified number of years. Even if the Board does recommend release, the case must still be considered by the trial judge, if available, or by the Lord Chief Justice, who will also make recommendations to the Secretary of State. Ultimately, the decision to release is for the Secretary of State.

Prisoners released from a life sentence are released on licence and are subject to recall at any time, even if they have not committed another offence. In England the position has been changed by the 1991 Criminal Justice Act, passed in response to a number of European Court cases, and prisoners may now challenge the lawfulness of their recall. Discretionary life sentence prisoners in England also have the right to know the "tariff" set by the sentencing judge and to a hearing where they are detained beyond the expiry of that tariff. However, these provisions do not apply in Northern Ireland.

Transfer of prisoners

Where prisoners who originally come from Northern Ireland are imprisoned in Great Britain they may apply to be transfered to Northern Ireland. They have no right to transfer in domestic law and the European Commission of Human Rights has stated that only in "exceptional circumstances" will failure to transfer breach the right to privacy and family life contained in the European Human Rights Convention.

Nevertheless there does exist a power to transfer prisoners between Northern Ireland and the rest of the United Kingdom. The authorities must consider all transfer requests and have indicated that they will grant them where the prisoner is sentenced and (1) has more than 6 months of his sentence still to serve,(2) was ordinarily resident in Northern Ireland before imprisonment or has close relatives in Northern Ireland and it is reasonably believed that he has a firm intention of taking up residence on release, (3) both sentencing and receiving jurisdictions are satisfied the prisoner will not be disruptive if transfered. However even if all of these three criteria are satisfied the guidelines allow transfer to be refused if it is believed that the prisoner is only seeking transfer to get a reduction in sentence or where so serious are his crimes he is "undeserving of public sympathy and should not benefit in any reduction in time to serve. (For offences committed between 1973 and 1989 those convicted in Northern Ireland generally have more favourable remission arrangements than people convicted of similar offences in Great Britain). The "undeserving of sympathy" requirement does not apply to temporary transfers as unlike permanent transfer release arrangements for prisoners on temporary transfer are governed by the law of the sentencing jurisdiction.

Chapter 8

Immigration and Freedom of Movement

Anne Grimes and David Bonner

United Kingdom immigration laws

Immigration law is the system of rules and laws which govern who can enter and live in the United Kingdom, under what conditions and for how long. The Immigration Acts 1971 and 1988 set out the system of immigration control and provide for officials to enforce it. Section 3(2) of the 1971 Act empowers the Secretary of State to make Immigration Rules. The current rules were made March 1990 and there have been several amendments since then. In addition the Asylum and Immigration Appeals Bill is due to be enacted during 1993. As we could not be certain about the effects of the Bill at the time this book went to press we have described the law as it currently exists. The Immigration Rules set out in detail the circumstances in which "leave" (*i.e.* lawful permission) to enter or remain in the UK is to be granted or refused to persons subject to immigration control. Immigration legislation applies uniformly throughout the UK.

Immigration control

Only certain people are subject to the control of the immigration system, and to differing degrees.

No control

Certain categories of people are not subject to immigration control and can freely enter and remain in the UK. These are:

- British citizens:
  Before 1 January 1983 all people born in the UK were British citizens. Since that date, children born in the UK are British citizens only if one of their parents is "settled" in the UK (*i.e.* has permission to reside in the UK indefinitely) or if one parent was a British citizen at the time of the child's birth. People who are not British citizens by birth may be registered or naturalised as British citizens in certain circumstances.

- People with the "right of abode" in the UK:
  Certain Commonwealth citizens have the "right of abode", *i.e.* those who (a) were born before 1 January 1983 and have a parent born in the UK, or (b) are women married before 1 January 1983 to a man who was either born, registered or naturalised in the UK or who is a Commonwealth citizen with a parent born in the UK:

- Irish citizens travelling from Ireland:
  The Republic of Ireland, the UK, the Isle of Man and the Channel Islands form a Common Travel Area (CTA). No system of immigration control exists for nationals of these areas travelling within the CTA. However Irish nationals can be refused entry to the UK if the Home Secretary directs that their exclusion is conducive to the public good in the interests of national security. Non-Irish citizens are governed by the Immigration (Control of Entry through Republic of Ireland) Order 1972. This provides that certain people travelling to the UK from Ireland are automatically given leave to enter for three months with a prohibition on employment. As there are no immigration officials at the border this will not be stamped on their passports but if they wish to stay longer they must apply to the Home Office for an extension of their leave to remain. This does not apply to visa nationals or people who have previously entered or remained in the UK. People who leave the UK for Ireland whilst having limited leave

to remain in the UK and whose leave expires whilst in Ireland are automatically given leave to enter the UK for seven days upon their return.

Limited control

European Community (EC) nationals are subject to limited control; they are free to enter the UK to exercise their community law rights to freedom of movement, *i.e.* to work or seek work, to enter into business or self-employment or to provide or receive services. They can be refused entry or deported on the grounds of public policy, public security and public health. An EC national may be accompanied by his or her family no matter what their nationality.

Full control

The following categories of people are subject to full immigration control and must, therefore, obtain leave to enter or remain in the UK:
- Commonwealth citizens without the "right of abode" (see page 108)
- British nationals who are not British citizens, *i.e.* British overseas citizens, British dependent territories citizens, British protected persons, British subjects and British nationals (overseas),
- aliens, *i.e.* all other nationalities.

Immigration control before entry

Prior to travelling, nationals of certain countries listed in the Appendix to the Immigration Rules ("visa nationals"), as well as people wishing to come to the UK for certain purposes (such as to settle as a spouse), are required to obtain entry clearance (often known as an entry certificate or visa) from a British Consular post overseas. The list of visa national countries consists mostly of third world countries and is regularly amended. Visa nationals who have already been granted leave to enter or remain in the UK for more than six months, or people who have been granted indefinite leave to remain and who are returning for settlement after an absence of two years or less, need not obtain visas when returning to the UK.

Another form of immigration control imposed by the Government is contained in the Immigration (Carriers' Liability) Act 1987. This provides for airlines to be fined for each passenger they bring to the UK who does not have the correct documentation, *i.e.* a valid passport and visa. Since July 1991 the fine has been £2,000 per passenger. This means that airline staff act as unofficial immigration officials. This provision has particularly affected refugees who wish to come to the UK to seek asylum. Often they are unable to obtain passports from their own governments and checks by airline staff effectively stop many refugees from getting to the UK where they could claim asylum. When many refugees have come to the UK from a particular country, the UK has made it into a visa country. People cannot get visas as refugees as they must be outside their own country in order to claim asylum.

Immigration control at time of entry

Immigration officers at the port of entry have the power to grant or refuse leave to enter the UK. Leave to enter is endorsed on the person's passport and may be limited in time and have conditions attached to it, *e.g.* a prohibition or restriction on employment.

Immigration control after entry

After entry to the UK limited leave to enter may be extended or varied by the Secretary of State at his or her discretion. In practice, the power is exercised by staff at the Immigration and Nationality Department of the Home Office at Lunar House, 40 Wellesley Road, Croydon CR9 2BY. The Home Office has a number of regional Public Enquiry Offices, one of which is at Olivetree House, Fountain Street, Belfast. Officials there deal with some applications for extensions of stay and with enforcement of immigration control at a local level. Applicants may apply for an extension of their "leave to remain" in the UK in the same category as their leave to enter was granted. They may also apply for a change of status. It is sometimes possible to switch from one category to another and to have time limits or other conditions changed. Applications may also be made for "settlement", *i.e.* a removal of all time limits and conditions attached to the applicant's leave. Applications for variation of leave should be made to the Home Office before the expiry of existing leave, otherwise the applicant becomes an "overstayer" and can be liable to prosecution. Additionally, if his or her application is refused, there is no right of appeal.

The Home Office will grant an application for variation of leave if the applicant satisfies all of the conditions for the particular category as set out in the Immigration Rules. The Secretary of State always has an overriding discretion to grant leave to remain despite the Rules, for instance when the applicant does not satisfy all of the requirements of the Rules or where there is no provision in the Rules for the granting of leave in the applicant's circumstances. In practice, any request for the exercise of that discretion is dealt with by the Home Office.

The Immigration Rules

Full details of the conditions for entry and stay in various categories are set out in the Immigration Rules. People can come to the UK for the following main reasons: for temporary purposes, to work, to join members of their family here, to seek asylum or for other purposes.

Temporary purposes

Only those people who are "visa nationals" (see page 109) require entry clearance from abroad to enter the UK in a temporary capacity. All others must obtain leave to enter from an immigration officer upon arrival. Those entering in a temporary capacity may sometimes, but not always, switch to another category.

- Visitors: The maximum period of a visit is six months; applicants must be able to support and accommodate themselves without working or claiming "public funds" (income support, housing benefit, family credit or housing under the homelessness legislation). They must intend to leave the UK at the end of their visit.
- Students who are enrolled in full-time private education must produce evidence of financial support without working or claiming public funds (see above). They must also intend to leave the UK upon completion of their studies.
- Trainees: Persons wishing to come to the UK for training or work experience may apply to come to the UK on a temporary basis. Again there must be an intention to leave the UK at the end of the period.

Training permits are obtained from the Department of Economic Development's Training and Employment Agency, ES2 Branch, Clarendon House, 9-21 Adelaide Street, Belfast BT2 8DJ.

- *Au pairs*: Unmarried women aged between 17 and 27 from certain countries (currently EC countries, Andorra, Austria, Cyprus, Czechoslovakia, the Faeroes, Finland, Greenland, Hungary, Iceland, Liechtenstein, Malta, Monaco, Norway, San Marino, Sweden, Switzerland, Turkey or Yugoslavia) may come to live in the UK for a maximum period of two years as *au pairs*. It is proposed to extend this category to young men.

- Working holidaymakers: Commonwealth citizens aged between 17 and 27 may come to the UK for a maximum period of two years on an extended holiday. They may work if it is incidental to their holiday. They must be in a position to support and accommodate themselves without claiming public funds.

Work

Work permits are obtained by the employer from the Department of Economic Development (see above for the address). They are granted only for certain categories of skilled employment where no other suitable candidates can be found in the UK or EC. Work permits are initially granted for a period of up to four years. After four years, a work permit holder may apply for "settlement", *i.e.* permission to reside in the UK indefinitely without any time limits or restrictions.

Certain jobs however do not require a work permit, *e.g.* Ministers of religion, missionaries or representatives of overseas newspapers. But applicants must obtain entry clearance from abroad before travelling.

Business people and the self-employed need to have at least £200,000 available for investment in business here and must show that employment will be created for people already settled here. They must also obtain entry clearance before travelling.

Writers and artists who can show that they will be able to support and accommodate themselves from their art, writing or savings and will not do any other work or claim benefits may be given entry clearance before travelling.

Joining family

Family members may apply to come to the UK to "settle" here. "Settlement" or "indefinite leave to remain" in the UK means that the person is legally in the UK without any time limits or restrictions on working. People coming to settle must obtain entry clearance before travelling. Sometimes people who are here in a temporary capacity may be allowed to change to a category leading to settlement.

- Spouses and fiancé(e)s: A spouse of a British citizen or of someone settled here can obtain leave to enter or remain for an initial period of 12 months and thereafter indefinite leave to remain. Both parties to the marriage must have met, they must be lawfully married and intend to live together permanently. The couple must be able to support and accommodate themselves "without public funds" (see page 111). They must also prove that the main purpose of the marriage is not to obtain settlement in the UK. This is known as the "primary purpose" rule and is one of the most difficult conditions to satisfy. Similar rules apply in respect of fiancé(e)s who must apply for entry clearance abroad. The primary purpose rule has been eased somewhat with the announcement in June 1992 that in principle an application from a spouse to enter or remain in the UK will be allowed where it is accepted that the marriage is genuine and subsisting and either the couple have been married for at least five years or a child of the marriage has the right of abode in the UK. A child has the right of abode if his or her father or mother is either a British citizen or settled in the UK at the time of the child's birth.

- Children: Children under 18 who are unmarried (and in certain circumstances daughters under 21) will be allowed to settle in the UK if both parents have been accepted with a view to settlement in the UK or are already settled here. The rule prohibiting public funds applies. In limited circumstances children may join one parent who is settled here.

- Parents and grandparents: Those over 65 who are wholly or mainly financially dependent on a son, daughter, grandson or granddaughter who is a British citizen or settled in the UK will be granted indefinite leave to remain here. Applicants must show that they have no close relatives in their own countries to turn to. Widowed mothers and grandmothers under 65 may also be admitted in this category.

- Other relatives must apply for entry clearance abroad and show that they are wholly or mainly financially dependent on their relative in the UK, that they have no other relatives in their own country to turn to, that they are living alone in the most exceptional compassionate circumstances and that they can be supported in the UK without claiming public funds.

Seeking asylum

Political asylum is granted to those who can show that they have a well-founded fear of being persecuted for reasons of race, religion, nationality or membership of a particular social group or political opinion and that they are therefore unwilling or unable to return home.

Applications for asylum are made to the immigration officer at the port of entry or, after entry, to the Home Office if the refugee has come into the country in another capacity (such as a visitor or student). Anyone who applies for asylum is entitled to have his or her claim considered by the Home Office and to remain in the UK pending a decision. However, people who come to the UK through a "safe" third country may be refused asylum without their claim being considered.

Those who apply for asylum on entry may be detained or given temporary admission. The Home Office takes many months, often years, to make a decision. During this time the asylum seeker may claim benefits and, after six months, he or she may request permission to work, which is normally granted. If the Home Office grants asylum the refugee's spouse and children can join the refugee. After four years a refugee may apply for settlement. Sometimes refugees are not granted asylum but are allowed to remain in the UK anyway. This usually takes the form of a grant of "exceptional leave to remain" which can be renewed on a yearly basis.

The Asylum and Immigration Appeals Bill which is being debated in Parliament at the time of writing proposes to make various changes to the procedures for claiming asylum. New Immigration Rules are also proposed. The main changes are that refugees seeking asylum in the UK will be finger-printed and if a person is refused asylum then any existing temporary immigration status, *e.g.* as a visitor or student, can be curtailed and the person can be deported. Rights of appeal will be given to all of those refused asylum however strict time limits will be introduced. Those who are refused asylum on entry to the UK will have two days to lodge an appeal, in all other cases of refusal of asylum the time limit for appealing will be 10 days. If the Secretary of State considers that the claim for asylum is without foundation the appeal must be heard within five days, in all other cases it must be heard within a maximum of 42 days from the date on which the appeal is lodged. In addition it is proposed that claims for asylum may be refused where there is a delay in claiming asylum or in disclosing material facts. Another ground for refusal is where the applicant has destroyed a passport or any other document of if there is any other part of the country from which he or she is fleeing to which he or she could be returned.

Other purposes

- UK born grandparents: Commonwealth citizens who have a grandparent born in the UK can be granted leave to remain for four years, following which they can be granted settlement.
- Returning residents: A person with indefinite leave to remain in the UK will generally be allowed back for settlement if he or she returns within two years of leaving. People with limited leave to remain in the UK of at least six months will generally be allowed back into the UK subject to the same time limits and conditions after an absence abroad.
- Persons of independent means: A person with close connections with the UK may come here if he or she has capital of at least £200,000 or a guaranteed income of at least £20,000 a year. He or she must obtain entry clearance before travelling and is prohibited from claiming public funds and from doing any work or business. Settlement can be obtained after four years in this category.
- There are a number of well-established practices within the Home Office which are not written in the Immigration Rules but where, in appropriate circumstances, leave to remain is normally granted. For example, it is well-established that people who have been in the UK legally for a period of 10 years may apply for settlement, and settlement is also normally granted to those who have been here for more than 14 years, even if some of their stay has been unlawful.

Enforcement of immigration law

There are a number of ways in which immigration laws are enforced.

Removal

Someone who has been refused leave to enter at a port of entry may be removed to his or her country of origin or to the country from which he or she travelled.

Deportation

This is removal after entry due to one of the following:

- a person has overstayed leave or breached a condition of leave;
- a person's removal is deemed by the Secretary of State to be conducive to the public good; or
- a criminal court recommends deportation following conviction of a crime punishable by imprisonment.

If the Home Office intends to deport someone a two stage process is followed. Firstly, a decision to deport is issued. For those who have been in the UK for less than seven years there is a limited right of appeal following a decision to deport, but they can win an appeal only if the facts on which the Home Office based its decision to deport were not correct. People who have been here continuously for more than seven years can put forward family, compassionate and other reasons at their appeal hearing. It is possible to apply to the Chief Immigration Officer or to an adjudicator for bail pending the appeal hearing. The second stage is the issuing of a deportation order. There is no further right of appeal against a deportation order except by way of an objection to removal to the destination named on the order. If one is made, it is not normally revoked for at least three years. Until it is revoked the person subject to the order may not return to the UK. If a man is or has been ordered to be deported, his wife and any children under 18 may be deported too. If a woman is or has been ordered to be deported, her children under 18 may also be deported, but not her husband. This power is clearly discriminatory on grounds of sex but it has not yet been successfully challenged in the courts.

Illegal entry

This is entry without leave or in breach of a deportation order. The definition of illegal entry has widened in recent years; it was originally thought to mean entering the UK without seeing an immigration officer at all, but it now encompasses the situation where someone sees an immigration officer who mistakenly fails to stamp the entrant's passport where the entrant has not deceived the immigration officer at all. In addition, recent court cases have decided that a person who has leave to enter which the Home Office alleges was obtained by deception, misrepresentation or non-disclosure will be treated as an illegal entrant. Alleged illegal entrants can be removed on apprehension without any formal right of appeal.

Criminal offences

The Immigration Acts create criminal offences for breach of the laws, *e.g.* overstaying or breaking conditions of leave. Suspected offenders can be arrested by immigration officers and the police. If convicted they can be fined, imprisoned and recommended for deportation.

Challenging decisions

There are a number of ways in which to challenge immigration decisions.

Reviews

The Secretary of State has discretion to reverse a previous decision to refuse leave to enter or remain or to deport someone and may direct the grant of entry clearance or leave to enter. The discretion is generally exercised only in exceptional or compassionate circumstances, however where there is no right of appeal, for instance where an application for leave to remain is made after the previous leave expires, it is still worth asking the Home Office to reconsider the decision.

Appeals

There is a two-tier system of appeal laid down in immigration law. An initial appeal lies to an Adjudicator, with a second appeal to an Immigration Appeal Tribunal on a point of law. Leave is required before taking a case to the Tribunal. The grounds for appeal are very limited: the appellant must show that the decision was wrong in law, was not in accordance with Immigration Rules or involved an exercise of discretion which should have been exercised differently.

Further limitations to the appeal procedure are as follows.

- There is no appeal within the United Kingdom against refusal of leave to enter if the appellant did not hold entry clearance.
- There is no appeal against an allegation of illegal entry until after departure.
- There is no appeal against the refusal of further leave to remain if the application was lodged after the expiry of the person's initial leave.
- There is a very limited right of appeal against a deportation decision for people who entered the UK less than seven years ago.
- There are very strict time limits for appeal. The current time limit for lodging an appeal to the Adjudicator against a refusal to vary leave to remain is 14 days; an appeal against the refusal of entry clearance must be lodged with three months and against the refusal of leave to enter within 28 days of departure from the UK.
- There is no legal aid available for representation at appeals.
- There is no right of appeal against a decision to deport on the grounds of national security or other reasons of a political nature. The person is not told details of the allegations against him or her and can only seek review of the decision by a three-person panel which makes recommendations to the Secretary of State.
- The Asylum and Immigration Appeals Bill 1993 proposes to abolish the right of appeal against refusal of entry clearance for visitors, students on courses of less than six months and prospective students.
- The 1993 Bill proposes to abolish visitors' rights of appeal against a refusal to extend the period of the visit beyond six months.
- The 1993 Bill proposes imposing very strict time limits for lodging and hearing appeals against the refusal of an application for asylum.

Judicial review

Judicial review (see chapter 2) is available against decisions of the immigration officers, the Secretary of State or the appellate bodies if such decisions are illegal or unreasonable.

Representations to the Secretary of State

Due to the limitations of the appeal procedures and judicial review, further representations to the Secretary of State are often the only remedy available to the applicant. The Secretary of State can consider such representations under his or her general discretion to reverse previous decisions or grant leave. It is possible to enlist the help of the appropriate Member of Parliament to take up the case with the Home Office Minister when all other appeals and reviews have been exhausted.

International laws on freedom of movement

Freedom of movement is recognised by a number of international instruments dealing with human rights. Article 13 of the Universal Declaration of Human Rights (1948) states that everyone has the right to freedom of movement and residence within the borders of each state and to leave and return to any country, including his or her own. Article 12 of the United Nations' International Covenant on Civil and Political Rights (1976) provides that persons lawfully within the territory of a state shall have the right to liberty of movement within it and the freedom to choose their residence. The Covenant goes on to say (in Article 13) that no one is to be arbitrarily deprived of the right to enter his or her own country and that an alien legally within the territory of a state can be expelled from it:

"only in pursuance of a decision reached in accordance with law and shall, except where compelling reasons of national security otherwise require, be allowed to submit reasons against his or her expulsion and to have his or her case reviewed by, and be represented for the purpose before, the competent authority or a person or persons especially designated by the competent authority ".

All these rights are to be secured regardless of race, colour, national, ethnic or social origin, gender, language, religion or opinion (Article 26), but, apart from that of nationals to enter their own country, they can legally be restricted where necessary to protect national security, public order, public health or morals or the rights and freedoms of others.

The most explicit recognition of freedom of movement in the European Convention on Human Rights (the ECHR) is in Protocol Four. The United Kingdom has not agreed to be bound by this, largely because it would require changes to the country's immigration laws and, arguably, to the Prevention of Terrorism (Temporary Provisions) Act 1989 (the PTA). However, several other provisions in the ECHR are also relevant to free movement:

- Article 3 prohibits inhuman and degrading treatment, which may come into play when someone is expelled from the country, or where returning someone to a particular state may seriously affect his or her safety;
- where the matter concerns the separation of families, the rights to respect for family life (Article 8) and to marry and found a family (Article 12) may be at issue;
- detention for the purposes of exclusion or expulsion could contravene Article 5, which guarantees liberty and security of the person subject to limitations to secure certain purposes (*e.g.* to prevent crime).

However, in time of war or other public emergency threatening the life of the nation, a government can derogate from these Convention obligations (other than those in Article 3) "to the extent strictly required by the exigencies of the situation" (Article 15).

European Community law

Article 48 of the Treaty of Rome guarantees the freedom of movement of workers within the (now 12) member states of the European Community (EC). There must be no discrimination between workers on the basis of their nationality. The protection extends to a worker's husband or wife and to his or her dependent relatives, who all have the right to reside with the worker in the state where he or she is working. There cannot be a system of work permits for EC workers. Even if someone does not yet have a job but wishes to look for one in another member state of the EC, he or she must be allowed to enter that state (and to draw unemployment benefit) for at least three months. People living in the Republic of Ireland but working in Northern Ireland, or vice-versa, should be issed with special permits by the state they are working in.

It is to be noted that Articles 48(3) and 48(4) of the Treaty of Rome allow states to discriminate against workers from other member states for reasons of public policy, public security, public health or whenever employment "in the public service" is in issue. These exceptions are narrowly interpreted by the courts, but there can be no doubt that service in the police or army would fall within them, as would discrimination on the basis of a person's previous (if recent) conviction of a terrorist offence.

The Treaty of Rome contains separate provisions to regulate the freedom of movement of self-employed persons within the EC. By Articles 52-57 individuals and companies must be allowed to set themselves up in business in any member state on the same conditions as nationals of that state. Similarly, by Articles 59-66, an EC national must be allowed to provide his or her services in any member state under the same conditions as those imposed by that state on its own nationals. Articles 55, 56(1) and 66 create exceptions to the rights of establishment and provision of services similar to those in Articles 48(3) and (4) for employed persons. These are also narrowly interpreted by the courts. The "public policy" exception, for instance, cannot be used by authorities in Northern Ireland to deny rights to an EC national if the conduct of that person would not be stiffly penalised within Northern Ireland if perpetrated by a British citizen.

Travel controls under the PTA

The PTA 1989 is exceptional legislation, especially because of its marked impact on freedom of movement, even on that enjoyed by full citizens of the United Kingdom. Its inroads are effected by travel controls and the power to make exclusion orders. The Act superimposes an immigration-type security control on the immigration control already exercised against most entrants, not having the right of abode, at United Kingdom ports of entry. This security control, however, also extends to journeys within the CTA including travel between Great Britain and Northern Ireland.

Powers of examination under the PTA

The PTA 1989 provides for the regime of travel controls in section 16 and Schedule 5. It creates a set of designated ports of embarkation and disembarkation, and equips examining officers with powers of search, examination of passengers and arrest and detention of terrorist suspects. Examining officers may be police officers, immigration officers or customs officials. In practice, most are police officers from the Special Branch of the local police force for the area. A person who knowingly contravenes or fails to comply with the travel controls commits an offence punishable with three months' imprisonment and a fine up to £1,000.

The powers have been little used within Northern Ireland but have been frequently applied to persons who are travelling on passenger transport from Northern Ireland or Ireland to Great Britain, and *vice versa*. The Act establishes a set of designated ports and airports listed in Schedule 6, including Heathrow, Gatwick, Manchester, Birmingham, Luton and East Midlands airports, and seaports such as Liverpool, Holyhead and Stranraer. The captains of ships, aircraft and hovercraft must ensure that passengers and crew embark and disembark in accordance with arrangements approved by examining officers.

Examining officers' powers

Passengers may be required to complete landing or embarkation cards. The extent to which this is enforced is variable (*e.g.* passengers to and from Heathrow tend not to have to do so). Cards will be supplied on the plane or boat but, if not, may have to be completed at the port or airport if an examining officer so requests.

Examining officers are given extensive powers to search baggage and cargo and they may authorise the search to be carried out by persons who are not examining officers, such as airport security staff. Anything found may be detained for examination and kept for seven days. If the examining officer considers that it may be needed for use as evidence in criminal proceedings or in connection with the exclusion order or deportation order processes, he or she may detain it until satisfied that it is in fact not needed.

Examining officers have wide powers to examine passengers who have arrived in or are seeking to leave Great Britain by ship, aircraft or hovercraft. The power to examine also extends to transit passengers and crew. Because of its land frontier with the Republic, in Northern Ireland the powers extend to those entering or leaving Northern Ireland by land. Furthermore, an examining officer can examine any person found in Northern Ireland within one mile of the border to ascertain whether he or she is in the course of entering or leaving. Rail passengers entering Northern Ireland may be examined at the first stop. These powers supplement already extensive powers of stop and search exercisable by the security forces under the Emergency Provisions Acts (see chapters 3 and 4).

Grounds for examination

In Great Britain, the power of examination may be exercised to determine:

- whether a person is subject to an exclusion order barring him or her from Great Britain or the United Kingdom;
- whether there are any grounds for suspecting that a person is in breach of an exclusion order ;
- whether the person is or has been concerned in the commission, preparation or instigation of acts of terrorism connected with Northern Ireland affairs or acts of international terrorism (we shall refer to this as"involvement in terrorism").

Exercise of the power requires no prior suspicion that a person fits any of these categories; it is there to ascertain whether he or she might do so. So long as the power is exercised in good faith, it is effectively a power of random examination of travellers and is not likely to be reviewed by the courts, although it has been said that in an extreme case a court might be prepared to interfere if the decision to examine a person was one that no reasonable person could have taken (*Re Boyle, O'Hare and McAllister*, 1980).

A person examined must give any information in his or her possession which the examining officer requires for the purpose of carrying out the examination. He or she must, if the officer requests, produce either a valid passport with a photograph or some other document which satisfactorily establishes his or her identity, nationality or citizenship. Technically, this imposes no obligation to carry a passport or any such document, but prudence and a desire to avoid delay might dictate that one should. If asked to do so, a person examined must also declare whether he or she is carrying documents of a type specified by the officer. The documents must be ones relevant to the officer's functions, but could include documents of a political nature. Refusal to comply with these requests would appear to amount to a criminal offence.

Powers of detention under the PTA

Examination of a person cannot last for more than 12 hours unless the examining officer has reasonable suspicion of the person's "involvement in terrorism". Where the officer has that suspicion, he or she may serve on the examinee a written notice requiring him or her to submit to further examination. No formal arrest is involved. Although reasonable suspicion is required, since it need not be of a specific criminal offence but only of something vaguer, the prospects for effective judicial review of the officer's decision are remote.

Once a notice has been served, anyone examined may be detained on the authority of an examining officer for up to 48 hours, pending consideration of whether to make an exclusion order. However, if a Secretary of State (in practice the Home Secretary or the Scottish Secretary) so authorises, that 48 hour period can be extended by a period up to five days. Within the initial 48 hour period, detention must be reviewed every 12 hours, by a senior police officer not directly concerned with the ground for the detention. He or she must check that matters are proceeding diligently and expeditiously and that there are still reasons for detention (Schedule 3). The person detained or a solicitor must have an opportunity to make representations to the review officer about the detention.

An examining officer can require the captain of a craft to prevent the disembarkation of a person who is subject to an exclusion order or whom the Secretary of State is considering for one. To do so the captain may hold such a person in custody on the craft. An examining officer can also order the removal from a craft of anyone liable to examination or to be considered for an exclusion order. Persons may be detained in such places as the Secretary of State from time to time directs, and examining officers, or persons acting under their authority, can convey in custody persons under examination from one place to another for purposes of examination and control. In practice, except at ports with proper detention facilities, most detentions for examination will be in nearby police stations.

Persons liable to be detained can be arrested without a warrant by an examining officer, and a warrant can be issued by a Justice of the Peace to permit a search of premises in order to carry out the arrest. Apparently, although in law not so restricted, these powers are aimed at persons who have entered Great Britain secretly, without going through the controls, rather than at persons being examined at a port, who may well not be formally arrested at all.

Do the powers contravene European laws?

In *McVeigh, Evans and O'Neill v UK* (1981), applied in *Lyttle v UK* (1987), the European Commission of Human Rights, whose opinion was affirmed by the Committee of Ministers of the Council of Europe, considered that these powers of examination and detention at ports were permissible under Article 5 (1)(b) of the European Convention on Human Rights, which allows "the lawful arrest and detention of a person ... in order to secure the fulfilment of any obligation prescribed by law". In this situation the legal obligation is to submit to examination at the ports. The Commission took into account that the obligation arose only in the limited circumstances of travel across a clear geographical or political boundary and:

> *"that the purpose of examination is limited and directed towards an end of evident public importance in the context of a serious and continuing threat from organised terrorism."*

The searching, questioning, fingerprinting and photographing of the applicants were said to be legitimate interferences with their right to private life, justified under Article 8(2) of the ECHR as measures which were necessary in a democratic society for the prevention of crime. The retention of fingerprints, photographs and information obtained from the suspects, kept separate from criminal records where the suspect did not have a criminal record and reserved exclusively for use in the fight against terrorism, was similarly held necessary in the interest of public safety and for the prevention of crime.

The refusal to allow two of the applicants to contact their wives was, however, a breach of the right to family life not justified under Article 8 (2). This defect was remedied by the enactment of a statutory right of contact (subject to delay in appropriate circumstances) in the Criminal Law Act 1977, which, however, did not extend to Northern Ireland. The matter is now regulated in Great Britain by sections 56 and 58 of the Police and Criminal Evidence Act 1984 (the PACE Act) and in Northern Ireland by sections 44 and 45 of the Northern Ireland (Emergency Provisions) Act 1991(see chapter 3).

The PTA powers may also conflict with the rights to free movement conferred by the Treaty of Rome (which created the EC). However, those rights to free movement can be limited or denied on grounds of public security or public policy, provided that this is based exclusively on the personal conduct of the person concerned (which may include his or her present associations with a particular group regarded as socially harmful

- *Van Duyn v Home Office*, 1974) and that the conduct constitutes a genuine and sufficiently serious threat to the interests of the society.

Exclusion orders

Powers to make exclusion orders are conferred by sections 4-8 and Schedule 2 of the PTA 1989. An exclusion order expels a person from a particular territory (the United Kingdom, Great Britain or Northern Ireland) or prohibits a person from entering it. Such an order can be made by any Secretary of State, but in practice the powers are mainly exercised by the Home Secretary in relation to persons in, or seeking to enter, Great Britain, and by the Northern Ireland Secretary in respect of those in, or seeking to enter, Northern Ireland. Orders have a three year life, but fresh orders can be issued at or before the end of each three year period. The powers can be used whether or not the persons are subject to deportation under the Immigration Act 1971, and can create a form of internal exile for British citizens within the United Kingdom.

Subjecting someone to an exclusion order constitutes a more drastic interference with his or her right of free movement and other human rights than does the application of the powers of examination at ports. Exclusion has an impact on the individual and his or her family markedly similar to that of imprisonment. While it is true to say that the person excluded is not necessarily confined to a particular territory as a result of exclusion, in practice that will often be the end result. Exclusion to Northern Ireland of a person resident in Great Britain, in particular, may involve loss of employment, problems of accommodation and separation from friends and loved ones. At the very least it will create heightened pressures on family life, transfer to a potentially hostile if not lethal environment, and the stigma of perceived "involvement in terrorism" which may make the person a target for paramilitary groups on the other side of the sectarian divide.

When the powers can be exercised

Persons subjected to exclusion orders will usually be held under the PTA, the majority being detained under the port powers. But they may also be held under other powers, such as persons arrested under ordinary police powers or serving a term of imprisonment. Indeed, there is no requirement that the person be in custody at all. Orders can be, and are, made against persons not in the relevant territory in order to keep them out of it.

The power to exclude may be used in "such way as appears to the Secretary of State expedient to prevent acts of terrorism connected with the affairs of Northern Ireland" (PTA, section 3). This suggests that the test for whether an order should be made against a person is whether it would be advantageous for this public policy goal rather than whether the order is necessary for that goal. The Secretary of State must be satisfied that the person :

- is or has been concerned in the commission, preparation or instigation of acts of terrorism connected with Northern Ireland affairs, or
- is attempting or may attempt to enter the territory with a view to being concerned in such activities.

In its Circular 27/1989, the Home Office set out its view of what is encompassed by this "involvement in terrorism" test. The Circular states that "the mere harbouring of a terrorist without actual involvement is not sufficient." It also indicates that the Secretary of State is principally concerned with the current threat which a person poses, but that past "involvement in terrorism", itself sufficient to ground exclusion, will be taken into account. The political implications of an order also appear relevant - hence the revocation of the order against Gerry Adams while he was a Westminster MP.

How an order is made

In Great Britain, applications to the Home Secretary for an exclusion order, which are made by police forces, are filtered through the National Joint Unit (NJU) at Scotland Yard. This is made up of Special Branch officers from the Metropolitan Police and provincial police forces. The NJU has a general co-ordinating role with regard to investigating and preventing acts of Irish terrorism. Applications are made in writing and should be received by the NJU not later than 48 hours before the end of the permitted detention period. If the applications survive the "filter" of the NJU, they will be considered in the Home Office by civil servants up to Deputy Secretary level, providing a further "filter" to weed out un-suitable applications. The submissions will then be presented to the Secretary of State by a junior minister. The final decision will be a personal one for the Home Secretary or, in his absence, another Secretary of State, duly briefed by Home Office officials. The Home Secretary's decision will still be made mainly on the basis of written information. A similar process, without the NJU, operates in Northern Ireland.

Consequences of an exclusion order

An order may expel the person from the territory or prohibit him or her from entering it. Where an individual is ordinarily resident in the territory, the Secretary of State must have regard to his or her connection with another territory and consider whether it is such as to make it appropriate that an order be made. What constitutes a sufficient connection for this purpose remains obscure.

Persons subject to an exclusion order may be held in custody pending its enforcement. An order is given effect by the Secretary of State giving directions to passenger carriers to secure the person's removal to the appropriate destination, in custody if necessary and at public expense.

Breach of the order is an offence punishable in the Crown Court with a maximum of five years' imprisonment and an unlimited fine or, in a magistrates' court, imprisonment not exceeding six months and a fine not exceeding £2,000 (section 8).

Exemptions

Certain individuals are exempt from exclusion from a particular territory. No British citizen may be excluded from the United Kingdom (section 7). Nor may a British citizen be excluded from Great Britain or Northern Ireland if he or she is at the time ordinarily resident in that part of the United Kingdom and has been throughout the preceding three years. In calculating periods of ordinary residence certain periods of imprisonment have to be disregarded, as do periods when a person was in that part of the United Kingdom in breach of an exclusion order or the immigration laws (see Schedule 2, para. 9). Neither can a British citizen be excluded from Great Britain or Northern Ireland if he or she is already subject to an order excluding him or her from the other of those places. Citizens of the Republic of Ireland not also holding British citizenship do not qualify for these exemptions, even though they may be exempt from deportation under the Immigration Act 1971.

Challenging an exclusion order

Sensitive material from informers and intelligence operatives will naturally be considered by the Secretary of State. Some of this will be hearsay. Much of it may be low-grade intelligence about the person's connections with paramilitary organisations and suspect individuals. Any reports from police interrogation of the suspect will be considered too. A suspect's silence may be used against him or her if the police conclude that it indicates training in techniques of resisting interrogation. The nature of all this material is clearly such as to warrant the most careful scrutiny within the police and the Home Office, as well as in any review proceedings open to the suspect.

Interviews with an adviser

Once served with an order, a person can make representations to the Secretary of State (see Schedule 2 of the PTA) and those representations must then be referred to an adviser appointed to assist the Secretary of State. The individual can have a personal interview with the adviser to discuss the case, and that interview can even take place after the person has consented to being removed in the meantime. The individual who consents to interim removal has 14 days in which to make representations and request an interview. The period is seven days where the person is awaiting removal. In practice, legal representation is permitted at the interview, but the review is not intended to be a judicial process in the sense of a court of law, with adversarial procedures and full disclosure of the case against the suspect. Rather it is a way of taking into account what the suspect wishes to say and it provides an independent second opinion of the case based upon the representations made, the interview and the written material seen by the Secretary of State.

The adviser can have regard to a file of his or her previous decisions in these sorts of cases, but apparently does not interview relevant police or intelligence officers or their sources of information. He or she may have some independent discretion as to how much information to disclose to the individual, but the latter's main problem lies in having to make representations without knowing the real substance of the case against him or her. In any event, the adviser's report is not binding on the Secretary of State, merely an element to be taken into account when reconsidering the original decision. However, the Secretary of State usually follows the advice. Discontent with such procedures for review may be one reason for the low take-up rate, though a one-in-three success rate is apparent from the statistics.

Taking court proceedings

A person affected by the exclusion order can test its legality in the courts. If the contention is that he or she falls within a category exempt from exclusion, then, provided he or she can prove this point, a court will have no difficulty in striking down the order. But if, as is more likely, the ground of challenge is that the person is not "involved in terrorism", the position is problematical. It is open to the court to review the decision, ask the Secretary of State to give the reasons for making the order, and consider whether he had sufficient basis in law for making the order. However, given the "security" context of the power, its subjective wording ("is satisfied that"), the status of its wielder (a principal Secretary of State responsible to Parliament), and the existence of a review mechanism in the legislation itself, the court is likely to be satisfied by a sworn statement that the decision was made personally by the Secretary of State on the basis of reports from trusted subordinates founded on information from intelligence operatives, the details of which cannot for security reasons be disclosed to the court. The court itself would be unlikely to probe behind that, the individual would not be able to identify from it any defect, and it would be impossible to establish that the Secretary of State had made the order and the statement in bad faith.

Any challenge on grounds of procedural fairness directed towards getting further reasons for the making of the order would similarly fail. In view of the "security" context, it is left to the Secretary of State to decide how much information can safely be disclosed to the individual (*Ex parte Stitt*, 1987). In many cases all the individual receives is a printed form stating the Secretary of State's satisfaction that he or she falls within the particular statutory criteria indicated on the form.

Do the powers contravene European laws?

While exclusion orders may contravene Protocol Four of the European Convention on Human Rights this does not help a person in the UK because the UK government has not signed that Protocol. Nor would claims made under Articles 5 or 8 of the Convention be likely to succeed, except perhaps on the ground that there are no effective means of challenging in a court the lawfulness of detention prior to the issue of an exclusion order.

Exclusion orders can have an impact on European Community nationals (especially Irish citizens) and their families, who are within the protection of Treaty of Rome provisions on the free movement of workers, the right of establishment and the right to provide and receive services (see page 120). The case of *R. v Saunders* (1979), however, suggests that the protection of those provisions does not extend to cover restrictions on the movement within the state of a state's own nationals, at least where the restriction is imposed as a form of punishment. Even if it did, exclusion orders against them or other Treaty-protected persons could probably be justified on public policy or public security grounds, in much the same way as was refusal of entry to a Dutch scientologist in *Van Duyn v Home Office* (1974).

Directive 64/221/EEC provides that measures taken on these grounds must be based exclusively on the personal conduct of the individual (though this may include his or her present associations with a particular group regarded as socially harmful) and that previous criminal convictions do not in themselves constitute grounds for taking such measures. The conduct must constitute a sufficiently serious threat to the fundamental interests of the society. Furthermore, unless it would be contrary to the security of the state concerned, the person must be informed of the grounds on which the decision has been taken. It is an open question whether the adviser system complies with the requirements of the Directive. All of these matters would be subject to final decision by the European Court of Justice at Luxembourg in an individual case. However, it is difficult to envisage its scrutiny of the reasons for individual orders going deeper than that likely to be employed in our own High Court in judicial review proceedings.

Chapter 9

Meetings and Demonstrations

Brice Dickson

As with many of the other "freedoms" dealt with in this book, there is no law in any part of the United Kingdom which expressly guarantees a person's right to associate with others or to be part of an assembly. The "freedoms" are what is left after the law has laid down preconditions on a person's ability to go wherever he or she pleases. In Northern Ireland there are more of these preconditions than in other parts of the United Kingdom. As a result the extent of the remaining freedom is not as wide as in Great Britain.

The law on this matter is intricate. There is not one set of rules for, say, holding a public meeting and another for organising a protest march. Instead there is a core of law which is relevant to all situations and in addition a few rules which are special to particular sets of circumstances. In Northern Ireland a lot of the relevant rules are laid down in the Public Order (NI) Order 1987, which updated and replaced the Public Order (NI) Order 1981. Many rules also derive from decisions of judges in reported cases (the common law). The European Convention on Human Rights must be borne in mind too.

European Convention law

Article 11 of the European Convention on Human Rights provides as follows:

> *"(1) Everyone has the right to freedom of peaceful assembly and to freedom of association with others, including the right to form and to join trade unions for the protection of his (sic) interests.*
>
> *(2) No restrictions shall be placed on the exercise of these rights other than such as are prescribed by law and are necessary in a democratic society in the interests of national security or public safety, for the prevention of disorder or crime, for the protection of health or morals or for the protection of the rights and freedoms of others. This Article shall not prevent the imposition of lawful restrictions on the exercise of these rights by members of the armed forces, of the police or the administration of the State."*

Article 17 of the Convention says that the Convention must not be interpreted so as to give any state, group or person the right to engage in activities aimed at limiting other people's rights.

To date, the European Commission and the European Court of Human Rights at Strasbourg have not had to interpret Article 11 very often, but when they have done so they have usually been reluctant to allow a government to rely on Article 11(2) in order to restrict either of the freedoms. Thus, in *Christians Against Racism and Fascism v UK* (1980), the Commission held that the right to assemble (in that case, to organise a demonstration) could not be taken away just because there was a possibility of a violent counter-demonstration. The thinking behind such a decision is that, in the long term, it is healthier for a society to allow all views to be expressed, even if their content is disgusting to the vast majority of the general public.

The European Commission also held in the *Christians against Racism* case, however, that it was permissible for the United Kingdom to have a law which in effect prevented the authorities from imposing bans on single processions but allowed them to ban all public processions, or a class of public procession, for a period not exceeding three months. That is the power which now exists both in England and in Northern Ireland (Public Order (NI) Order 1987, article 5). It is difficult to understand how blanket bans of this nature can, within the terms of Article 11(2) of the European Convention, be "necessary".

Most of the cases taken to Strasbourg on Article 11 have involved the activities of trade unions. As with other matters, however, it is difficult to discern a definite pattern in the judgments handed down. On the one hand, the European Court has said that Article 11 "safeguards freedom to protect the occupational interests of trade union members by trade union action, the conduct and development of which the Contracting States must both permit and make possible". On the other hand, it has pointed out that the Article "does not secure any particular treatment of trade unions, or their members, by the State, such as the right that the State should conclude any collective agreement with them". Nor does the Article guarantee the right to strike.

The European Commission was involved in the GCHQ case - *Council of Civil Service Unions v Minister for the Civil Service* (1987) - where workers at Government Communications Headquarters at Cheltenham were banned from belonging to certain trade unions. The unions involved were unsuccessful in persuading the English appeal courts of the justice of their case. They also lost at the European level, where the European Commission held that their complaint could not be considered because the ban was a "lawful restriction" necessary in the interests of national security.

In an earlier case (*Young, James & Webster v UK*, 1983) the European Court placed a general query over closed shop agreements between employers and one or more trade unions. In *Sibson v UK* (1993) the Court held that an employer could require an employee belonging to a particular union to work at a separate site from that used by employees belonging to a different union.

Associating with others

The effect of the various rules concerning freedom of association in Northern Irish law is to confer upon individuals the right to associate with whomsoever they please. There are, however, some exceptions to this, and these are outlined below.

Apart from these four exceptions, the right freely to associate is absolute. Of course, people who feel that they are being harassed or unduly annoyed by another person's company may well have a remedy in the law of trespass (which is an intentional interference with someone else's land, person or property), or they may qualify as the victims of other specific civil wrongs or crimes, but these are all wrongs which can be committed just as much by individuals as by people acting in consort. Members of groups distinguishable by their gender or by their religious or political beliefs are protected against some forms of discrimination by laws such as the Fair Employment (NI) Acts 1976 and 1989 and the Sex Discrimination (NI) Order 1976: see chapters 12 and 13. Deplorably, there are not yet any laws against racial discrimination in Northern Ireland, nor against discrimination based on a person's homosexuality, physical or mental disability or age.

(1) An association to plan the commission of a crime

It must not be an association to plan the commission of a crime. This would amount to the offence of conspiracy, which is committed (under article 9(1) of the Criminal Attempts and Conspiracy (NI) Order 1983):

> *"if a person agrees with any other person or persons that a course of conduct shall be pursued which, if the agreement is carried out in accordance with their intentions, either (a) will necessarily amount to or involve the commission of any offence or offences by one or more of the parties to the agreement, or (b) would do so but for the existence of facts which render the commission of the offence or any of the offences impossible."*

Under article 9(3) there is an exception for acts that are to be done in contemplation or furtherance of a trade dispute, provided the offence is a minor one triable only before magistrates. A husband and wife cannot alone be charged with conspiracy, nor can a person be charged with conspiring with a person under 10, but a person can be, and often is, charged with conspiracy with a person unknown. Incitement or attempt to conspire are not punishable as crimes. Conspiracies to commit a minor offence are punishable by an unlimited fine; conspiracies to commit a serious (*i.e.* "indictable") offence can be punished with the same maximum term of imprisonment as the indictable offence itself (article 11 of the 1983 Order).

Actually associating in a crime, as opposed to a plan for a crime, makes a person guilty of aiding, abetting, counselling or procuring the crime. In Northern Ireland the idea of counselling and procuring has sometimes been interpreted by the judges in a way which attributes guilt even to people involved at an early stage in an incident. In 1990 three men were convicted of counselling and procuring the murder of two British soldiers because the men were said to be part of a "common purpose" or "joint enterprise" which culminated some time later in the soldiers being killed at a different location (*R v Kane, Kelly and Timmons*).

(2) An association specifically banned by legislation

It must not be an association which has been specifically banned by legislation. An example is the ban imposed at GCHQ by the Civil Service Order in 1982. In Northern Ireland several associations are banned (or "proscribed") by section 28 and Schedule 2 of the Northern Ireland (Emergency Provisions) Act 1991. These are the Irish Republican Army, the Irish National Liberation Army, the Ulster Defence Association, Ulster Volunteer Force, the Ulster Freedom Fighters, the Red Hand Commandos, Saor Eire, Cumann na mBan and Fianna na hEireann. In England and Wales only the first two of these are proscribed. In Northern Ireland the maximum penalty for belonging to a proscribed organisation, or for inviting support for it, is 10 years' imprisonment and an unlimited fine. If the support invited relates to money or other property, the maximum penalty is 14 years' imprisonment and an unlimited fine.

It is also unlawful to be a member of a quasi-military organisation (section 7(1) of the Public Order (Amendment) Act (NI) 1970) and any person who is a member of the association or who takes part in the control of the association is guilty of an offence. There is an exemption for employment by the organisers of any lawful public procession or meeting of a reasonable number of people as stewards to assist in the preservation of order. The maximum penalty for membership of a quasi-military association is three months' imprisonment and a fine of £100; that for managing or training such an association is five years' imprisonment and a fine of £1,000. See too the Unlawful Drilling Act 1819 (page 151).

(3) Unlawful assembly

The association must not be an "unlawful assembly" under judge-made law. In Northern Ireland the old common law offence of unlawful assembly remains. A person is guilty of it if he or she is a member of an assembly of three or more people which is either causing a disturbance or giving rise to a reasonable apprehension of a breach of the peace. "Breach of the peace" means conduct causing a reasonable apprehension (to someone present) of violence against persons or property. The offence can be committed both on private property and in public places, and the assembly be densely packed in order to be unlawful: illegal occupants of 70 houses have been held to constitute an unlawful assembly over a five week period (*McKibben v Belfast Corporation*, 1936).

(4) Association forbidden by order

The associating in question must not have been forbidden by administrative or judicial order. These orders can be called exclusion orders. One notorious variety is that issued by a Secretary of State under the Prevention of Terrorism (Temporary Provisions) Act 1989 (see chapter 8). Another type can be issued by magistrates in cases of domestic violence, in order to exclude one person, usually a man, from premises occupied by that person's spouse or cohabitee.

Controls on private meetings

It is necessary to distinguish between private and public meetings. As regards the latter, it is also important to distinguish between public meetings in general and those held in the open-air. Election meetings and council meetings are in a special position too.

Meetings on private premises and restricted to a "private" group are virtually uncontrolled by the law. They are never unlawful, unless one of the exceptions mentioned at pages 135-137 above is relevant or unless certain offences are committed during the meeting. If, for example, a breach of the peace is being committed, the police can enter private premises in order to break up a meeting. The police can also enter private premises in order to arrest a suspected criminal, which is why groups of after-hour drinkers in public houses are at risk.

Members of the public have no right to attend private meetings unless they are invited or given express permission to enter. "Gate-crashers" will be guilty of trespass, which is not a crime if it takes place on private premises but it allows the occupier of the premises to sue in the civil courts for compensation even if the trespassing has caused no damage. Even when permission to enter has been granted, it may later be withdrawn. If a club or society holds a meeting and tries to exclude certain members, those members, if they have the opportunity, are entitled to apply for a court order (called an "injunction") to compel the organisers to grant them admission.

Public meetings in general

In 1936, the Lord Chief Justice of England said that "English law does not recognise any special right of public meeting for political or other purposes" (see *Duncan v Jones*). This principle continues to apply in both England and Northern Ireland. All public meetings are subject to the rules set out below, but open-air public meetings are subject to even further restrictions. Meetings on public highways are particularly susceptible to controls. A speaker at any meeting must also "take the audience as he or she finds it": if the audience is hostile, the speaker must be careful not to "occasion" disorder.

A "public meeting" is defined by article 2 of the Public Order (NI) Order 1987 as including any meeting in a public place and any meeting (even in a private place) which the public or any section of the public is permitted to attend, whether on payment or otherwise. In turn, "public place" is defined as meaning any street, road or highway and any place to which the public or any section of the public has access, on payment or otherwise, as of right or by virtue of express or implied permission. "Meeting" is also defined in the same article: it means a meeting held for the purpose of discussing matters of public interest. A few points need to be made about these definitions:

- They apply only to the defined words when they are used in the 1987 Order; it would be possible for a judge or a law-enforcement officer to place a different interpretation on those words when they appear in another piece of legislation or in a law laid down by judges.

- Whereas "public place" and "meeting" are given exclusive definitions, "public meeting" is defined only so as to *include* certain categories of meeting. It is conceivable that a judge or law-enforcement officer could make the term embrace other categories of meeting as well, such as meetings run by an organisation for its own members and their friends.

- In the definitions of "public meeting" and "public place", the phrase "public or any section of the public" is used. In English cases on the Race Relations Acts this phrase has been interpreted so as not to cover clubs and societies with some form of membership system. To get round this interpretation Parliament had to amend the Acts in 1976 so that they could extend to many of these clubs and societies. It remains to be seen whether a court in Northern Ireland will take as restrictive a view of the meaning of this phrase as the English courts have done, though even if they do, because of the point made in the preceding paragraph, it may not make the 1987 Order inapplicable.

- The definition of "meeting" certainly excludes most of those meetings held merely for the purpose of discussing the internal matters of a particular group or association. The internal workings of a large political party may be a matter of public interest, but not perhaps the discussions of a parent-teacher association. Whether a matter is or is not of public interest is a question which can ultimately be tested in court. Comparisons with other areas of the law, such as contempt of court and defamation, would suggest that virtually any matter could, in the proper circumstances, be of public interest.

- A meeting can consist of two or more people; there is no higher minimum number required, as there is for "assemblies" in England (where there have to be at least 20 people).

Offences connected with public meetings

Needless to say, any behaviour which constitutes an offence in a private setting will not be any less criminal simply because it occurs at a public meeting. There are also some offences which can be committed only at public meetings (just as there are other offences, especially those concerning indecency and sexual relations, which can only be committed in public places). Under article 7(2) of the Public Order (NI) Order 1987, a person is guilty of an offence, punishable in a magistrates' court by up to six months in prison and a fine up to £2,000, if he or she at a lawful public meeting "acts in a disorderly manner for the purpose of preventing the transaction of the business for which the meeting was called together".

Two other offences currently regulated by the Public Order (NI) Order 1987 need to be mentioned. Under article 19 it is an offence "at or in relation to any public meeting" (or indeed in any public place) if a person:

> "(a) uses threatening, abusive or insulting words or behaviour, or (b) displays anything or does any act, or (c) being the owner or occupier

of any land or premises, causes or permits anything to be displayed or any act to be done thereon, with intent to provoke a breach of the peace or by which a breach of the peace or public disorder is likely to be occasioned (whether immediately or at any time afterwards)".

The House of Lords has said that behaviour does not qualify as threatening, abusive or insulting just because it gives rise to a risk that immediate violence will be provoked, nor is it enough that the behaviour gives rise to anger, disgust or distress: *Brutus v Cozens* (1972), where the defendant had merely run on to the No. 2 court at Wimbledon Lawn Tennis Club and distributed leaflets.

In England it is an offence to display "any writing, sign or other visible representation", while in Northern Ireland it is an offence to display "anything". Some would argue, therefore, that in England it could not be a criminal act, *e.g.*, for a Protestant to wear or carry an orange lily in a strongly Catholic area at a time of sectarian tension (since the lily is real and not just a sign or representation), but this could clearly be a crime in Northern Ireland. Conversely, Northern Ireland has no direct equivalent to section 5(1) of England's Public Order Act 1986, which outlaws threatening, abusive or insulting behaviour "within the hearing or sight of a person likely to be caused harassment, alarm or distress thereby."

Article 21 of the 1987 Order prohibits a person in any public place or at any public meeting from wearing a uniform signifying an association with any political organisation or with the promotion of any political object. The Chief Constable of the RUC may, with the Secretary of State's consent, permit exceptions to this prohibition, but only for ceremonial, anniversary or other special occasions. There is no definition of "uniform" in the 1987 Order, so the courts will have to decide whether, for instance, wearing a beret or some kind of sash is enough to constitute a uniform. In the English case of *O'Moran v DPP* (1975) it was held that the wearing of dark berets, dark glasses, dark pullovers and other dark clothing, when escorting the coffin of an IRA supporter through London streets, could be regarded as a uniform.

It is also necessary to note that, under section 29 of the Northern Ireland (Emergency Provisions) Act 1991, it is an offence for any person in a public place to dress or behave in such a way as to arouse reasonable apprehension that he or she is a member or supporter of a proscribed organisation (see the list at page 136). The maximum penalty is one year's imprisonment and an unlimited fine. This same maximum penalty applies to offences under section 33 of the Act, which prohibits the wearing without lawful authority or reasonable excuse in a public place or dwelling-house (other than the person's own residence) of any hood, mask or other article which has been made, adapted or used for concealing the identity or features. It remains uncertain what constitutes a reasonable excuse for wearing a mask; presumably it is permissible to put on a funny face at Hallowe'en or when performing a play!

Public meetings on private premises

The definition in article 7 of the 1987 Order makes it clear that a meeting may constitute a public meeting even though it is held on private premises, whether outdoors or indoors. Police officers can attend such meetings in a purely private capacity, but their right to be there in a professional capacity is not certain. One well-known English case, *Thomas v Sawkins* (1935), suggests that the right exists in situations where the police reasonably apprehend a breach of the peace. But whether the police's apprehension is reasonable could be tested in the courts.

Election and council meetings

Some special rules apply to election meetings by virtue of the Electoral Law Act (NI) 1962 and the Representation of the People Act 1983. Under Schedule 9, para 13, of the 1962 Act, a person who acts in a disorderly manner for the purpose of preventing the transaction of business at a local election meeting is guilty of an "illegal practice", which is an offence punishable with a fine of £100. The same kind of disturbance at a meeting connected with a forthcoming election for a Westminster seat is punishable with a fine not exceeding £400. At election times in Great Britain all candidates have the right to use certain schools and halls for public meetings free of charge, and to inspect the list of halls available in the area. In Northern Ireland these rights do not appear to exist.

By law, all meetings of district councils in Northern Ireland, and all meetings of committees of those councils, are open to members of the public whether or not they reside in that council area (section 23 of the Local Government Act (NI) 1972). By the same section, a council may decide by resolution to exclude the public when publicity would be prejudicial to the public interest because of the confidential nature of the business or for other special reasons. The power to exclude persons from a meeting in order to suppress or prevent disorderly behaviour also exists (section 27(a)). Newspapers can require copies of the agenda to be sent to them in advance of meetings (section 24), but no person can insist on being allowed to take photographs at, or to record or relay, the proceedings (section 27(b)). (See too page 179.)

Open-air public meetings

Controls on open-air public meetings are stricter in Northern Ireland than in England. The Public Order Act 1986 allows the police in England to impose conditions on the holding of such meetings, but does not permit them to be banned. In Northern Ireland the police's power to impose conditions has existed since 1951 and the grounds for imposing them were extended by the 1987 Order. The power to ban open-air public meetings was first introduced by the Stormont Parliament as a reaction to the troubles of 1969-71 (see the Public Order (Amendment) Act (NI) 1971). At that time the banning power was vested in the Minister of Home Affairs, but now it is vested in the Secretary of State.

Public open spaces are usually regulated by bylaws issued by the relevant district council or public body; these bylaws may completely disallow public meetings in those spaces or require prior special permission. (See the reference to the Town Police Clauses Act 1847, page 149 below.)

Conditions

The power to impose conditions on open-air public meetings is at present conferred by article 4(2) of the Public Order (NI) Order 1987. This requires a senior police officer reasonably to believe that the meeting may result in:

- serious public disorder;
- serious damage to property;
- serious disruption to the life of the community; or
- that its purpose is the intimidation of others with a view to compelling them not to do an act they have a right to do or to do an act they have a right not to do.

The officer may then impose such conditions as to the place where the meeting may be held, its maximum duration, or the maximum number of persons who may constitute it, as appear necessary to prevent such disorder, damage, disruption or intimidation.

The directions given by the "senior officer" must be in writing, except in cases where people are already assembling for the meeting. A person who knowingly fails to comply with a condition imposed under article 4 is punishable with up to two years in prison and an unlimited fine. It is a defence for the accused to prove that the failure arose from circumstances beyond his or her control.

Bans

The power to prohibit open-air public meetings is now conferred by article 5(1) of the Public Order (NI) Order 1987, which requires the Secretary of State to be of the opinion that the meeting is likely to:

- cause serious public disorder,
- cause serious disruption to the life of the community, or
- make undue demands upon the police or military forces.

The Secretary may then make an order prohibiting for up to three months the holding in that area of all or specified open-air public meetings.

The 1987 Order provides that a statement made by the Secretary of State as to the need to prohibit a meeting "shall be conclusive evidence of the matters stated therein" (article 5(3)). This probably means, alarmingly, that the reasonableness of the Secretary of State's opinion cannot be challenged in court by judicial review. This distinguishes Northern Irish law from English law, where there is no equivalent to article 5(3) as far as the imposing of conditions on public meetings is concerned.

The 1987 Order does not impose a requirement to notify the police that a public meeting is scheduled to take place, unlike in the case of public processions (see page 144). Nor does the legislation require the consent of the Chief Constable or of the Police Authority before a banning order is issued; the Police Authority is, wherever practicable, merely to be "consulted" (article 5(2)). A person who knowingly organises or takes part in a banned open-air public meeting is guilty of an offence for which the maximum penalty is two years in prison and an unlimited fine.

Picketing

Some of the rules on picketing are described in chapter 17. For the present it is necessary to note that if two or more pickets are acting together they may well constitute a public meeting and so be subject to the rules set out above. In England and Wales this will be the case only if the numbers picketing are 20 or more, because only then will they constitute an assembly in English law.

One of the tests which the police must consider before deciding to impose conditions on an open-air public meeting in Northern Ireland is whether its purpose is the intimidation of others (article 4(2)(b) of the 1987 Order). This is clearly aimed at the control of picketing and "intimidation" will therefore be interpreted as it has been under the Conspiracy and Protection of Property Act 1875, section 7 of which first imposed specific controls on picketing (expanded for Northern Ireland by the Trade Disputes and Trade Unions Act (NI) 1927, section 3). That gives it a wider meaning than the one attributable to the same term in section 1 of the Protection of the Person and Property Act (NI) 1969 (see page 150). However, in a case arising out of the News International dispute at Wapping, an English court held that abuse, swearing and shouting did not of itself amount to intimidation (*News Group Newspapers Ltd v SOGAT '82*, 1986).

Controls on public processions

The laws on association and on public meetings will normally also be relevant to public processions. But in some respects the rules vary a little and there are, in addition, other rules which are relevant only to processions.

Article 3 of the Public Order (NI) Order 1987 requires a person organising a public procession to give not less than seven days' notice to the police. This applies regardless of whether the procession consists of people walking, running, cycling or motoring. The notice must specify the following information:

- the date and time when the procession is to be held;
- its route;
- the number of persons likely to take part in it;

- the number and, where reasonably practicable, the names of any bands likely to take part in it;
- the arrangements for its control being made by the person proposing to organise it; and
- the name and address of the organiser.

The obligation to give notice does not apply if the procession is a funeral procession (see page 146) or is of a description specified by the Secretary of State. There is no exemption just because the procession is one commonly held in the area in which it is proposed to be held. "Traditional" marches organised by the Orange Order or the Ancient Order of Hibernians therefore have to be notified. But less than seven days' notice can be given if it is not reasonably practicable to give the full notice. This means that spontaneous demonstrations are still lawful. It will ultimately be up to the law-enforcement agencies to decide whether the failure to give notice in a particular case was "not reasonably practicable".

A person who organises or takes part in an unnotifed public procession is punishable with up to six months in prison and a fine up to £2,000 (articles 3(5) and (8) of the Public Order (NI) Order 1987). It is, however, a defence to prove that the accused did not know of, and neither suspected nor had reason to suspect, the failure to satisfy the notice requirements (article 3(6)). If the alleged offence relates to a failure to keep to the notified date, time or route for the procession, it is also a defence to prove that the failure arose from circumstances beyond the accused's control. In England and Scotland, only the organisers of, not the participants in, unnotified processions can be guilty of offences, and the maximum punishments are less severe.

People taking part in a public procession in Northern Ireland are given a certain amount of protection by article 7(1) of the Public Order (NI) Order 1987:

"A person who for the purpose of preventing or hindering any lawful public procession or of annoying persons taking part in or endeavouring to take part in any such procession hinders, molests, obstructs or acts in a disorderly manner towards, or behaves offensively and abusively towards, those persons or any of them shall be guilty of an offence."

There is no equivalent to this offence in English law. It is punishable, in a magistrates' court only, with a maximum of six months' imprisonment and a fine up to £2,000. Northern Ireland law has no equivalent to sections 4 and 5 of England's Public Order Act 1986. Section 4 makes it an offence to use threatening words or signs with intent to cause a person to believe that immediate unlawful violence will be used against him or her. By section 5 it is an offence to use threatening words or signs within the hearing or sight of a person likely to be caused harassment or distress. These offences can be committed in private places but not private homes.

The powers to impose conditions or bans on public processions arise in the same circumstances as the powers concerning public meetings, except that the conditions which can be imposed include those which re-route the procession or prohibit it from entering any place specified in the police directions. If the Scottish law is followed by judges in Northern Ireland, a court may uphold a ban on a public procession if it is based on the likelihood of disorder emanating from opponents of the procession: *Loyal Orange Lodge No 493 v Roxburgh District Council* (1979). However a court will interfere with a senior police office's discretion on whether to allow a procession only if there is evidence that he or she failed to consider proper matters, considered irrelevant matters or reached a decision which no reasonable person could make. Opposition to the procession will not be enough to re-route it unless there is also a belief on the part of the police that the result may be (at the very least) serious disruption to the life of the community: *In re Murphy's Application* (1991).

Funerals

Funeral processions are exempted from the notice requirements of the Public Order (NI) Order 1987. Nevertheless, under regulations made in 1991, the police can require mourners to travel in vehicles.However, at the point where, or when, a funeral procession loses its connection with the interment or cremation of a body, it will be liable to the controls laid down in the 1987 Order for other types of public processions.

Bands

Northern Ireland also has a unique provision for the control of bands, which are defined as "a group of two or more persons who carry for the purpose of playing or sounding, or engage in the playing or sounding of, musical or other instruments". Article 6 of the Public Order (NI) Order 1987 allows the Secretary of State to require bands to be registered and anyone knowingly parading with an unregistered band would be guilty of an offence punishable with up to six months' imprisonment and a fine up to £2,000. In fact, no registration requirement has yet been made and there would be great difficulties in creating one which could not be easily evaded. It is, in any event, open to question whether restrictions on band-playing are necessary in Northern Ireland. Even if article 6 did come into effect, it would not apply to bands playing at a public meeting rather than in a public procession.

Additional public order offences

Many of the offences which might be committed during the course of meetings or processions have already been referred to. It is now necessary to describe some further offences:

Riot (or riotous assembly)

In Northern Ireland this is still a common law offence committed whenever three or more people, in execution of a common purpose, use force or violence which alarms or terrifies at least one person "of reasonable firmness", and with an intent to assist one another, by force if necessary, against any person who may oppose them. The maximum penalty is life imprisonment.

Rout

This is a common law offence which is more serious than unlawful assembly but less serious than riot; it is virtually never prosecuted these days and has been expressly abolished in England and Wales by the Public Order Act 1986.

Affray

This too is still a common law offence in Northern Ireland. It consists of unlawful fighting, or a display of force, in such a manner as to terrify a person "of reasonable firmness" (who does not have to be present at the scene). It can be committed by one person acting alone, but is commonly charged whenever the police break up street fights or pub brawls. The maximum theoretical penalty is life imprisonment, though the Northern Ireland courts may follow the sentencing guidelines issued by the English Court of Appeal in *R v Keys and Others* (1986), where it was said that the leaders and organisers of serious affrays can anticipate sentences of seven years' imprisonment or more.

Riotous, disorderly or indecent behaviour

In what is a partial re-enactment of the Criminal Justice (Miscellaneous Provisions) Act (NI) 1968, section 9, it is an offence under article 18 of the Public Order (NI) Order 1987 for a person in any public place to use behaviour which is riotous, disorderly or likely to occasion a breach of the peace. The maximum penalty is six months' imprisonment and a fine of £2,000. In *Clinton* v *Watts* (1992) the Northern Ireland Court of Appeal held that words alone can constitute disorderly behaviour (*e.g.* swearing and shouting) and that it is enough if the behaviour is seen by a police officer; the behaviour does not have to be directed towards any particular person provided it at least seriously infringes the values of orderly conduct held by right-thinking people. The amended version of section 9 of the 1968 Act (see Schedule 1, para 3 of the 1987 Order) criminalises, in addition, indecent behaviour in any public place and behaviour, on premises where intoxicating liquor is sold, which is riotous, disorderly, indecent or likely to occasion a breach of the peace.

Obstructive sitting etc in public places

Under article 20 of the 1987 Order a person is guilty of an offence - maximum penalty one month's imprisonment and a fine of £400 - if he or she sits, stands, kneels, lies down or otherwise conducts himself or herself in a public place so as wilfully to obstruct traffic or to hinder any lawful activity.

There is also the offence known as obstruction of the highway (see article 47 of the Roads (NI) Order 1980):

"Any person who, without lawful authority or reasonable excuse, in any way wilfully or negligently obstructs the free passage along a

road shall be guilty of an offence and liable on summary conviction to a fine not exceeding £50".

Breach of council bylaws

The district councils and some other authorities have power to issue bylaws (requiring confirmation by the Secretary of State) to regulate activities in public places. Council bylaws can be inspected free of charge at council premises and generally speaking the maximum penalty for contravening them is a fine of £20, plus £2 for each day that the offence continues after conviction (Local Government Act (NI) 1972, section 92).

Persons employed by the district council and members of the RUC may be authorised by the council to secure the enforcement of bylaws. Under section 21 of the Town Police Clauses Act 1847, still in force in Northern Ireland, it is an offence (punishable now with a fine up to £400) wilfully to breach an order made by a local authority "for the route to be observed by all ... persons, and for preventing obstruction of the streets, ... in all times of public processions, rejoicings or illuminations ...". The maximum penalty for a taxi driver plying for hire without a licence is now £1,000.

Carrying offensive weapons in public places

Under article 22 of the 1987 Order a person is guilty of an offence if, without lawful authority or reasonable excuse (proof of which lies on the accused), he or she has in any public place an offensive weapon, meaning "any article made or adapted for use for causing injury to the person, or intended by the person having it ... for such use ... " The maximum penalty is two years' imprisonment and an unlimited fine.

Offences in relation to public buildings

Under article 23 of the 1987 Order, it is a criminal offence to be a trespasser in a public building (a term which is widely defined and includes the Stormont Estate) or knowingly to interfere with the carrying on of any lawful activity in any public building. The maximum penalty is two years' imprisonment and an unlimited fine.

Obstructing a police officer

Obstructing or impeding a police officer in the due execution of his or her duty is an offence under section 7 of the Criminal Justice (Miscellaneous Provisions) Act (NI) 1968. The obstruction must be intentional, but virtually any act qualifies if it makes the job of the police more difficult to carry out. A police officer can himself or herself be guilty of the offence, especially if he or she colludes with a suspect to mislead an investigation (*Clinton* v *Kell*, 1991). However, a refusal to give information is not obstruction (though it may amount to a separate offence: see chapter 3). If a police officer is exceeding his or her duty at the time, no obstruction can occur in law. It is also an offence, under the same section, to assault a police officer in the due execution of his or her duty. For the purposes of these offences a traffic warden is classified as a police officer. The maximum penalty is two years' imprisonment and an unlimited fine.

Intimidation

By section 1 of the Protection of the Person and Property Act (NI) 1969 it is an offence if a person unlawfully causes another in any way whatsoever to do or refrain from doing any act. This widely worded provision carries a maximum penalty of five years' imprisonment and an unlimited fine. Participants in a provocative and disorderly demonstration can be prosecuted under it if their actions cause someone, *e.g.*, to stay indoors all day. As so often, the impact of the section depends greatly on the prosecution policies of the police and the Director of Public Prosecutions. (See also page 155.)

Breach of the peace

According to Lord Justice Watkins in *R.* v *Howell* (1982), a breach of the peace arises:

> *"whenever harm is actually done or is likely to be done to a person or in his (sic) presence to his property or a person is in fear of being so harmed through an assault, an affray, a riot, unlawful assembly, or other disturbance"*.

It can occur on private premises even though no member of the public outside the premises is involved: *McConnell v Chief Constable of the Greater Manchester Police* (1990).

A breach of the peace is not itself a criminal offence, but it can very easily constitute some other offence and therefore the police and courts have significant powers to prevent breaches of the peace. A magistrate has power under article 127 of the Magistrates' Courts (NI) Order 1981 (and under the Justices of the Peace Act 1361) to "bind over" any person to keep the peace and/or be of good behaviour for a period up to two years, on pain of paying a sum of money if he or she fails in this duty. If this sum is not paid, the court may send the person to prison for up to six months. The time and money specified in a binding-over order must be reasonable (usually the time period is 12 months); appeals can be made to the Crown Court and judicial review proceedings may be taken in the High Court (see chapter 2).

There have been many attempts to have the law on breach of the peace abolished or reformed, because it represents a grave risk to basic freedoms. As yet all such attempts have been unsuccessful.

Unlawful drilling

Parts of the Unlawful Drilling Act 1819 are still in force in Northern Ireland. Section 1 prohibits:

> *"all meetings and assemblies of persons for the purpose of training or drilling themselves, or of being trained or drilled to the use of arms, or for the purpose of practising military exercise, movements, or evolutions, without any lawful authority from His Majesty, or the lieutenant, or two justices of the peace of any county."*

The maximum penalty for persons conducting the training is seven years in prison; for those being trained it is two years. Prosecutions have to be brought within six months of the commission of the offence (section 7). Training in the making or use of firearms or explosive substances is also an offence under section 32 of the Northern Ireland (Emergency Provisions) Act 1991, the maximum penalty being 10 years' imprisonment and an unlimited fine.

Chapter 10

Freedom of Expression

Steve Mcbride

Freedom of expression is one of the most widely invoked human rights. Because communication is such a fundamental aspect of our humanity, protecting the right to speak freely is vitally important. However, defining what is meant by freedom of expression is difficult, and setting the proper limits to what should be protected by the law can be especially so. This is even more the case in Northern Ireland, where the language of politics is often extreme.

As with other human rights, the exercise of one person's right may conflict with the same or other legitimate rights of other individuals or of society as a whole. Drawing the right line between art and pornography, between free debate and mere insult, between investigative journalism and invasion of privacy, between protecting democracy and protecting those who want to overthrow it, is not easy. A realistic assessment of the position may be that it is essential for democratic society that there should be as little restraint as possible on the free discussion of ideas and of current events, but that certain restraints may be imposed in order to protect the rights of others.

The legal background

Article 19 of the Universal Declaration of Human Rights states that:

> *"Everyone has the right to freedom of opinion and expression; this right includes freedom to hold opinions without interference and to seek, receive and impart information and ideas through any media and regardless of frontiers".*

The United Kingdom and Ireland are both signatories to the Universal Declaration, although it has no standing in domestic law.

Article 10 of the European Convention on Human Rights states that:

> *"1. Everyone has the right to freedom of expression. This right shall include freedom to hold opinions and to receive and impart information and ideas without interference by public authorities and regardless of frontiers. This Article shall not prevent States from requiring the licensing of broadcasting, television and radio.*
>
> *2. The exercise of this freedom, since it carries with it duties and responsibilities, may be subject to such formalities, conditions, restrictions or penalties as are prescribed by law and are necessary in a democratic society, in the interests of national security, territorial integrity or public safety, for the prevention of disorder or crime, for the protection of the reputation or rights of others, for preventing the disclosure of information received in confidence, or for maintaining the authority and impartiality of the judiciary."*

The European Convention cannot yet be directly relied upon in British or Irish courts, but the decisions of those courts can be appealed to the European Commission and Court of Human Rights. In spite of the extensive qualifications in the second paragraph of Article 10, a number of aspects of British and Irish law have been successfully challenged, including the rules on telephone tapping and contempt of court. The status of Article 10 and of freedom of expression in general were recently extensively discussed in the English courts in *Derbyshire County Council v Times Newspapers Ltd* (1992), where the House of Lords held that there was a vital public interest in protecting the right to criticise official bodies.

The law within Northern Ireland relating to freedom of expression must be sought in a wide variety of sources.

* The criminal law punishes various offences which involve threatening or inciting comments, prohibits comments deemed to be offensive to public morals, and penalises breaches of official secrecy or the prejudicing of court proceedings.

- The civil law, though the rules on defamation, (*i.e.* libel and slander) allows an individual to protect his or her reputation and also provides remedies for, amongst other things, breach of confidence and breach of copyright.

Not only individuals but also the mass media are subject to most of these restraints, and the mass media are in some cases subject to additional constraints.

Criminal offences

Incitement

It is an offence under judge-made law to incite another person, whether by threats or encouragement, to commit any criminal offence. The incitement may be by words or conduct. There must be an intention that the other person commit the offence but it is irrelevant whether or not the offence is actually committed.

Conspiracy

It is an offence under article 9 of the Criminal Attempts and Conspiracy (NI) Order 1983 to agree with any person to commit any criminal offence. Conspiracy is committed as soon as there is such an agreement; it need not be formal, explicit or detailed.

Threats

A threat to kill someone, communicated to that person or another, is a criminal offence, carrying a sentence of up to 10 years' imprisonment. It is also a crime, carrying the same maximum sentence, to threaten without lawful excuse to damage or destroy the property of another. There are specific criminal offences of procuring sexual intercourse by threats or false pretences, and of obtaining entry into any premises by violence or the threat of violence.

Intimidation

Section 1 of the Protection of the Person and Property Act (NI) 1969 provides that a person shall be guilty of an offence if he or she:

"unlawfully causes, by force, threats, or menaces or in any way whatsoever, any other person (a) to leave any place where that person is for the time being resident or in occupation; or (b) to leave his employment; or (c) to terminate the services or employment of any person; or (d) to do or refrain from doing any act".

There is a penalty of up to five years' imprisonment for such intimidation (see also page 150).

Incitement to hatred

Article 9 of the Public Order (NI) Order 1987 makes it an offence to use or display threatening, abusive or insulting words or behaviour, with intent to stir up hatred or fear of a section of the Northern Ireland community, or where such fear or hatred are likely to be stirred up. The fear or hatred must be directed against a group of persons defined by religious belief, colour, race, nationality or ethnic or national origins. It is not an offence to use such words or behaviour in a private dwelling, provided that the person concerned has no reason to suppose that the words or behaviour will be seen or heard outside.

It is similarly an offence under articles 10 and 11 of the Public Order (NI) Order to publish, distribute, play or show written or taped material which is threatening, abusive or insulting, with the intention of stirring up fear or hatred or where such fear or hatred is likely to be aroused. It is an offence under article 13 to possess such material with a view to publishing, displaying or distributing it.

Rumours

Article 14 of the Public Order (NI) Order 1981 makes it an offence to publish or circulate any statement or report likely to stir up hatred or fear of any section of the public in Northern Ireland on the basis of race, religion, or national origin, knowing that report or statement to be false and intending to provoke a breach of the peace at any time.

Poison pen letters

The Malicious Communications (NI) Order 1988 makes it an offence to send or deliver articles with the intention of causing distress or anxiety.

Bomb hoaxes

It is an offence under article 3 of the Criminal Law (Amendment)(NI) Order 1977 intentionally to cause or communicate a false bomb warning. The maximum penalty is five years' imprisonment.

Support for proscribed organisations

It is an offence under section 28 of the Northern Ireland (Emergency Provisions) Act 1991(the EPA) to solicit or invite support for an organisation proscribed (*i.e.* prohibited) under the EPA. It is also an offence to organise or address a meeting knowing that it is to support or further the activities of such an organisation or that it is to be addressed by a person professing to belong to a proscribed organisation.

Public order offences

These are covered in chapter 9.

Sedition

The old offence of sedition (also called seditious libel) makes it a crime to speak or publish words which are likely and intended to provoke public disorder and violence against the monarch, government or constitution of the United Kingdom. In practice, conduct which might once have been charged as sedition is now likely to be dealt with under one of the other headings mentioned here.

Incitement to disaffection

The Incitement to Disaffection Act 1934 makes it an offence punishable by two years' imprisonment to endeavour to seduce any member of the armed forces from his or her duty or allegiance to the Crown, while the Mutiny Act 1797 makes it an offence punishable by life imprisonment to incite any member of the armed forces to mutiny or commit traitorous acts. The 1934 Act also criminalises possession of a document inciting disaffection with the intention of using it for that purpose.

Defamation

The law of defamation causes a great deal of difficulty for journalists and others making public comment. Defamation is essentially the publication of a statement about someone which is both untrue and likely to be damaging to his or her reputation. Publication simply means the communication of the statement to another person (other than the person defamed) and the statement need not be in words; a drawing or cartoon may suffice.

Defamation may be either libel or slander; libel is defamation in a permanent form, notably in printed form, but also including film, tape, television and theatre. Slander is defamation in non-permanent form, usually unrecorded speech. There is only one important difference between the two forms of defamation: for slander, but not for libel, there is a need to prove financial loss. The exceptions are slanderous words concerning a person's competence in his or her trade or business, or suggesting that a woman is 'unchaste' or that a person has a contagious disease or has committed a criminal offence. In these cases loss need not be proved.

Three unusual aspects of suing for defamation discourage the making of such claims and encourage the settlement of those that are made. They mean that defamation actions are usually a risky business for all concerned.

- Legal aid is not available either to take or to defend a defamation action.
- Defamation actions for more than £1,000 can be taken only in the High Court, with consequently higher costs.
- Defamation is now one of the very few civil issues which must be tried with a jury (unless both parties agree to trial by judge only). The jury (consisting of seven people) will have to decide whether the plaintiff (*i.e.* the person bringing the action) has been defamed and, if so, the amount of damages to be awarded. The issues involved may be very complex, making for an uncertain outcome and a long and expensive trial. The amounts awarded by juries for defamation may

vary from the colossal (£1.5 million in one recent case) to the contemptuous (60p in another).

In 1991 the Neill Committee Report recommended a number of amendments to the law aimed at simplifying and speeding up defamation actions. These included an extended form of the "innocent defamation" defence (see page 159) which would allow newspapers to offer corrections and apologies and to have damages set by a judge on that basis. The Lord Chancellor indicated in December 1992 that he intended to introduce some of the Committee's proposals, but at the time of going to press no further action has been taken.

Proving defamation

A person who alleges defamation must show that the comments in question diminish his or her reputation in the eyes of "right thinking members of society". The judge must decide whether the statement is capable of bearing a defamatory meaning, but the jury must decide whether it actually does carry such a meaning and whether it could reasonably be taken to apply to the plaintiff.

The intentions of the person making the statement are normally irrelevant; in most circumstances it will be no defence to say that no defamatory meaning was intended, or that the statement was not intended to be taken as referring to the plaintiff. Nor need the plaintiff show that anyone did in fact read such a meaning into the statement, or thought any less of the plaintiff because of it. It is enough if they might have done.

The court is entitled to consider innuendoes and hidden meanings, and it is not necessary for the defamation to be obvious to the general public: it is sufficient if some other person with particular knowledge is able to identify the plaintiff as the subject of a defamatory statement. A statement about a broad group, such as a racial grouping, will not normally be actionable, but a statement about a specific grouping, or an unidentified member of such a grouping (such as a committee) will be actionable by any member of that group.

Defences to defamation

It is a defence to prove that on the balance of probabilities the statement was true (this is known as the defence of "justification"). But it is not enough that the defendant believed that the statement was true, or had reasonable grounds for believing that it was true, or was merely repeating what he or she had been told by someone else. It is also a defence to prove that the statement was fair comment, *i.e.* that it was the expression of an opinion held honestly and without malice by the defendant on a matter of public interest. The statement must be an expression of opinion, not of fact, and the facts on which it is based must be substantially correct. Matters of public interest include politics, books and plays.

As regards the defence of "privilege", the law permits people in some circumstances, both public and private, to be free to communicate without fear of being sued for defamation. "Absolute" privilege covers statements made in Parliament, in parliamentary papers or in court, and fair, accurate, and contemporaneous newspaper reports of judicial proceedings; the makers of such statements and reports cannot be sued for defamation. "Qualified" privilege, which means that the maker of a statement cannot be sued provided that the material is published without malice, attaches to a wide variety of other situations, including reports of parliamentary proceedings and non-contemporaneous reports of judicial proceedings. Fair and accurate reports of public meetings or meetings of a range of public or semi-public bodies, including local authorities, and reports of the decisions of trade, professional, religious, educational and sporting bodies are protected by qualified privilege, provided that anyone aggrieved by such a report is given a reasonable right of reply. Qualified privilege also covers situations where one person is under a moral or legal duty to give information and another to receive it. This might cover complaints to the police, to social workers or to an employer about an employee.

Section 4 of the Defamation Act 1952 provides a defence for a publisher, who, after exercising all due care, did not know and could not reasonably have known that a statement was defamatory. The defence applies only where the offer of a correction and apology has been made, and would be relevant only in rare cases, the classic example being where a fictional character bears an unfortunate resemblance to a real person. The Libel Act 1843 provides a defence for a publisher of a newspaper or magazine who can show that the libel was not published maliciously or with gross negligence, and that an apology has been published and payment made in compensation.

In general, all those involved in the publication of a libel may be compelled to pay compensation. In the case of a newspaper this could include the writer, editor, owner and printers. Distributors, wholesalers, newsagents and others involved in the distribution of a newspaper or magazine have a defence to a libel action if they can show that they exercised due care and had no reason to know that a publication contained libellous material.

Anyone who anticipates that a defamatory statement will be published about him or her may apply for an injunction to prevent publication. The courts, however, acknowledge the importance of protecting free speech, and will not normally grant such an injunction where the defences of justification or fair comment are likely to be pleaded.

Malicious falsehood

There may be occasions when people suffer damage through incorrect statements being made about them, even though those statements do not strike at their reputation and hence are not defamatory. For example, a professional person may lose business through an incorrect report that he or she has retired or gone on a long holiday. Anyone in such a position may be able to sue for malicious falsehood where it can be shown that the person making the statement acted from malicious or improper motives. In *Kaye v Robertson* (1990) an injured actor successfully sued a tabloid newspaper under this heading.

Criminal libel

Libel is also a crime if it is so serious as to require criminal prosecution in the public interest. Proceedings against a newspaper or periodical can be initiated with the consent of a High Court judge. It is not a sufficient defence to prove that the alleged libel was true; it must also be shown that its publication was for the public benefit.

Broadcasting and television

Broadcasting in the UK, and hence in Northern Ireland, requires a government licence under the Wireless Telegraphy Acts. All television broadcasting in Northern Ireland is under the authority of either the BBC or the Independent Television Commission (the ITC), a regulatory and supervisory body which grants the franchises under which all independent television companies operate, and which was set up in 1990 to replace the former Independent Broadcasting Authority. The Independent Radio Authority has a similiar role in respect of independent radio stations, and the Cable Television Authority deals with cable television. Satellite television based in the UK is subject to the authority of the ITC, with the Home Secretary having a power to proscribe any unacceptable foreign satellite service.

The BBC was established by Charter and the ITC by the Broadcasting Act 1990. Both have ultimate responsibility for programmes broadcast under their authority. The ITC is under a statutory duty to ensure that news reporting is fair and impartial and that nothing is broadcast which offends against good taste or decency or which is likely to incite crime or disorder or be offensive to public feelings. The BBC has bound itself to a similar standard. Unlike its predecessor the ITC does not have the right to call in programmes for pre-transmission vetting, but it does have significant sanctions in respect of independent television companies, including the power to impose financial penalties.

The 1990 Act makes the Obscene Publications Act and, in Northern Ireland, the incitement to hatred laws (page 155 above), applicable to broadcasting. In Northern Ireland a senior police officer, suspecting that an offence has been or is likely to be committed under the incitement to hatred laws, has the right to demand access to any relevant scripts, films or tapes.

The Broadcasting Standards Council

The 1990 Act gives the Broadcasting Standards Council, set up in 1988, statutory powers to monitor broadcasting and to draw up codes of practice in respect of sex, violence, good taste and decency in broadcasting. Broadcasting bodies are under an obligation to take account of the Council's codes when establishing their own practices. The Council has the power to receive complaints about standards in broadcasting and to initiate complaints itself. It can also require broadcasting bodies to publicise its findings in respect of such complaints. The address of the Council is:

- 7, The Sanctuary, London SW1P 3JX (tel: 071 233 0544).

The broadcasting ban

Both the BBC and the ITC are subject to reserved government powers. These include the power, vested in the Home Secretary, to order both bodies to include or exclude specific matters in their broadcasts and this power was invoked in October 1988 when Douglas Hurd, the then Home Secretary, instructed the BBC and the IBA to:

> *"refrain at all times from sending any broadcast matter which consists of or includes any words spoken, whether in the course of an interview or discussion or otherwise, by a person who appears or is heard on the programme in which the matter is broadcast (a) where the person speaking the words represents or purports to represent an organisation specified below, or (b) the words support or solicit or invite support for such an organisation".*

The notice then specifies eight organisations proscribed under emergency legislation including:
- the Irish Republican Army
- the Irish National Liberation Army
- the Ulster Volunteer Force
- the Ulster Freedom Fighters and
- the Red Hand Commandos

as well as three otherwise legal organisations:
- Sinn Fein
- Republican Sinn Fein
- the Ulster Defence Association (made illegal in 1992).

The notice also states that the ban does not apply during election campaigns or to words spoken in Parliament.

This ban has posed considerable difficulties of interpretation. The Home Office has indicated that it does not prevent the showing of still or moving pictures of an affected speaker while a reporter reads a paraphrase or even a word-for-word report of what the speaker is saying. It has also said that there is nothing to prevent direct reports of anyone speaking in a personal capacity or purely in his or her capacity as a member of an organisation which does not fall under the notice. This appears to protect coverage of elected representatives speaking on constituency matters, but the distinction between speaking as an MP or councillor and speaking as a member of a political organisation is a vague one. The ban has also caused particular difficulties in respect of live and phone-in programmes. It has had the absurd effect of preventing the broadcasting of historical and archival material, including programmes which have previously been televised without comment or controversy.

Because the broadcasting ban is simply a matter of the Home Secretary exercising powers under existing legislation, it is not readily subject to legal challenge or clarification. One legal challenge has already been rejected by the House of Lords (*R v Home Secretary, ex parte Brind*). Decisions on the implementation of the ban are in the final analysis a matter for the broadcasting authorities. With the government holding the ultimate authority with regard to broadcasting and appointments to the broadcasting authorities, it is hardly surprising that there has been a tendency, especially in England, to err on the side of safety. Members of the public, persons affected by the ban, and even journalists and programme makers have very little means of redress over any particular decision.

In favour of the ban, it has been argued that the presence of spokespersons or apologists for violent organisations on television causes widespread public outrage, and that it is a necessary and legitimate means of combatting the greater evil of terrorism. It is also pointed out that the Republic of Ireland has had similar but more comprehensive provisions since 1971. The European Commission of Human Rights has held that the Irish legislation does not contravene Article 10 of the European Convention (*Purcell v Ireland*, 1990). Against the ban, it has been argued that it is ineffective and irrelevant to the fight against terrorism, has given a propaganda victory to the terrorists and diminished the credibility of broadcasters as independent reporters , and that the exclusion of otherwise legal organisations from the electronic media is a dangerous precedent for government interference in the process of political debate.

Newspapers and periodicals

There are no licensing requirements for the publishing of newspapers or periodicals; the phrase "registered with the Post Office as a newspaper" relates only to postal rates.

Complaints against newspapers can be made to the Press Complaints Commission (the PCC), which was set up in 1991 following the Calcutt

Report of 1990. The PCC has published a code of practice covering issues such as accuracy, the right to reply, invasion of privacy, harassment and misrepresentation, but like the Press Council which it replaced its powers are very limited. Continuing complaints about the conduct of some sections of the press led to a second Calcutt report in 1993 which recommended the scrapping of the PCC and the creation of a statutory press tribunal with the power to order the publication of apologies and to impose fines on errant newspapers. At the time of writing the government appears to have rejected the idea of the tribunal.

Advertising

Complaints about advertisements may be made to the Advertising Standards Authority (Brook House, 2-16 Torrington Place, London WC1E 7HN; tel: 071-580-5555). This is an independent body sponsored by the advertising industry itself and it has published a Code of Advertising Practice, among the requirements of which are that advertisements should be legal, decent, honest and truthful. The ASA rules on complaints and in extreme cases may instruct subscribing media organisations not to accept the advertisement. The ITC applies similar rules in respect of advertising on commercial television and radio.

Films and videos

The British Board of Film Classification censors and classifies films and video tapes. In respect of video tapes it has statutory powers under the Video Recordings Act 1985, which allows massive fines for selling or distributing videos which have not obtained a Board classification. Most local authorities, which have a licensing role in respect of cinemas in their areas, make it a licensing requirement that no film can be shown which does not have a BBFC certificate but they have the right to ban even films which do have a classification. Local authority licensing requirements do not apply to private cinema clubs.

Copyright

Copyright law prevents the use of protected material without the copyright owner's consent. Material protected may include original literary works (very broadly defined and including almost anything written down), artistic and musical works, photographs, films, sound and video recordings, and television and radio broadcasts. It is not a breach of copyright to make fair use of a copyrighted work for the purposes of criticism or reporting of current events, provided that the author of the work is properly acknowledged. Use of copyright material may also be justified where the public interest is best served by publication.

Obscenity

In England and Wales the judge-made law on obscenity was largely superseded by the Obscene Publications Act 1959, but that legislation has never been extended to Northern Ireland. The common law still applies here, making it a criminal offence to publish what is technically called "an obscene libel."

The common law test of obscenity is whether the material in question has a tendency to "deprave or corrupt" those who are likely to see it. Whether a particular publication is obscene is for the jury (if there is one) or the judge to decide, applying the current standards of ordinary decent people. "Deprave or corrupt" means something which is more than merely shocking or offensive. Although obscenity is normally taken to apply to pornographic matter it can cover other material as well, such as publications advocating drug-taking or glorifying violence.

To break the law it is sufficient, as in defamation, to "publish" the material to one other person, but it is not necessary to prove that any person has actually been depraved or corrupted. Having an intention to publish, knowing that the material would have a tendency to deprave or corrupt, is enough. The Obscene Publications Act provides a specific defence for publications if they are for the public good in that they are in the interests of science, literature, art or learning or other objects of general interest. The common law position is less clear, but there is probably a basis for an essentially similar defence.

Indecency

A variety of statutes and local bylaws deal with indecent behaviour, publication or display. "Indecent" lacks any clear legal definition but would seem to include anything offensive to the standards of ordinary reasonable people, though lacking the element of depravity necessary for obscenity (see too chapter 15).

The customs and excise authorities have wide powers to seize indecent or obscene material brought into the United Kingdom, though the effect of a ruling by the European Court of Justice has been to restrict these powers to material which would be deemed obscene rather than merely indecent. The Post Office Act 1953 makes it an offence to send any indecent or obscene article through the post, while the Unsolicited Goods and Services (NI) Order 1976 prohibits the posting of unsolicited sexual publications. The British Telecom Act 1981 criminalises telephone calls which are grossly offensive, indecent, obscene or menacing. The Protection of Children (NI) Order 1978 makes it an offence to take, distribute or possess indecent photographs of children.

Blasphemy

The judge-made law on blasphemy once made it a crime to deny the truth of the Christian religion. In its modern form, however, blasphemy simply covers comment which amounts to an insulting or abusive attack on the Christian religion. The intention of the person making or publishing the comment is irrelevant; it is only necessary to show that he or she is responsible for comments which the court deems to be sufficiently offensive.

The offence remains extremely vague and unsatisfactory. As has been confirmed by a case arising out of the Salman Rushdie affair (*Ex parte Choudhury*), it does not protect non-Christian religions, and there is even doubt as to whether it extends beyond protecting the doctrines of the Church of England. With modern legislation now providing racial and religious groups with some measure of protection against abuse, it would be best if the crime of blasphemy were either abolished altogether or limited, as the Law Commission has recommended, to disruptive or abusive behaviour at a religious service or on church premises.

The Elected Authorities Act

The Elected Authorities (Northern Ireland) Act 1989 provides that any candidate for election to a district council or to the Northern Ireland Assembly (currently suspended) must sign a declaration on submitting his or her nomination papers, and again, if elected, before taking his or her seat. The declaration states that:

> *"if elected, I will not by word or deed express support for or approval of (a) any proscribed organisation or (b) acts of terrorism (that is to say, violence for political ends) connected with the affairs of Northern Ireland."*

This requirement does not apply to elections to Westminster.

The declaration covers comments at public meetings or in circumstances where the person concerned can reasonably be expected to know that his or her comments will become public knowledge. The relevant test is whether the comments can reasonably be understood to express support or approval for an illegal organisation or for acts of terrorism.

The Act states that a district council, or any member of that council or any elector for that council, may take legal proceedings in the High Court for a judicial determination that a member of that council is in breach of the declaration. If such a ruling is granted, that member will be disqualified from holding office and will not be permitted to stand again for election for a period of five years. No such proceedings have yet been taken.

Contempt of court

The law on contempt of court protects the fair and impartial administration of justice. It is particularly concerned with preventing juries from being exposed to prejudicial comment. The modern law is largely to be found in the Contempt of Court Act 1981, which was passed after criticism of existing United Kingdom law by the European Court of Human Rights in the *Sunday Times* case (1979).

The 1981 Act makes it an offence to publish anything which creates a substantial risk that the course of justice in any particular case will be substantially impeded or prejudiced. This covers any speech, writing or broadcast addressed to the public or any section of it, and the rule applies when any proceedings are "active" (*i.e. sub judice*, to use the old phrase). Criminal proceedings are active from the time when someone is arrested or an arrest warrant or a summons has been issued. Civil proceedings are active from the time when a date is set for trial. Appeals are active from the time when leave to appeal is applied for or notice of appeal lodged.

Liability is "strict", *i.e.* the intention of the publisher is not normally relevant. It has recently been held, however, that the 1981 Act has not affected the common law position concerning material published *with the intention* of prejudicing or interfering with court proceedings: it can still be contempt to publish such material, even when no proceedings are active (*Attorney -General v News Group Newspapers*, 1988).

Publication of an accused's criminal record or comment on his or her character or that of a witness, or linking an accused to other offences, would probably constitute a substantial risk of prejudice, as would publication of a photograph of an accused where identification may be an issue. But fair, accurate and contemporaneous reports of proceedings in court cannot be contempt and discussion in good faith of public affairs or matters of public interest is not contempt if any risk of prejudice to particular proceedings is only incidental to the discussion.

Any attempt to bribe, intimidate or otherwise improperly influence witnesses, jurors or judges would be contempt of court. Abusive criticism of judges, or accusations of prejudice or partiality against them, may amount to the old form of contempt known as "scandalising the court", though the Court of Appeal has said that criticism in good faith of a judgment, however vigorous, should not constitute contempt.

Section 8 of the 1981 Act completely outlaws any approaches to jurors, however innocuous. It declares it to be contempt of court to obtain, disclose or solicit any particulars of statements made, opinions expressed, arguments advanced or votes cast by members of a jury during their deliberations.

Contempt of court also covers disorderly behaviour in court, failure to comply with court orders or to observe an undertaking given to the court, and obstructing court officers in the course of their duties. It was held in the course of the "Spycatcher" litigation that a newspaper could be in contempt of court for publishing material which was the subject of injunctions preventing publication by other newspapers. In *Home Office v Harman* (1983) a solicitor allowed a journalist to see some documents concerning prisons which the court had ordered the Home Office to disclose to the court. The House of Lords decided that this behaviour was contempt, but when the solicitor took the case to the European Commission of Human Rights the government agreed to settle it. Under the terms of this settlement the government promised to change the law so that it would no longer be a contempt to disclose documents already produced in court pursuant to a court order.

Other restrictions on court reporting

Most legal proceedings in Northern Ireland take place in open court, and can be reported by the press. The press and public can be excluded from prosecutions taken under official secrets legislation and in a number of circumstances where publicity would defeat the interests of justice, such as blackmail cases. Similarly, the Contempt of Court Act 1981 allows courts, in exceptional circumstances, to order that the names of parties or witnesses, or other relevant information, must not be mentioned in open court or the press.

There are a number of other circumstances where press reporting of court proceedings is subject to limitations. The names of rape victims are protected from publication by the Sexual Offences (NI) Order 1978 (see chapter 15). Only very limited factual information can be published about committal proceedings in magistrates' courts (which precede criminal trials), unless the defendant asks for reporting restrictions to be lifted. In a jury trial the press cannot report legal arguments heard in the absence of the jury. Juvenile court proceedings can be reported on condition that the identity of the defendant or witnesses is not revealed. Most matrimonial proceedings are held in private and are subject to substantial reporting restrictions.

Journalists' sources

The Contempt of Court Act 1981 provides a measure of protection for journalists' sources. Section 10 says that a court can order a journalist or editor to disclose a source only where such disclosure is necessary in the interests of justice or of national security, or for the prevention of disorder or crime.

The police may in some circumstances seize documents and other journalistic material. Under the Police and Criminal Evidence (NI) Order 1989 they may obtain a court order granting access to such material where they can satisfy a judge that the necessary conditions have been met (see chapter 3). They may also be able to obtain such material, including films and photographs, under section 18 of the Prevention of Terrorism (Temporary Provisions) Act 1989, which requires the disclosure of any information which may be of assistance in preventing terrorism. This law was first used against Channel Four after it broadcast a programme in 1992 concerning alleged collusion between RUC officers and Loyalist paramilitaries (*DPP. v Channel Four Television Co. Ltd*).

Official secrets

Official secrecy has been the subject of very considerable controversy in recent years. Section 1 of the Official Secrets Act 1911, which is still in force, makes what would commonly be called spying an offence; it deals with collecting or revealing information likely to be useful to an enemy, for any purpose prejudicial to the safety or interests of the state. Under the Official Secrets Act 1989, which came into force in March 1990, it is an offence to communicate or receive any government information whatsoever without permission.

The new Act essentially creates two kinds of offence.

- It makes it an offence for any member or former member of the security services, or anyone associated with security or intelligence activities, to disclose any information about such activities. The Home Secretary may by "notification" make anyone who comes into contact with intelligence activities subject to this restriction. Journalists who assist or encourage such disclosure, or who publish such information with grounds for believing that it has been disclosed without permission, may be prosecuted as accomplices.

- It is an offence to disclose other kinds of government information where damage is caused or likely to be caused by unauthorised disclosure. The categories of information covered include anything which would endanger British interests abroad, prejudice the capabilities of the armed forces, or impede the work of the police. Confidential information obtained from another state or international organisation is protected. Where information about intelligence, security, defence or international issues has been communicated to other governments or international organisations and has been leaked abroad it is an offence to repeat it in the United Kingdom.

Section 5 of the 1989 Act makes it an offence for journalists or editors to publish information where they know it to be protected by the Act and have cause to believe that publication would be damaging to the national interest. The Act does not allow any defence of acting in the public interest: unauthorised disclosure, and in some cases publication, of protected information is a criminal offence even though it may expose criminal activities, corruption or serious government malpractice. The absence of such a public interest defence is a particular cause for concern, even though there was no such defence in the old Act, but it may be that scrutiny in the courts and the common sense of juries will tend to keep a check on any abuse of the new provisions.

The absolute prohibition on unauthorised disclosure of information by those involved in the security services is also a matter of considerable concern. Given the extremely wide authority given to the security services by the Security Services Act 1989, and the lack of any parliamentary scrutiny of their activities, the absence of any means whereby members of the security services can bring even the most serious abuse of power to the attention of the public (or even of Parliament) is a very serious omission.

Unauthorised disclosure of government information outside the areas specified in the Official Secrets Act 1989 is not a criminal offence, but it may well expose the culprit to internal disciplinary procedures. The government may also use the civil law to obtain injunctions against publication or to claim damages.

"D Notices"

The "D Notice" system is an informal system which acts as a restraint on press coverage of sensitive defence and security topics. The notices are issued by the Defence, Press and Broadcasting Committee, a body composed of officials from government departments concerned with national security and representatives of broadcasting organisations and the press. The Committee gives guidance on the publication of material which is sensitive on national security grounds, and from time to time issues notices warning that publication of certain stories may be harmful to national security. The system lacks legal force: the Committee cannot prevent publication and prior clearance from the Committee is no defence to prosecution under the Official Secrets Acts.

Chapter 11

Access to Information

Gerry McCormack

The main justification for giving someone access to information held by others is that informed citizens are the basic ideal upon which a free and democratic society is premised. But there are more specific grounds as well. A person may want to check the accuracy of information held about him or her. There is the fear that if government is allowed to operate in secrecy it will abuse the powers entrusted to it and its officials will become corrupt. Allow people access to official information and they will be able to participate more effectively in law-making and administration.

In this chapter, the way the law *restricts* and *confers* access to information is examined. The final section argues the need for a Freedom of Information Act.

Laws restricting access

Broadly speaking, there are seven ways in which the law in Northern Ireland may *restrict* access to information. Three of these - the rules on contempt of court, disclosure of official secrets and "D notices" - have already been discussed in chapter 10.

Contracts

There may be a contract in existence, one of whose terms prevents a contracting party from disclosing information to a non-contracting party. This is common in employment contracts, which often prohibit employees from revealing information acquired during the course of their employment. It also exists in contracts between banks and account holders.

Breach of confidence

In certain circumstances the law imposes an obligation not to disclose information received in confidence. It is generally necessary that the recipient has expressly or impliedly acknowledged the obligation, but he or she will not be held to it if the information is already in the public domain. This defence was upheld in a 1978 case where John Lennon tried unsuccessfully to prevent the *News of the World* from publishing an article by his former wife about their married life. Lord Denning said that the relationship of the parties had ceased to be their private affair. Similar arguments prevailed in the "Spycatcher" case, where the House of Lords concluded that publication of Peter Wright's memoirs in Britain could not be prevented because it had been published and much publicised throughout the world.

A second possible defence to an action for breach of confidence is the public interest. The courts take this to mean that no-one can be prevented from disclosing information which indicates the commission of a crime. If a journalist wishes to reveal details of misconduct confided to him or her by someone involved in the misconduct, he or she cannot be prevented from doing so (see *British Steel Corp. v Granada Television Ltd*, 1980).

Privacy

There is no general right to privacy in the law of Northern Ireland. Various Private Members' Bills have been put forward to create the right, but none of these has yet been enacted by Parliament. However the law relating to trespass, nuisance, defamation and malicious falsehood does provide a degree of protection. For instance, where a private detective posing as a post office engineer obtains entry to a building and places a bugging device in a telephone receiver, this would be trespass to land as well as trespass to goods. The persons in possession of the land and telephone could sue for compensation. The damages awarded would be increased in cases of insolent or oppressive behaviour ("aggravated" and "exemplary" damages). But it has been held that an owner of land does not possess all of the air above the land, so he or she cannot sue an aerial photographer who flies over the land to take pictures of it. Constant overhead surveillance might constitute what the law terms a nuisance, as would the making of persistent telephone calls to a person's home or office.

The law relating to malicious falsehood proved of assistance to a person whose privacy had been infringed in *Kaye v Robertson* (1990). This is a case where a well-known actor obtained a court order preventing a paper from publishing photographs and an interview which it had acquired through deception. To do so would have constituted the wrong of malicious falsehood.

As regards invasions of privacy by the press it may be that the only effective remedy is a complaint to the Press Complaints Commission. This body was established in 1991 following the recommendations of the Calcutt Committee and in place of the Press Council which had existed since 1953. The Press Complaints Commission has an independent chair and 15 other members, but of these only 5 are not drawn from the press or the media in general. Anyone may complain to the Commission about an invasion of privacy, whether personally affected or not. The Commission may censure a newspaper or journalist but it has no power to fine or to award compensation. While newspapers are expected to publish an adverse adjudication they are not legally compelled to do so. In these respects the powers of the Press Complaints Commission mirror those of the Press Council which it replaced. On the other hand, the Commission, unlike the Press Council, does not require a complainant to give up any legal right of action.

Where it is alleged that a TV or Radio broadcast has infringed a person's privacy there is an opportunity of making a complaint to the Broadcasting Complaints Commission. This body consists of at least 3 members and was established under the Broadcasting Act 1990. If it considers that there has been an unwarranted invasion of privacy, the Commission may require the broadcasting body to publish an apology in, for example the *Radio Times* or to broadcast a summary of the complaint and the Commission's findings.

Telephone tapping and tampering with mail

In the *Malone* case an English court confirmed that a person had no right not to have his or her telephone tapped by state authorities. There was nothing to make the practice unlawful, therefore it had to be tolerated. Mr. Malone then took his case to Strasbourg, where the European Court of Human Rights decided in 1984 that the United Kingdom's law was in breach of Article 8 of the European Convention on Human Rights (*Malone v UK*, 1984). Article 8 guarantees the right to respect for everyone's private and family life, home and correspondence. The Court said that the United Kingdom's law did not indicate with sufficient clarity the scope and manner of exercise of the relevant discretion conferred on the public authorities.

The Interception of Communications Act 1985 was passed in order to comply with the European Court's judgment in the *Malone* case. It is now an offence for anyone to intercept communications sent by post or by means of a public communications system. The offence is committed, however, only where the interception is intentional and intention may be difficult to prove in a particular case. For instance, in 1992 there was no prosecution when details of a private telephone conversation allegedly involving the Princess of Wales were published. Moreover, interception remains permissible if it is consented to (*e.g.* when someone wishes to trace offensive telephone calls) or if it is carried out under a warrant issued by the Secretary of State, who must not issue one unless he or she considers that the warrant is necessary:

- in the interests of national security;
- for the purpose of preventing or detecting serious crime; or
- for the purpose of safeguarding the economic well-being of the United Kingdom.

The Prime Minister appoints a Commissioner to supervise the issuing of the warrant and there is a tribunal to investigate complaints. If the tribunal finds that the Act has been violated it must inform the complainant and the Prime Minister and it may cancel the warrant, order the intercepted material to be destroyed and direct compensation to be paid. If the tribunal finds no violation of the Act, the complainant is told this but not whether interception has in fact been carried out. There is therefore still no absolute right to know whether your telephone is being tapped and no figures have been released on the number of taps authorised in Northern Ireland.

The 1985 Act does not deal with surveillance by electronic bugging devices. The use of such devices is not of itself a crime, though physically placing an electronic bug may give rise to a civil action for trespass. In any event, more sophisticated modern devices are capable of listening in on conversations from a considerable distance.

Laws conferring access

Data Protection Act 1984

This Act was passed in order to comply with the Council of Europe's 1981 Convention for the Protection of Individuals with regard to Automatic Processing of Data. It compels users of data to register with the Data Protection Registry, non-registration being a criminal offence. The Registrar can issue enforcement or de-registration notices against registered users who violate the Act's data protection principles. To check whether these principles are being maintained the Registrar has powers of entry and inspection. There is a Data Protection Tribunal to hear appeals against decisions taken by the Registrar.

A user of data is defined by the Act as a person who "controls the contents and use of the data" which are part of a collection processed or intended to be processed by that person or by someone on his or her behalf.

The core of the Act is the part giving "data subjects" the right of access to stored data. Upon request in writing (for which a charge of up to £10 can be made) a data user must within 40 days state whether he or she has any personal data relating to the person making the request and must supply that person with a copy of such data. The data subject must be an identifiable living person, not a company. If damage or distress is caused as a result of an inaccurate entry, compensation is payable by the data user unless he or she can prove that such care was taken as was reasonably required in all the circumstances to ensure the accuracy of the data at the time. A court can order inaccurate data to be rectified, erased or supplemented.

Exemptions

Three important matters are exempt from registration :
- personal data required for the purpose of safeguarding national security;
- payroll and accounting data;
- data held for domestic or club purposes.

Matters exempt from the subject access provisions are:
- the three items already listed;
- personal data held for the prevention or detection of crime;
- personal data held for the assessment or collection of any tax or duty;
- personal data relating to the physical or mental health of the subject;
- data held subject to legal professional privilege or for the making of judicial appointments;
- data held in confidence for statistical or research purposes.

Data protection principles

The data protection principles which all data users must adhere to are laid out in Schedule 1 of the 1984 Act.
- The information to be contained in personal data must be obtained and processed fairly and lawfully.
- The personal data must be held only for one or more specified and lawful purposes.
- Personal data held must not be used or disclosed in any manner incompatible with the purpose(s) for which it is held.
- Personal data held must be adequate, relevant and not excessive in relation to the purpose for which it is held.
- Personal data must be accurate and, where necessary, kept up to date.
- Personal data must not be kept for longer than is necessary.
- An individual is entitled at reasonable intervals and without undue delay or expense to be informed by any data user whether he or she holds personal data about that individual, and to have access to any such data.
- An individual is entitled, where appropriate, to have personal data corrected or erased.

- Computer bureau must take appropriate security measures against unauthorised access to or alteration, disclosure, loss or destruction of personal data.

Non-computerised personal files

The Data Protection Act does not apply to data kept elsewhere than on computer. Such non-computerised files are often very detailed. In England, the Access to Personal Files Act 1987 went some way towards plugging the gap in the law. It gave power to the Home Secretary to make regulations conferring on people a right of access to information about themselves on local authority records. To date regulations have been made covering housing, social work and education records. The Act does not, however, permit access to employment records, government benefit and immigration records, or bank, building society and credit records. Similarly, the Access to Medical Reports Act 1988 provided a very limited right of access to non-computerised medical records. The rights conferred by these two Acts were eventually extended to Northern Ireland by the Access to Personal Files and Medical Reports (NI) Order 1991. The comparable Access to Health Records Act 1990 is soon to be extended to Northern Ireland by the Access to Health Records (NI) Order 1993, though the health authorities claim that they already have procedures in place which comply with the disclosure requirements imposed by that legislation. For access to school records, see chapter 16.

Company and land records

The Companies (NI) Order 1986 requires companies incorporated in Northern Ireland to supply certain information to the Companies Registry. This may then be examined by members of the public on payment of a fee. The companies must also disclose certain facts and figures in their annual reports (and any prospectuses issued prior to the issue of shares to the public).

The Land Registration Act (NI) 1970 provides for the registration of the ownership of property in the Land Registry, details of which may be consulted by the public. This scheme applies principally to rural property. The Registration of Deeds Act (NI) 1970 provides for the registration of "memorials" (i.e., shortened versions of certain documents of title to land), a scheme which particularly covers urban property and which again allows for public access.

Registration of births, deaths and marriages

The registration of births and deaths is provided for under the Births and Deaths Registration (NI) Order 1976. Article 34 requires the Registrar General to keep an index for each register and this is open for inspection by the public. Any individual may obtain a certified copy of an entry in the register upon payment of a fee.

The picture regarding marriages is similar. All marriages, with the exception of Roman Catholic marriages, are governed by sections 68-71 of the Marriages (Ireland) Act 1844, which permit searches in the registers. Much the same effect is achieved for Roman Catholic marriages by section 19 of the Registration of Marriages (Ireland) Act 1863, as amended.

Local authority records

Section 23 of the Local Government Act (NI) 1972 requires meetings of a local authority to be open to the public, a right of access which extends to the Fire Authority of Northern Ireland but not to Education and Library Boards or to Health and Social Services Boards. A copy of the agenda at local authority meetings must be supplied on request to any newspaper.

The 1972 Act permits a council to pass a resolution excluding the public from a meeting whenever publicity would be prejudicial to the public interest:

- by reason of the confidential nature of the business to be transacted; or
- for such special reasons as may be specified; one such special reason may be the need to receive advice from a non-council source in private.

There is also a power to exclude disorderly or misbehaving members of the public and to ban photographs or recordings (section 27). In England, the right of access is greater in that it extends to meetings of committees and sub-committees within the local council (see the Local Government (Access to Information) Act 1985). The right to inspect the minutes covers all such meetings held during the preceding six years (Local Government Act 1972, section 100C).

Public records

Public records relating mainly to Northern Ireland are stored at the Public Records Office (NI), which was established under an Act of Parliament in 1923. By section 3, records are to be delivered to the office 20 years after their making. Access to members of the public is possible 30 years after a document has been made, but this period may be extended in three situations:

- if the papers are exceptionally sensitive, their disclosure being contrary to the public interest on security or other grounds;
- if the documents contain information supplied in confidence, the disclosure of which might constitute a breach of faith; or
- if the documents contain information about individuals, the disclosure of which would cause distress or danger to living persons or their descendants.

Discovery of documents

After a court action has been started the parties to it can be compelled to disclose the existence and contents of certain documents, a process known as "discovery". For county court actions, discovery is regulated by Order 15 of the County Court Rules (NI) 1981; for High Court actions the relevant provision is Order 24 of the Rules of the Supreme Court (NI) 1980, as amended. A court order for discovery is required only if the parties do not volunteer the information themselves. A court would need to be convinced that production of the documents in question is necessary for disposing fairly of the case or for saving costs.

Generally speaking, there is no power to order discovery against someone who is not a party to the proceedings. The correct procedure is to call that person as a witness to give oral testimony. But the House of Lords held in *Norwich Pharmacal Co. v Customs and Excise Commissioners* (1974) that, where a person through no fault of his or her own gets mixed up in another person's wrongdoing, he or she may incur no personal liability in law but is under a duty to assist the victim of the wrongdoing by giving him or her full information. In a further decision, *British Steel Corp. v Granada Television Ltd* (1980), the House of Lords stressed that an applicant's interest in obtaining information so as to detect and punish wrongdoing must be shown obviously to outweigh the public interest in protecting the source and ensuring the free flow of information to the media. Moreover, no order can be issued against a stranger who is completely uninvolved in the suspected wrongdoing.

A further important law is the Administration of Justice Act 1970. Section 31 permits what is called "pre-trial" discovery: a person who is likely to be a party to legal proceedings concerning injury or death can apply for an order of discovery against another likely party. The disclosure of documents might then enable the applicant to discover whether he or she has a case worth starting in the courts. Section 32 of the 1970 Act enables a claimant in a personal injury or fatal accident case to obtain discovery of, for instance, medical records. This provision is to be generously interpreted in the plaintiff's favour (see *O'Sullivan v. Herdmans Ltd*, 1987).

Limitations to obtaining discovery

There are two important limitations to the right to obtain discovery of documents:

- the claim of legal professional privilege protects all confidential communications between a client and his or her lawyer, as well as some confidential communications between either of these people and a third party;
- public interest privilege allows the minister who is at the head of a relevant government department to contend that disclosure of the documents in question would be injurious to the public interest, either because of their contents or because of the class of documents to which they belong. In recent years the courts have made it clear that if a public interest claim is asserted by the government the judges can inspect the documents to see whether in fact the public interest does lie in their being kept secret.

The need for a Freedom of Information Act

As can be seen, there is a mishmash of legislation providing a right of access to information in limited circumstances. There is no general law conferring such a right, as there is in other countries. Sweden has the longest established system of access, dating back to the Constitution of 1766. But the American experience is the one most often referred to. In 1946 the Administrative Procedure Act was passed there to establish a right of access to government records, but only in relation to proceedings taking place before an administrative body. A more far-reaching Freedom of Information Act was passed in 1966 and it has given rise to a great deal of litigation. Canada, Australia and New Zealand each enacted a Freedom of Information Act in 1982.

A number of schemes have been proposed in the United Kingdom for affording the public a right of access to government-held information. A Green Paper in 1979 concluded that a major step forward would be the production of a Code of Practice to guide ministers in reacting to requests for information. Mr. David Steel put forward a private members' Bill in 1984, but it failed to gain enough Parliamentary support. The Bill would have established an Information Commissioner to exercise investigatory powers and to order access to be granted. Appeals would have gone to an Information Appeal Tribunal. A Labour MP introduced a similar Bill in the 1992-1993 parliamentary session but again it failed to achieve the necessary support.

The present government has no plans to introduce or support a Freedom of Information Bill though the Minister with responsibility for the Citizens' Charter has promised greater voluntary disclosure of information. Opposition parties, on the other hand, would very much like to see such a law. It is unlikely that legislation, if it comes, will be confined to a part or parts of the United Kingdom, but the change in Northern Ireland's law may not be as liberal as that in England because of the ever-present security considerations affecting this part of the world.

Chapter 12

Religious Discrimination

Stephen Livingstone and Austin Magill

Discrimination on grounds of religion or political belief has been a central civil liberties issue in Northern Ireland's history. From the beginnings of the Northern Ireland state a public commitment was given to preventing religious discrimination, in that section 5(1) of the Government of Ireland Act 1920 provided that the Parliament of Northern Ireland could not:

"give a preference, privilege or advantage, or impose any disability or disadvantage, on account of religious belief".

However, expressing a commitment to the absence of discrimination is one thing, devising the mechanisms to eradicate it is another. By the 1960's the civil rights movement and a number of studies, notably the government-appointed Cameron Commission, had established the existence of significant discrimination in housing and employment. Most legislative action to counter this has been in the area of employment but there have been anti-discrimination measures in other fields too.

Complaints of employment discrimination

If people feel they have not been selected for an interview, job or promotion because of their religion or political views, they will succeed in a claim of discrimination if they can prove a number of points:

- that they have been the victim of either *direct* or *indirect* discrimination;
- that the discrimination was carried out by a relevant body;
- that the discrimination related to a "relevant matter";
- that the discrimination is not protected by any of the exceptions in the legislation.

Direct discrimination

The legislation defines direct discrimination as occurring where a relevant body treats a person less favourably than other persons would be treated on grounds of religion or political opinion (section 16(2) of the Fair Employment Act (NI) 1976, as amended by section 49 of the 1989 Act). This is probably what most people think of when they consider what discrimination is, namely deliberately refusing a job or promotion to someone because he or she is a Catholic or Protestant. However, direct discrimination is not limited to such malicious or deliberate action: an employer will still be liable even if the discrimination is applied out of concern for the person, or the views of others. In the case of *Neilly v Mullaghboy Private Nursing Home* the employer was found to have discriminated where she dismissed a cook from her nursing home job because the residents of the home said they did not want a Catholic cook from the Irish Republic. This was discrimination even though the employer did not share the residents views.

Direct discrimination also occurs where decisions are based on generalised assumptions about people of a particular religion or political opinion, *e.g.* where a brewery refuses to employ a member of the Free Presbyterian Church because of an assumption that the abstentionist policy practised by that church would mean that its members would not be loyal and enthusiastic brewery employees. The employer would need to establish that the attitudes of that particular applicant would not be likely to make him or her a good employee. The fact that the definition states that less favourable treatment need only be based on "grounds of religion or political opinion" means that discrimination occurs whenever religion or political opinion becomes one factor in the decision. It would therefore be discrimination to dismiss an employee because his wife was a Catholic, even though the employee was not.

The number of cases in which religion is explicitly given as a reason for a decision is likely to be small. However, a person may feel that, though he or she has been refused a job or promotion on grounds that do not obviously involve religion or politics, the "real" reason for the decision was their religion or political opinions. The courts have recognised that deciding claims of discrimination will often involve making inferences and attempting to unearth facts not immediately available. A number of things may help a person claiming direct discrimination to bring these facts into the open:

- Where an application is made to the Fair Employment Tribunal (discussed below) the rules on "discovery" of documents applicable to county court actions will apply (see page 180). The Tribunal has indicated that even confidential documents relating to interviews and selections can be discovered where it is in the public interest that they be available for the applicant's case. In addition, the applicant may serve a prescribed form on those alleged to be discriminating which contains questions about their reasons for doing any act or about any other relevant matter. The replies can be used in evidence in any tribunal hearing. If the alleged discriminator fails to reply within a reasonable time, or if the tribunal finds the reply to be evasive, it may draw whatever inferences it considers just and equitable.

- The courts and the Tribunal have indicated that a *prima facie* case of discrimination will exist where a better qualified person of a different religion is not shortlisted, appointed or promoted. At this point the employer is called upon to explain the non-discriminatory reasons why this person was not shortlisted etc.(*Fair Employment Agency v Craigavon Borough Council*, 1980). Indeed, in *Department of the Environment v Fair Employment Agency* (1989) the Northern Ireland Court of Appeal indicated that this inference could be drawn where the applicants were equally qualified. Other cases show that, if the reasons the employer puts forward to explain the different treatment of the person complaining from that of someone of a different religion are vague or subjective, the Tribunal is entitled to conclude that the "real" reason was discrimination. In one case the Tribunal was satisfied there was discrimination when a better qualified person was passed over for a job and there was no evidence as to what criteria were adopted in short-listing and making appointments. The Tribunal decisions to date indicate that an employer's case will be be greatly weakened if he or she has failed to adhere to the Code of Practice. Failure to use objective criteria, train interviewers, retain notes or remove the display of sectarian emblems have all been referred to by the Fair Employment Tribunal as factors which have been taken into account in the process of drawing inferences

Indirect discrimination

This occurs where one of the "relevant bodies applies a condition or requirement" equally to all applicants or employees but where the "proportion of persons" of a particular religious belief or political opinion who "can comply" with this condition or requirement is "considerably smaller" than those not of that belief or opinion. The condition or requirement must be to the detriment of the person complaining of discrimination because he or she cannot comply with it and the person or body applying the condition or requirement "cannot show [it] to be justifiable irrespective of the religious belief or political opinion of the person to whom it is applied".

What this rather convoluted formulation means is that employers may be liable for discrimination where their employment decisions are based on criteria which may have nothing to do with religion or political opinion but whose effect is to reduce substantially the number of members of a particular religious or political group who could be considered for the employment in question. If the use of such criteria does have this effect the employer will be liable for discrimination unless he or she is able to show that the criteria are important for the job in question.

Examples of indirect discrimination are:

- an employer requiring all employees to live in East Belfast;
- recruiting all employees from a particular youth club which is run by the Catholic church;
- recruiting on the recommendation of current employees where the current workforce is overwhelmingly of one religion;
- promoting only people with particular qualifications which are generally unavailable to people from one community, or promoting only people with a certain length of service where members of a

particular religious group are under-represented among those with that length of service.

This notion of indirect discrimination was introduced into Northern Ireland's fair employment law for the first time by the Fair Employment (NI) Act 1989. However, it has been employed for some time in sex discrimination law throughout the United Kingdom and in race discrimination law in Great Britain. Its use there has given rise to certain areas of doubt:

- The first of these concerns the use of the phrase "condition or requirement". The English Court of Appeal, in *Perera v Civil Service Commissioner* (1983), indicated that the condition or requirement in question had to be a "must", *i.e.* that a person would be entitled to the job etc only if he or she complied with it. But other cases indicate that the phrase should be read broadly, bearing in mind that the objective of the legislation is to outlaw practices which have a discriminatory effect. The courts in Northern Ireland have yet to rule on this question.

- The second issue is the reference to "can comply". This appears to mean "can comply in practice", so it would not be a valid argument for an employer to say that Catholics could comply with a requirement that employees must live in East Belfast.

- Thirdly, the proportion in question must be "considerably smaller". There is no clear indication as to what proportion is sufficient. In a recent English case the Employment Appeal Tribunal indicated that 95.3% of men in the economically active population who are not in receipt of an occupational pension is a considerably smaller proportion than the 99.4 % of women who are similarly situated. In the *McCausland* case the Fair Employment Tribunal stated that a difference of 2% of Protestants to 1.5% of Catholics being able to be appointed via an internal civil service trawl was not "considerably smaller". There is also little law on the question of what "pool" of employees or potential employees is relevant for comparison. It seems that one looks to the pool of people from the complainant's community who are qualified for the job in question on all the criteria the employer uses, apart from those challenged as indirectly discriminatory. Thus, if the job is a relatively low skill one, the pool might be the entire Protestant or Catholic population. If it requires high skill, the pool might be Protestant or Catholic workers with a particular qualification (where the requirement of that qualification is not itself being challenged as discriminatory).

- The fourth issue is what employers must show if they argue that a condition or requirement is "justifiable". The Fair Employment Tribunal has adopted the approach developed in the race discrimination context. These indicate that there has to be an "objective balance between the discriminatory effect of the condition or requirement and the reasonable needs of the party who applies the condition" (*Hampson v Department of Education and Science*, 1989). These reasonable needs may include economic or administrative needs. This suggests that it is not enough for an employer to produce just any reason, but nor does it require the employer to prove that the condition or requirement was necessary for performance of the job. The tribunal must carry out a balancing test.

"Relevant bodies"

Employers are the main body against whom claims of discrimination may be brought. But five other bodies are mentioned in the Fair Employment Acts. These are:

- persons with statutory power to select employees for others;
- employment agencies;
- vocational organisations;
- persons providing training services; and
- persons with power to confer qualifications which might facilitate employment; this has been held to include planning permission or government benefits where such benefits enable someone to be employed or to employ others.

Employers are prohibited from discriminating against both applicants for employment and those they already employ, including "contract workers" supplied by someone else.

"Relevant matters"

Complaints may be made in respect of:

- being refused a job or promotion;
- dismissal or redundancy arrangements;

- the terms on which employment is offered;
- "the arrangements made for determining employment" (which includes shortlisting interview procedures or application forms);
- "access to benefits";
- being "subjected to any other detriment"; the courts have indicated that someone will be subject to a "detriment" if a "reasonable worker would or might take the view that they had been disadvantaged" (*De Souza v Automobile Association*, 1986).

The Fair Employment (NI) Act 1976 (as amended) gives the Fair Employment Commission (FEC) power to seek "injunctions" (i.e. prohibitions) against advertisements which indicate an intention to discriminate directly against someone.

Under section 16 (3) of the 1976 Act it is unlawful to discriminate against anyone because he or she is or has been involved in proceedings under the Act, either as complainant or witness. It will not be unlawful, however, where the allegations in question are false and not made in good faith.

Exemptions

There are three general exemptions from unlawful discrimination.
- section 41 of the 1976 Act exempts acts done to comply with a statutory requirement passed before the 1976 Act came into force;
- section 42 of the 1976 Act indicates that where the Secretary of State issues a certificate indicating that an act was done for the purpose of safeguarding national security, public safety or public order it is exempt from challenge as discriminatory;
- section 57(3) of the 1976 Act states that discrimination on the grounds of a person's political opinion will not be unlawful where that opinion includes approval or acceptance of the use of violence for political ends connected with Northern Ireland.

There are also specific exemptions for particular jobs:
- employment or occupation as a minister or priest;
- employment for the purposes of a private household;
- employment as a teacher in a school;

- actions by employers may in addition be exempt if they are taken as one of the *affirmative action* provisions provided for in the Fair Employment Acts; these are discussed below (see page 195).

The Fair Employment Tribunal

If someone feels that he or she has been the victim of direct or indirect discrimination an application should be made within three months to the Fair Employment Tribunal. The Tribunal will send the copy of the application to the Labour Relations Agency, which is under a duty, if requested by both the applicant and the body being complained against, to try to achieve a settlement without the application being heard by the Tribunal. The Agency can also intervene of its own accord if, after considering the application, it feels it could achieve a settlement with a reasonable chance of success.

If a Labour Relations Agency settlement is not attempted, or if it proves unsuccessful, the application will be heard by the Fair Employment Tribunal. This is organised along the same lines as an industrial tribunal and the President of the industrial tribunals is also President of the Fair Employment Tribunal. The applicant may represent himself or herself in person before the Tribunal or may be represented by a lawyer, but legal aid is unavailable. The applicant may, however, apply to the Fair Employment Commission both for initial advice on making an application and for free representation before the Tribunal. The Commission has a discretion to grant assistance in representation where it feels that the case raises an issue of principle or is too complex for the applicant to deal with unaided or where any other special circumstances are present.

The Tribunal hearings will normally take place in public but the Tribunal can sit in private to hear certain categories of evidence. These include:

- evidence which the Tribunal feels it may be against the interests of national security or public order to be heard in public;
- evidence which consists of information given in confidence;
- information which might cause substantial injury to the undertaking which employs the person giving it;
- evidence which would create a substantial risk of exposing someone to physical attack or sectarian harassment.

Remedies

If the claim of discrimination is accepted by the Tribunal, various remedies are available. The Tribunal may:

- make a declaration of the parties' rights;
- recommend that the discriminating party should take specified action within a prescribed period to eliminate the effects of discrimination; in one case the Tribunal ordered that the employer post a sign to the effect that the applicant had been discriminated against; or
- award damages; awards may include compensation for injured feelings, exemplary damages or aggravated damages. In the case of *Duffy v EHSSB* all three categories were invoked and a total of £25,000 was awarded.

There is an upper limit on the total compensation the Tribunal may award in respect of any one complaint (£30,000) and no damages will be available for unintentional indirect discrimination. If the Tribunal makes a recommendation and the discriminating party fails to comply within a reasonable period, the Tribunal may subsequently make an award of damages if it did not do so before, or increase the damages awarded up to the £30,000 maximum. An appeal on a point of law can be made against any aspect of the Tribunal's decision to the Court of Appeal.

Actions to ensure equality of opportunity

The measures already explained are all targeted at preventing employers and other relevant bodies from using discriminatory criteria in respect of jobs, promotions, benefits and qualifications. However, they are of limited effectiveness, as they begin to "bite" only when employers receive applications for jobs, promotions etc. In Northern Ireland, for a variety of historical reasons, the perception has grown up that certain jobs are essentially reserved for one religion and that there is little point in people from another religion bothering to apply for them. Hence applications are not forthcoming from the under-represented group and substantial imbalances in workforces remain. Anti-discrimination provisions are unlikely alone to achieve the aim of the legislation that employment, qualifications and promotions are genuinely open to all, regardless of religion or political opinion. For this reason the legislation contains other measures aimed at ensuring "equality of opportunity" and "fair participation".

The definition of "equality of opportunity" is given in section 20 of the 1989 Act. This states that a person has equality of opportunity with a person of any other religious belief if he or she has:

"in any [employment] circumstances the same opportunity ... as that other person has or would have in those ... circumstances, due allowance being made for any material difference in their suitability".

This definition is similar to that previously contained in section 3 of the Fair Employment (NI) Act 1976. The Standing Advisory Commission on Human Rights has observed that the Fair Employment Agency (the body replaced by the Fair Employment Commission) interpreted section 3 to mean that equality of opportunity was denied if practices adopted by employers operated to exclude members of a community under-represented in the workforce or discouraged applications from that community. Such practices include those now described as "indirect discrimination", *e.g.* word of mouth recruiting. But the Agency's interpretation seemed to go further. It included practices, such as allowing sectarian displays at workplaces or advertising only in newspapers not generally read by the under-represented community, which had the effect of discouraging applications from that community.

On some occasions the Agency also recommended the taking of positive steps to remedy past under-representation, such as setting goals and timetables for minority representation in the workforce or establishing training programmes targeted at the under-represented community. There remained some doubt as to whether recommending positive steps, as opposed to recommending the removal of barriers to recruitment, was within the definition of equality of opportunity. Some ambiguity about the scope of the concept remains. However the 1989 Act also introduced a new term, "fair participation", which employers can in some circumstances be required by the Fair Employment Commission to attain. "Fair participation" is not defined in the legislation but the Code of Practice issued by the Department of Economic Development indicates that what is fair depends on the circumstances and that:

"employers should be making sustained efforts to promote [fair participation] through affirmative action measures and, if ap-

propriate, the setting of goals and timetables. It does not mean that every job, occupation or position in every undertaking in Northern Ireland must reflect the proportionate distribution of Protestants and Roman Catholics in the province".

What this appears to be aiming at is that if the employer is or should be aware (through monitoring) of significant under-representation of one community in the workforce, and is not taking steps to counteract this, a failure to ensure fair participation exists.

The legislation does not place employers under a specific duty to ensure equality of opportunity or fair participation but does give the Fair Employment Commission powers to require action where an employer is failing to ensure either. It also places a number of other specific duties on employers which are designed to assist the ensuring of equality of opportunity.

Monitoring

The Fair Employment (NI) Act 1989 requires all employers with a workforce of more than 25 employees (more than 10 after the 1989 Act has been in force for two years), which are not public authorities as certified by the Department of Economic Development (DED), to register with the Fair Employment Commission. Failure to register exposes an employer to a fine not exceeding £2,000. Any new employer taking over a registered concern must apply within a month to the Commission to change the registration. To any proceedings in respect of non-registration there is a statutory defence of having a reasonable excuse for failing to make an application.

The DED has power to certify a body as a public authority in a number of specified circumstances - a Westminster or Northern Ireland Department, a body created by statutory provision or "a person appearing to the Department to exercise functions of a public nature". Lists of bodies already certified can be found in the Fair Employment (Specification of Public Authorities) Order (NI) 1989. Although public authorities are exempt from registration requirements they are not exempt from the requirements placed on registered concerns to provide information.

Registered employers (and public authorities) are required to monitor the composition of their workforce by religion. As the Code of Practice states, such monitoring is less concerned with a person's religious beliefs than with ascertaining his or her "community background", Protestant or Catholic. The exact information which the employer has to collect and the methods by which it is to be collected are spelt out in the Fair Employment (Monitoring) Regulations (NI) 1989. Guidance for employers is also provided in the Code of Practice.

To ascertain a person's community background an employer can use one of three "principal methods". These are:

- asking what primary school the employee attended;
- asking for all the schools the employee attended;
- directly asking which community employees perceive themselves as belonging to.

The DED has published a schools list, "The Classification of Schools for Monitoring Purposes", which is to be used along with questions about schools attended to classify an employee's community background.

If none of the three principal methods establish to which community an employee belongs, an employer can fall back on the "residuary method". This allows an employer to use a variety of information about an employee or applicant, including his or her name, membership of clubs or societies and sporting or leisure pursuits, in order to determine to what community he or she belongs. Employers must inform employees which community they have been classified as belonging to. After being so informed, employees have seven days to challenge what they see as inaccuracies.

Registered concerns (and public authorities) are required to submit a monitoring return each year to the Fair Employment Commission on the composition of their workforce. The information must be broken down by sex and job category. Employers of over 250 people, and public authorities, are also required to produce monitoring returns (similar to those for employees) regarding applications for employment. All registered employers must obtain information regarding the community background of applicants for employment and retain this for three years. Failure to produce a monitoring return without reasonable excuse exposes an employer to a fine of £2,000, while sending in a monitoring return which is not prepared in accordance with the regulations can lead to a fine of up to £10,000. Employees or anyone else who provides false information, knowing it will be used for a monitoring return, also commit an offence.

Information provided for the purposes of monitoring is confidential and anyone who discloses it is guilty of an offence and liable to a fine up to £2,000. There are exceptions for disclosure which is necessary for legal proceedings, disclosure to the Fair Employment Commission and disclosure to someone else in the business or public authority whose duties reasonably require such information.

Periodic reviews

Employers are required to carry out reviews of workforce composition at no more than three year intervals after registration. These are directed at discovering whether members of each community have fair participation in the workplace. If the employer determines that they do not then the employer should determine what affirmative action, if any, would be appropriate. Affirmative action may include the setting of goals and timetables regarding the composition of the workforce and applicants.

General affirmative action measures

Section 58 of the 1989 Act defines affirmative action as "action designed to secure fair participation in employment by members of the Protestant or Roman Catholic community in Northern Ireland". This may include:

- abandonment of practices which discourage participation;
- adoption of practices which encourage participation.

Abandoning practices

Modifying or abandoning restrictive practices means dealing with the kinds of things that the provisions on indirect discrimination are aimed at, *e.g.* looking at the educational qualifications normally set for a job and deciding whether these are really necessary for that job and whether they are likely to have a discriminatory effect. It could include considering the means by which jobs are advertised or abandoning informal methods of recruitment, such as by word of mouth.

Adopting practices

As regards measures to encourage participation, the basic rule is that an employer can do anything which does not itself turn out to constitute either direct or indirect discrimination (unless it is specifically exempted as discussed below). Thus, an employer cannot, under the guise of an affirmative action programme, set aside a certain percentage of jobs for members of a particular religious group. The provisions do not allow for "quotas" or for "preferential hiring". However, an employer may establish a target and timetable for improving the participation of a certain section of the community in the workforce, or carry out a monitoring scheme even where this is not required by the legislation.

Specifically exempted affirmative action

The legislation specifically exempts certain actions from challenge as directly or indirectly discriminatory if taken as part of an affirmative action programme. These are:

- provision of training facilities;
- redundancy;
- encouraging applications from the under-represented community.

Provision of training facilities

The first of these is provided for in the new section 37A of the 1976 Act. This exempts the provision of training facilities in a particular place or to a particular class of people, provided that the class is not a "class framed by reference to religious belief or political opinion". Unfortunately, the legislation is not a model of clarity here. It does not allow the provision of training only to members of a particular religious group, unlike the affirmative action provision in article 48 of the Sex Discrimination (NI) Order 1976, which allows the setting up of "women only" or "men only" training schemes in specified circumstances. But it is not clear whether, provided that an employer does not expressly refer to religion or political opinion in establishing criteria for training, a training scheme will be immune from challenge. If this is the position then an employer who wished to offer training specifically to Catholic staff, and discovered that the secretarial staff were all Catholic, would be protected by the legislation if training were offered only to the secretarial staff. On another interpretation such action would be unlawful as the criteria for training, although not expressly referring to religion, had been chosen with religion in mind; if it had been "framed by reference to religious belief".

Of these two interpretations it seems that the former must be correct. If the latter prevailed then the whole object of the legislation would be undercut. If an employer is prohibited from taking religion into account at any level in deciding upon criteria for training it is almost impossible to see how an employer could utilise the provision of training as part of an affirmative action strategy designed to ensure the fair participation of an under-represented community. Yet by enacting the provision Parliament clearly intended that training could be used to this end.

A further problem for employers is how this provision relates to sex discrimination law. For instance, some of the criteria which employers might use in selecting people for training could indirectly discriminate against women by being based on age, years of employment or full-time status in the organisation. Schedule 2 of the 1989 Act amends the Sex Discrimination Order to ensure that training schemes for men or women only will not be challengeable under fair employment law by reason that they indirectly discriminate against a particular religious group, but there is no comparable exemption from the requirements of sex discrimination law.

Redundancy

A second exempt form of affirmative action, contained in the new section 37B of the 1976 Act, is any affirmative action practice adopted with regard to redundancy. The comments made above about the interpretation of "by reference to religious or political opinion" in section 37A apply here too.

Encouraging applications from the under-represented community

A final exempt form of affirmative action, contained in the new section 37C of the 1976 Act, are measures taken to encourage applications from an under-represented community for employment or training. This permits employers to strengthen contacts with minority schools with a view to encouraging applicants, or to advertise primarily (or perhaps even exclusively) in one sector of the press. It would seem lawful for employers to advertise the fact that they have set goals and timetables for minority representation in their workforce as a means of encouraging minority applicants to apply. What the section would not seem to permit is "encouraging applications" by actually discriminating in favour of the under-represented community when selecting people for employment or training. However, if merely having a "preference" for people from a particular locality or with particular qualifications or experience (even where this is not shown to be job-related and is compliable with by a substantially smaller section of one community) is not indirectly discriminatory (assuming that a "preference" would not be a "condition or requirement") then it would appear to be lawful to advertise such a preference as part of an affirmative action programme.

FEC directed affirmative action

The above discussion concerns circumstances where an employer voluntarily adopts an affirmative action plan. In some circumstances the Fair Employment Commission may impose an affirmative action plan on an employer. Section 12 of the 1989 Act empowers the FEC to issue directions to employers if, after a formal investigation (see page 200), the Commission concludes that an employer is not affording equality of opportunity and is unable to secure an undertaking from the employer that it will take steps to ensure equality of opportunity. Such directions may include the setting of goals and timetables.

If the directions have not been complied with "within such period as the Commission considers reasonable" the FEC can apply to the Fair Employment Tribunal (FET) for an enforcement order. If the FET upholds the FEC application it may make an order setting out what steps should be taken to give effect to the directions and specifying that the employer must report what action has been taken to the FET within a certain time. Failure to comply with any part of this order renders the employer liable to pay a fine to the DED of up to £30,000. Employers have a right of appeal to the FET at the time the directions are issued on the grounds that they are already affording equality of opportunity or that the directions are inappropriate. A right to appeal to the Court of Appeal on a point of law exists regarding any of the FET's decisions.

The FEC also has power to make recommendations of affirmative action where an employer's review discloses that members of a particular community are not enjoying or are not likely to continue enjoying fair participation in employment. However, it does appear that the recommendations are themselves legally enforceable.

Contract compliance

The term "contract compliance" is borrowed from American experience of government contracting. There, however, it works as an incentive system whereby government grants and contracts are made more available for those with affirmative action programmes. The Northern Irish provisions are more like a penalty scheme, where grants and contracts may be lost for proven failure to afford equality of opportunity.

The provisions deal with limitations on the award of public grants and contracts. These are significant in that over 40% of private sector concerns in Northern Ireland are in receipt of some form of public funds. The Act indicates that public authority contracts and government financial assistance should be denied to "unqualified people". There are four circumstances in which a concern can become unqualified:

- after conviction of an offence relating to failing to register;
- after conviction for failing to rectify the register when a new employer has taken over the concern;
- after conviction of an offence relating to failure to return a monitoring return;
- as a result of receiving a penalty after failing to comply with a Tribunal order to enforce an employer's undertaking or FEC directions.

Where any of these conditions is satisfied, the FEC may issue a notice stating that such a person is unqualified and the FEC can take all reasonable steps to bring this to the attention of public authorities. Employers have rights of appeal against this notice to the FEC, thence to the FET and eventually to the Court of Appeal on a point of law. Public authorities are disbarred from entering into contracts with or accepting tenders from unqualified persons. Northern Ireland government departments may also refuse to pay any grant or discretionary assistance to unqualified persons. The FEC has enforcement powers by injunction from the High Court if it feels that a public authority is likely to breach its duty not to give contracts to disqualified persons, but no such powers exist in respect of government grants.

The Secretary of State may exempt contracts if he or she certifies that the work is necessary or desirable for the purposes of safeguarding national security, public safety or public order. A Northern Ireland department may also exempt a contract if it certifies that the work could not otherwise be done without disproportionate expense.

The Fair Employment Commission

The role of the Fair Employment Commission is central to the fair employment legislation. Some of its powers and functions have been highlighted in earlier parts of this chapter but others have not yet been mentioned. The address of the Commission is:

• Andras House, 60 Great Victoria Street, Belfast BT2 79B (tel: 0232 240020).

Information

In general the FEC has an educational role in relation to the legislation. It is empowered to provide training courses, hold conferences, undertake research, disseminate information and establish services for giving advice on equality of opportunity. It is also specifically required to recommend affirmative action when appropriate and to maintain a Code of Practice for the promotion of equality of opportunity. The Code is to be taken into account in any Tribunal proceedings even though failure to observe its requirements does not of itself render anyone liable to proceedings. For the time being, the current Code is that produced in December 1989 by the DED.

Assistance with complaints

Any person complaining of unlawful discrimination is entitled to advice from the Commission unless the complaint is frivolous. The Commission is also empowered to give assistance, including legal representation, to any complainant where the case raises an issue of principle or its complexity makes it unreasonable to expect the complainant to deal with it unaided.

Investigation

Under section 11 of the 1989 Act, the FEC may conduct an investigation for the purpose of establishing whether a body is affording equality of opportunity. Before beginning an investigation the FEC must serve a notice on those it intends to investigate, indicating the scope and purpose of the investigation. The investigation must take place in private and those investigated must have an opportunity to comment on the matters referred to in the notice. The Commission has the same powers as the High Court as regards the compelling of witnesses and the production of documents. Any obstruction without reasonable excuse of the Commission's investigation can be referred to the High Court, which can deal with it as though the offence had been committed in relation to that Court.

Monitoring

The Commission must maintain a register of employers containing the names and addresses of all concerns which qualify. All registered concerns are required to serve a monitoring return on the Commission, which is under a general duty not to disclose any information from which the religious belief of any individual could be discovered.

Enforcement

The Commission has a variety of powers concerning enforcement:

- The FEC has the ability to secure undertakings and to obtain directions when, having carried out a formal investigation, it concludes that a concern is not affording equality of opportunity. Any undertakings obtained or directions issued may be subsequently enforced by an application to the Fair Employment Tribunal.
- The FEC may ensure that concerns carry out monitoring and reviews of employment practice satisfactorily. Again there is power to seek enforceable undertakings or issue directions if this is not done.
- The Commission has enforcement powers in respect of access to public grants and contracts. It is under an obligation to publicise the names of those concerns ineligible for public contracts and may seek injunctions to prevent public authorities from entering into contracts with unauthorised concerns.
- The Commission has enforcement powers in respect of discriminatory advertisements. It is empowered to seek an injunction to restrain publication of any advert which indicates an intention directly to discriminate against anyone on the grounds of his or her religious belief or political opinion.

Other provisions against discrimination

Northern Ireland Constitution Act 1973

By section 19(1) of the Northern Ireland Constitution Act 1973, acts by government and public bodies which are discriminatory on political or religious grounds are made unlawful and actionable in the courts. Even Orders in Council can be challenged under this heading. Only a small number of cases have so far invoked the Act, perhaps because it is generally assumed that "discrimination" in the Act refers only to "direct discrimination".

Standing Advisory Commission on Human Rights

The 1973 Act also established the Standing Advisory Commission on Human Rights, which has the function of advising the Secretary of State for Northern Ireland on the adequacy and effectiveness of the law preventing discrimination on the grounds of religious belief or political opinion. The address of the Commission is:
* 55 Royal Avenue, Belfast BT1 1FX (tel: 0232-243987).

The Ombudsman

As explained in chapter 2, the function of the Ombudsman is to deal with complaints from members of the public who claim to have suffered injustice by reason of "maladministration" by those bodies which fall within her jurisdiction. Maladministration includes discrimination and since the fair employment legislation largely covers issues of employment discrimination the Ombudsman restricts her attention to cases falling outside the remit of the FEC (*e.g.* cases where a national security certificate has been issued, or complaints of discrimination in the provision of public services).

Stirring up hatred or arousing fear

It is an offence under the Public Order (NI) Order 1987 to engage in certain activities which are intended or likely to stir up hatred against, or arouse fear of, any section of the population in Northern Ireland (defined by religious belief, ethnic or national origins, colour, race or nationality). The activities in question are:

- the use of threatening, abusive or insulting words or behaviour;
- the display, publication or public distribution of written material which is threatening, abusive or insulting;
- the public distribution, showing or playing of any recording containing material which is threatening, abusive or insulting.

It is a defence for a person who did not intend to stir up hatred or arouse fear to show that he or she did not intend the material or activity to be threatening, abusive or insulting (or was not aware of the content of the material) and did not suspect that it might be. Anyone convicted under the legislation is liable to an unlimited fine and up to two years' imprisonment.

Chapter 13

Sex Discrimination

Beverley Jones

L egislation to eliminate discrimination between the sexes was introduced into Northern Ireland in the mid-1970's. It followed
developments in Great Britain, which were in turn influenced by
the American civil liberties movement of the 1960's. In addition, the
United Kingdom was seeking membership of the European Community
and the Treaty of Accession required the introduction of equal pay for
equal work between men and women.

European Community law and Northern Ireland law

European Community law plays a crucial role in the interpretation of
the domestic legislation governing equal treatment between men and
women in Northern Ireland. It takes precedence over conflicting
provisions in the domestic laws of member states. It is interpreted and
enforced by the European Court of Justice in Luxembourg by way of cases
brought before it either by the EC's Commission or through references
from the national courts of member states.

Article 119 of the Treaty of Rome 1957 (which created the Community) requires equal pay for men and women engaged in equal work.
"Equal pay" means:

- pay for the same work at piece rates must be calculated on the basis of the same unit of measurement, and
- pay for work at time rates must be the same for the same job.

In 1975 the Equal Pay Directive (75/117/EEC) further defined the concept as meaning:

"for the same work or for work to which equal value is attributed, the elimination of all discrimination on grounds of sex with regard to all aspects and conditions of remuneration. In particular, where a job classification system is used for determining pay it must be based on the same criteria for both men and women and so drawn up as to exclude any discrimination on grounds of sex."

In 1976, another Directive (76/207/EEC) was passed aimed at achieving equality in respect of access to employment, vocational training, promotion and other working conditions. Similar Directives have been passed concerning social security, occupational pension schemes and the protection of self-employed women and spouses who work for the self-employed during pregnancy and motherhood.

The Equal Pay Act (NI) 1970 was amended by the Sex Discrimination (NI) Order 1976 and both pieces of legislation came into effect in July 1976. The two laws are supposed to be read as an "harmonious code", though such a reading is difficult since their language is different and they cover mutually exclusive areas. The equal pay legislation, which was further amended in 1984, governs only sex discrimination which arises in terms and conditions of individual contracts of employment concerning pay. The Sex Discrimination (NI) Order 1976, as amended by recent Orders, was intended to eliminate discrimination in other aspects of employment. In addition, the Order has provisions outlawing discrimination on the grounds of sex in the field of education and in the provision of goods, facilities and services to the public.

The equal pay legislation

Between 1976 and 1984 a woman (or a man) was entitled to equal pay only where she was employed on "like work" with, or work rated as equivalent to, that done by a colleague of the opposite sex. In the case of

Commission of the European Communities v UK (1982), the European Court of Justice held that the Equal Pay Act (NI) 1970 did not comply with the requirements of Article 119 nor with the Equal Pay Directive since there was no provision enabling a woman doing work of *equal value* to a man undertaking a different job to claim equal pay. The government was held to be in breach of its European obligations and was required to introduce amending legislation.

The Equal Pay (Amendment) Regulations (NI) 1984 provide a statutory right for women undertaking work of equal value with men to claim equal pay. However, the procedure for such a claim is complex and lengthy. By October 1992 only two equal value claims had been successfully concluded in Northern Ireland (*Tennants Textile Colours Ltd v Todd* and *Winton v NIE*). However settlements had been secured in a number of cases, including company and sectoral agreements to review a complete pay system.

Making an equal value claim

Claiming is regulated by the Industrial Tribunal (Rules of Procedure) (Equal Value Amendment) Regulations (NI) 1984. First, at a preliminary hearing the tribunal considers whether it is reasonable to compare the applicant's job with one with which she wishes it to be compared. It is the applicant who chooses the comparator, who must work either at the same place or for the same employer at a different place but under the same terms and conditions. The tribunal will also consider at this stage whether the claim should be dealt with as a "like work" or "rated as equivalent" claim.

The fact that there are men doing the same work as an applicant, and who are paid the same, does not preclude an equal value claim with comparators engaged in different jobs (*Pickstone v Freeman's Mail Order Ltd*, 1988). It may, however, be relevant at a later stage of the proceedings when the employer is entitled to raise the defence that the difference in pay is due to a "genuine material factor" not based on sex. At the same time, where the employer is alleging that the jobs being compared are the subject of a job evaluation scheme, the tribunal will consider whether such a scheme is "analytical" and whether it is tainted with sex discrimination. An analytical scheme is one which compares jobs under headings such as skill, effort, responsibility and decision-making, rather than making whole job comparisons. In the case of *Bromley v H*

& J Quick Ltd (1988), the Court of Appeal in England set out guidelines for the requirements which must be met if the scheme is to preclude an equal value claim. In *McAuley and Others v EHSSB* (1990) the Court of Appeal of Northern Ireland held that the job evaluation scheme which applied to all health service ancillary workers in Great Britain could not preclude an equal value claim in Northern Ireland, because the scheme had never been applied to Northern Ireland.

Once the tribunal is satisfied that the claim is reasonable and has excluded the application of a job evaluation scheme, the matter is referred to an independent expert who prepares a report on whether the jobs compared are of equal value. There is a small panel of independent experts who are appointed by the Labour Relations Agency in Northern Ireland specifically for this purpose. Recently, the European Court of Justice confirmed that equal value means *at least* equal value (*Murphy v Bord Telecom Eireann,* 1988).

At this point the employer may raise any matters which he or she believes constitute "a genuine material factor" defence. The House of Lords in *Rainey v Greater Glasgow Health Board* (1987) held that a difference in pay which was objectively justifiable would defeat a claim for equal pay. At a European level, in *Von Hartz v Bilka Kaufhaus GmbH* (1986) the court in Luxembourg has confirmed the need for objectivity in justifying differential access to pay and benefits. The tribunal can accept, reject or adjourn consideration of the "genuine material factor" defence. If the defence is accepted, the claim fails. If it is rejected or adjourned, the independent expert prepares a report for the tribunal. The average time for the preparation of reports is approximately two years, even though the Regulations contemplated a much shorter period (seven weeks).

Once the report is completed the tribunal is reconvened. If the tribunal decides to admit it as evidence, the facts on which it is based cannot be disputed. If the report is not admitted as evidence, the tribunal must appoint a second expert to prepare a report. A tribunal can accept or reject an expert's findings and the parties themselves are entitled to call their own expert evidence to refute the independent expert's report. In practice this is a hard task, though not impossible.

In the case of *Hayward v Cammell Laird Shipbuilders Ltd* (1988), the employer argued that, even though the applicant did work which was of equal value to her male comparators, she was not entitled to an increase in pay because her overall terms of employment were no less satisfactory than those of the men, since she enjoyed access to pension rights and sick pay which they did not. The House of Lords ruled that she was neverthe-less entitled to the increase in pay, as she could compare a specific less favourable term of her contract with a similar term contained in the males' contracts. The court ruled that it was not required to consider the value of the overall package of terms and conditions enjoyed by the applicant and her male colleagues. In 1991 the European Court of Justice in Luxembourg upheld this approach in *Barber v Guardian Royal Exchange Assurance Group.*

If the "genuine material factor" defence fails, the applicant will be entitled to an equality clause in her contract of employment. She will then be entitled to equal pay which can be back-dated for up to two years.

Difficulties with the legislation

It is arguable that the current legislation still fails to provide women with the machinery necessary to obtain proper redress. Commentators have argued that the amended legislation does not comply with European law in a number of important respects. The processing of cases is inor-dinately lengthy, with claims in Northern Ireland taking an average 46 months. Without expert advice and legal representation throughout, it is unlikely that any claim will succeed. Absolute bars to claims, under the job evaluation and genuine material factor provisions, may contravene individual rights of review.

Given the substantial differentials in pay between men and women, employers have every reason to seek to defeat equal pay claims, particular-ly where industries predominantly employ female workers. It remains unclear what genuine material factors can defeat a claim. In *Fleming & Others v Shorts plc* (1991) it was argued unsuccessfully by the company that the separate collective bargaining structure accounted for the pay differential between men and women. The tribunal found that this merely explained why there was sex discrimination. The issue of separate collec-tive bargaining as a defence to equal value claims was referred to the Luxembourg Court in *Enderby v Frenchay Health Authority and the Secretary of State* and a decision is awaited. There are instances of employers changing the duties of applicants or comparators in order to circumvent the law, as well as threats of dismissal or redundancy if claims are pursued. The Confederation of British Industry has recently called for the repeal of the legislation arguing that it places too heavy a burden on industry. There is, however, little evidence of employers reviewing their pay structures to ensure implementation of the principle of equal pay. Indeed, many employers are adopting a policy of doing nothing until faced with a claim. Despite these difficulties the Equal Opportunities Commission for Northern Ireland continues to receive a growing number of equal pay complaints each year. Indeed in 1991-1992 the claims rose from around 50 to over 600.

The sex discrimination legislation

The Sex Discrimination (NI) Order 1976, as amended, provides limited protection against unequal treatment of men and women in the fields of employment, education and the provision of goods, facilities and services to the public. There are a number of important exclusions which restrict the scope of the legislation, but unlike the equal pay legislation the Order contains definitions of what constitutes discrimination. In addition, the Order sets up the Equal Opportunities Commission for Northern Ireland (the EOC).

While the terms are not specifically used, two forms of discrimination are defined in the Order: "direct" and "indirect".

Direct discrimination

Direct discrimination means treating an individual less favourably than a person of the opposite sex (and, at work, a married person less favourably than a single person). For example, if girls have to obtain higher marks than boys to secure a grammar school place then a *prima facie* case of unlawful discrimination arises, under the education provisions of the Order. Unless it can be shown that the reason for the less favourable treatment is unrelated to the sex of the children, it will be unlawful. The motive for the treatment is irrelevant, even if it is intended for perceived good reasons (*In re EOC for Northern Ireland,* 1988). It is for the court to determine whether the reason provided for the less favourable treatment is not based on sex. In the case of *Wallace v South Eastern Education and Library Board* (1980), the Northern Ireland Court of Appeal recognised that there was rarely clear evidence of sex discrimination and that unless the court was able to draw an inference of unlawful discrimination from the circumstances of the complaint the purpose of the legislation would be largely defeated.

Indirect discrimination

Indirect discrimination is the application of a requirement which a considerably smaller proportion of one sex than the other (and, in employment cases, married as opposed to single people) can comply with. For example, a height requirement of five feet six inches excludes more women than men and so unless the requirement is justifiable it will amount to unlawful discrimination.

Proving indirect discrimination is difficult. The applicant must first establish that there is a requirement which constitutes a barrier. The courts have generally interpreted this liberally, though in a race discrimination case in England the Court of Appeal held that the requirement must constitute an "absolute bar" (*Perera v Civil Service Commission*, 1983). This judgment fails to appreciate that many conditions which appear to be optional operate as barriers in practice. Fortunately, Court of Appeal judgments in England are not binding in Northern Ireland and it is to be hoped that the Northern Ireland courts will not follow the narrow approach adopted in *Perera*. It appears that the European Court takes a less technical approach to the issue (see the *Bilka* case, above page 207).

Whilst the legislation does not stipulate the need to prove statistically that the condition has an adverse impact on one sex, courts have generally required such evidence, which may be difficult to obtain. Recently, in *NE Education and Library Board v Briggs* (1990) the Northern Ireland Court of Appeal held, however, that a tribunal is entitled to conclude adverse impact, without statistical evidence, from its own knowledge of the position of men and women generally. Once the adverse impact has been proved, the onus shifts to the employer to justify it. In the *Bilka* case (see page 207) the European Court laid down the definitive test for justifiability. The condition must be both necessary and proportionate to achieve the required objective without sex discrimination. Finally, the complainant is required to show that the requirement has operated to his or her detriment before it will be held unlawful.

Victimisation

The legislation defines and prohibits victimisation. It aims to protect a person from being less favourably treated because he or she has asserted a right under the equality laws. There has not been a definitive judgment on the scope of this provision in Northern Ireland, but in a race relations case before the Employment Appeal Tribunal in England (*Aziz v Trinity Street Taxis* Ltd, 1988) it was held that the appellant had failed to show victimisation since he had produced no evidence to suggest that he would have been treated any differently had he complained under other legislation.

Sex discrimination in education

Articles 24-29 of the 1976 Order make it unlawful for a body responsible for the provision of education to discriminate against girls or boys. This applies to both schools and the Education and Library Boards, but the Order does not cite the Department of Education as a "body responsible". The reason for this appears to be that the Department is expected to ensure that schools and Boards do not offend the legislation. In *In re EOC for Northern Ireland and others* (1988) the Department marked "11 plus" papers, adjusting the scores for boys and girls differentially. It then separated the sexes, taking the top 27% of boys and the top 27% of girls as eligible for free grammar school places. The effect of this practice was to exclude some girls with better marks than some boys from free places. The High Court held that the practice constituted unlawful discrimination and that the Boards had contravened the Order by implementing the Department's decision. The Department itself was found to have contravened article 40 of the Order ,which prohibits the issuing of unlawful instructions.

It should be noted, however, that the Order contains special exemptions for single sex schools.

Provision of goods, facilities and services

Article 30 of the 1976 Order requires that goods, facilities and services must be available to both sexes "in the same manner and on the same terms as are normal in relation to men". Whilst there are no definitions of "goods", "facilities" or "services" in the Order, access to loan facilities and service in a public bar have been held to fall within these provisions, but in *R v Entry Clearance Officer, Bombay, ex parte Amin* (1983), the House of Lords held that the provision of vouchers allowing entry into the United Kingdom did not constitute a "facility" under the English section equivalent to article 30 in Northern Ireland's law.

The Court also held in *Ex parte Amin* that the section applies only to "market-place activities", *i.e.* activities which can be undertaken by a private individual. To a large extent this appears to exclude the state from liability for discrimination and to prevent scrutiny of the operation of government policies in the areas of social security and taxation. However, European law can in some instances provide protection from state discrimination. The failure to pay invalid care allowance to a married woman who gave up work to nurse an infirm relative owing to discriminatory assumptions made by the Department of Health and social security was found to be contrary to the European social security Directive in *Drake v Chief Adjudication Officer* (1985). This case led to many married women becoming eligible for the benefit.

Another exemption which limits the scope of article 30 is that governing private clubs. Under this, women are often denied equal access to sporting facilities, and the denial can extend to the use of public facilities, such as at golf clubs. In *Bateson v YMCA* (1980) the Northern Ireland High Court held that a temporary day membership card, which allowed access to a snooker table, did not make the facility a private club, so to deny women access to it amounted to unlawful discrimination.

Sex discrimination in employment

The 1976 Order makes it unlawful for employers to discriminate in the selection of employees and in the treatment of their workforce. This covers training and promotion opportunities, benefits, facilities, services, dismissals or "any other detriment" (article 8).

Only if there is a "genuine occupational qualification" is it lawful for an employer to seek specifically to employ a man (or woman), or to consider one sex only for training or promotion (article 10). In some circumstances, however, employers and training bodies can provide under-represented groups with the skills necessary for work which they may not have done traditionally (articles 17, 48 and 49). Courses can be run in companies trying to encourage applications for particular posts where there have been few or no women (or men) in the previous 12 months. Training bodies can provide courses limited to one sex or to persons who may have been away from employment because of domestic responsibilities.

Firms employing less than six employees, and private households, used to be excluded from the 1976 Order. But in the case of *Commission of the European Communities v UK*(1983), the European Court of Justice held that these exclusions were unjustified. It did, however, recognise that there might be instances when an employer could seek a person of a particular sex for employment in a private household. The Sex Discrimination (NI) Order 1988 (which parallels the 1986 Act in Great Britain) implemented the European Court's ruling.

Sexual harassment

"Sexual harassment" is now recognised as behaviour which can amount to unlawful discrimination. It encompasses unwelcome sexual advances and sexually explicit comments as well as physical assault. An industrial tribunal in Belfast upheld the first claim in the United Kingdom in the case of *M. v Crescent Garage Ltd* (1982). Subsequently, in *Porcelli v Strathclyde Regional Council* (1984) the House of Lords established conclusively that a campaign of unpleasant and lewd comments by the applicant's male work colleagues, which resulted in her seeking a transfer, constituted unlawful sex discrimination. The fact that the behaviour was not sexually motivated was not considered relevant, since the complainant was subjected to treatment to which a man would not have been subjected.

Pregnancy

Employers are allowed to provide preferential treatment for women in connection with pregnancy and maternity but the Order provides no specific protection against *less* favourable treatment on these grounds. Because the legislation compares like with like in determining "less favourable" treatment, an early claim of unlawful discrimination on the ground of pregnancy failed (*Turley v Allders Department Stores Ltd*, 1980). As a man could not become pregnant, said this decision, the failure to promote, or the dismissal of, a pregnant woman was not unlawful. An industrial tribunal in Northern Ireland was the first court to disagree with this interpretation. In *Jordan v Northern Ireland Electricity Service* (1984) the tribunal, appreciating the inadequacy of the Order in dealing with one of the fundamental grounds for discrimination against women, held that the reason for the failure of the employer to promote Mrs Jordan was that she was pregnant and that this amounted to sex discrimination. The tribunal did not address the question of the need for a comparison. In England the approach to such claims has been, generally, to compare pregnant women with sick men in order to bring the claim within the scope of the Order.

To compare pregnancy with sickness is clearly a most unsatisfactory state of affairs. However this is the approach which has been adopted in *Webb v Emo Cargo Ltd* (1992) in the House of Lords. By contrast, tribunal decisions in Northern Ireland have continued to develop an interpretation of the Order which construes unfavourable treatment on the grounds of pregnancy as unlawful discrimination without the need for a comparison (*Donley v Gallagher Ltd*, 1987 *McQuade v The Lobster Pot*, 1989). In the *Dekker* and *Hertz* cases (1991) two decisions of the European Court adopted the approach taken by the industrial tribunals in Northern Ireland. Despite these definitive rulings the courts in Great Britain persist in the comparative approach.

In 1992 the Court of Appeal in Northern Ireland decided to refer to the European Court the question whether a reduction in pay to a woman during maternity leave was unlawful (*Gillespie & Others v DHSS and Others*). In October 1992 the European Council of Ministers adopted a Directive on maternity leave and this is partly implemented in Great Britain by the Trade Union Reform and Employment Rights Act 1993. However, in providing for pay comparable to sickness benefits it is arguable that the Directive contravenes existing Community law. In the same way as the Directive on occupational pensions was so found in the *Barber* case (above, page 208). Despite this radical interpretation, the failure of the legislation specifically to protect pregnant women from discrimination remains a major barrier to the achievement of equality in the workplace. There should be clear statutory protection for all pregnant working women. It is also now clear that the domestic law is contrary to European law in its failure to outlaw discrimination on the ground of "family status", referred to in the Equal Treatment Directive.

Retirement

Matters relating to "death or retirement" fall outside the scope of the 1976 Order. However, in the case of *Marshall v Southampton and S W Hampshire Area Health Authority* (1986) the European Court held that, whilst discrimination in the state pension age was lawful, the domestic legislation could not preclude protection against *dismissal* at different ages for men and women, even though they were based on the age at which people became entitled to the state pension. Though the Sex Discrimination (NI) Order 1988 limits the scope of this exclusion, successful challenges to the exclusion continue (*Barber v Guardian Royal Exchange Assurance Group,* 1990).

Collective agreements

In *Commission of the European Communities v United Kingdom* (1983), the failure to provide a remedy against discrimination appearing in non-binding collective agreements between unions and employers was found to be contrary to European Community law. The government argued unsuccessfully that, since the agreements were unenforceable, there was no necessity to provide a remedy. It was held that, irrespective of the legal effect of these agreements, they did in fact regulate working conditions and industrial relations. The 1988 Order makes void any term of a contract of employment which arises from discrimination in a collective agreement, but does not provide a mechanism to challenge the actual agreement. The European Commission is currently considering infringement proceedings against the United Kingdom for this failure.

National security certificates

Until 1988 there could be no consideration of matters covered by the 1976 Order whenever a certificate asserting that they were matters of national security had been issued by the Secretary of State. In *Johnston v Chief Constable of the Royal Ulster Constabulary* (1986), the applicant was one of 39 female reservists in the RUC whose three-year contracts of employment were not renewed, whilst those of male colleagues were. When the women challenged the decision, the Secretary of State issued a national security certificate. The case was referred to the European Court of Justice, which held that the failure to provide in Northern Irish law for judicial review of the national security certificate was a breach of Community law. The Sex Discrimination (Amendment) (NI) Order 1988 implemented the Court's ruling.

Protective legislation

Article 52 of the 1976 Order allows for the retention of many discriminatory pieces of legislation. In March 1988 the government issued a consultative document seeking views on the repeal of discriminatory protective health and safety legislation which precludes women from certain types of work and hours of employment (*i.e.* mining and night-shifts in factories). This document followed an opinion from the European Commission which required member states to review the need for such legislation in the light of progress towards equal treatment between men and women. The government's proposals for repeal appear to be fuelled by a commitment to deregulation rather than the achievement of equality. Much of the discriminatory protective legislation was indeed repealed early in 1990.

Remedies

The EOC has expressed considerable disquiet at the inadequate remedies afforded to individual complainants under the employment provisions of the 1976 Order. The industrial tribunal can issue a declaration that the employer has unlawfully discriminated against the applicant. It can also recommend that the employer should reduce the effect of the discrimination on the applicant. Finally, the tribunal can, in cases of direct discrimination, award compensation up to a maximum of £10,000. With the passage of the Fair Employment (NI) Act 1989 and its compensation level of £30,000, the remedies for sex discrimination are now wholly unacceptable as a guarantee for gender equality. Indeed the Equal Opportunites Commission for Northern Ireland argues that this disparity is contrary to Community law.

The failure to provide the tribunal with powers to issue injunctions (*i.e.* orders to do or not do something) means that the remedies of the court are often inappropriate, especially in sexual harassment cases. In addition, the powers of the tribunal to recommend means of redressing the impact of discrimination are very limited and the level of compensation rarely covers the economic or emotional cost of discrimination. In the *Marshall* case (see page 214), the industrial tribunal ignored the maximum level of compensation which it was empowered to award and, applying European law, awarded the complainant more than £19,000 (plus interest) to reflect her loss of earnings arising from the discrimination. This case is currently awaiting a hearing before the European Court in Luxembourg.

The Equal Opportunities Commission for Northern Ireland

The EOC was set up by the 1976 Order to work towards the elimination of discrimination, promote equality of opportunity between men and women and keep the relevant legislation under review. To carry out this remit the Commission was given powers to undertake research, initiate educational campaigns and enforce the legislation.

Its statutory enforcement powers are three-fold:

- the Commission can, in certain circumstances, assist individual complainants to pursue legal cases (article 75); this has formed the bulk of the Commission's enforcement work since its establishment;

- it can undertake formal investigations where it believes that there may be widespread discrimination (article 58); the complex provisions and the lack of resources required for these investigations have meant that only two have been completed during the Commission's existence;

- in very limited circumstances the Commission is empowered to take legal action in its own name (articles 38-42).

A radical change in the powers of the Commission is required if it is to have the necessary tools to combat discrimination. It should be given wider investigative powers together with greater scope to pursue legal actions. Since discrimination affects groups of people, class or representative actions are the necessary weapons to combat unlawful behaviour.

Conclusion

A comprehensive piece of legislation on sex discrimination and equal pay is urgently needed. It should require positive action by employers and state institutions, as the mere prohibition of discrimination is insufficient to secure equality.

The failure of the state to provide a comprehensive system of child-care facilities, combined with the lack of positive protection for pregnant working women, means that the burden of domestic responsibilities continues to rest upon women's shoulders. Stereotypical attitudes persist. Equal pay will not be won until sex segregation in employment is removed and women have equal representation in higher managerial grades.

Strengthening the law to provide a coherent enforceable set of rights manifests the commitment of the state towards the principle and practice of equality. Its importance is in setting the standard to be followed by society.

Chapter 14

Rights of Disabled People

Ray Geary and Laura Lundy

The term "disability" has a number of different meanings in law, depending upon what the legislation is meant to achieve. Thus a person may be considered to be disabled for the purposes of employment but not for social security benefits. But it can generally be defined as follows :

> *"Any restriction or lack of ability (resulting from an impairment) to perform an activity in the manner or within the range considered normal for a human being."*

On the basis of this definition the Policy, Planning and Research Unit of the Northern Ireland Office, in its 1992 study "The Prevalence of Disability in Northern Ireland", found that 17.4% of the adult population is disabled, a figure which is 20% higher than corresponding statistics in Great Britain. The object of this chapter is to look at the provision which has been made for disabled people living in Northern Ireland in five key areas, namely:

- employment
- housing
- social services
- access to buildings
- transport

The legal entitlement of disabled people to special education and to social security are considered in chapters 16 and 19 respectively.

Employment

Access to employment can have a significant impact on a disabled person's ability to achieve independent living. However, difficulties may arise for disabled people in both obtaining and retaining employment.

Obtaining employment

The object of the Disabled Persons (Employment) Act (NI) 1945 is to assist disabled persons to obtain employment or to undertake work on their own account. For these purposes, section 6 of the Act established a Register of Disabled Persons. Those eligible for registration are persons who on account of injury, disease or congenital deformity are substantially handicapped in obtaining or keeping suitable employment or work on their own account, and whose disability is likely to last at least twelve months. A disabled person who wishes to register should contact the Disablement Employment Adviser at any local office of the Training and Employment Agency (their address and telephone number can be obtained from the telephone directory under "Government"). Registration is voluntary but the advantage of registering is that there are various statutory provisions and schemes which are intended to assist persons who have registered as disabled to obtain employment. They are as follows:

Training schemes

Section 2 of the 1945 Act gives the Department of Economic Development ("the DED") the power to provide disabled people with vocational training and rehabilitation. The general policy on the training of the disabled is one of integration. Most disabled people will therefore be offered places in the Youth Training or Job Training Programmes. However, where integration is not possible, specialist training is also available. Details on the various training schemes can be obtained from the Disablement Employment Adviser at one of the local offices of the Training and Employment Agency.

The Designated Employment Scheme

The DED has the power to designate an occupation so as to reserve further entry into it for registered disabled persons. By virtue of the Disabled Persons (Designated Employments) (NI) Order 1946, two employments have been designated in this way, namely car park attendant and lift attendant. An employer may only employ a person who is registered disabled as a car park or lift attendant, unless the employer receives a permit from the DED. The duty applies to all employers of car park attendants and lift attendants except where the attendant spends less than half of his or her total weekly working hours with the one employer.

Aids to employment

Registered disabled persons may benefit from a number of schemes intended to make it easier for disabled people to get and keep employment. For instance, disabled persons who cannot use public transport and who do not have their own car may receive grants to cover their travelling expenses to work under the Fares to Work Scheme. Technical aids to employment such as adapted typewriters and special chairs are available on free permanent loan under the Special Aids to Employment Scheme. Blind or partially sighted people may be given assistance with the cost of employing a part-time reader at work. Moreover, employers who need to adapt their premises or equipment in order to employ a disabled person may receive capital grants of up to £6,000. Details on all these forms of assistance can be obtained from the Disablement Employment Adviser at any local office of the Training and Employment Agency.

The statutory quota

Section 9(1) of the Disabled Persons (Employment) Act (NI) 1945 places a statutory duty on employers employing more than twenty employees to employ a certain quota of persons (3%) who are registered disabled. It is not a criminal offence for an employer simply to be employing fewer disabled persons than the quota. However, where the employer is below the quota, he or she must take on a registered disabled person for any vacancies that occur unless a permit of exemption has first been obtained from the DED. Failure to comply with the duty amounts to a criminal offence. If prosecuted, the employer could receive a fine not exceeding £400 and/or a maximum of three months in prison (section

9(6)). In 1991 72% of registered employers did not meet the quota. However, there have been no prosecutions for failure to comply with the quota in Northern Ireland. This may be because a prosecution must be instigated by the DED. A disabled person who feels that he/she has not been hired because of his/her disability is not given an individual right to enforce compliance with the duty. The only possible remedy arises where the employer is a public body, in which case action may be taken by an individual by way of judicial review (see chapter 2). One such case was recently initiated for an alleged breach of the equivalent Great Britain legislation, *i.e.* the Disabled Persons (Employment) Act 1944.

Disabled people looking for employment may meet with prejudice from some employers who are uninformed about the nature of their disability. Yet, in spite of pressure from disability action groups, there is no legislation prohibiting employers from discriminating against disabled persons in recruitment or promotion exercises. The Government's approach to the issue of discrimination against the disabled is to encourage employers to voluntarily employ disabled people rather than to introduce anti-discrimination legislation. The DED have issued a Code of Practice on the Employment of Disabled People. The Code encourages the adoption of positive policies on all aspects of the employment of disabled people and provides practical guidance on how such policies might be implemented. Copies of the Code are available from the Disablement Employment Adviser at the local offices of the Training and Employment Agency.

Sheltered employment

Section 15 of the 1945 Act gives the DED the power to provide employment for registered disabled people whose disability is such that they could not otherwise find employment in the open market. The Department exercises this power in several ways. Firstly, it funds the Sheltered Placement Scheme ("SPS"). The SPS enables employers to employ severely disabled people at a reduced rate, which is broadly equivalent to their capacity for employment. For example, if the disabled person's capacity is assessed at 50%, the employer only has to pay 50% of the normal wages for the job. The remaining portion of the wages is made up by one of three sponsoring organisations, Ulster Sheltered Employment Ltd, Disability Action and the Industrial Therapy Organisation. Secondly, the Department also funds one sheltered workshop. This is based in Belfast and managed by Ulster Sheltered Employment Ltd. Finally, the DED runs the Job Introduction Scheme, which offers a weekly premium to employers who provide a trial period of six weeks' employment to disabled people. Details on the sheltered employment schemes can be obtained from the Disablement Employment Adviser at the local offices of the Training and Employment Agency.

Retaining employment

The statutory quota

By virtue of section 9(5) of the Disabled Persons (Employment) Act (NI) 1945, an employer must not discharge a registered disabled person without "reasonable cause" if he/she is below his/her statutory quota or if the discharge would bring him/her below it. Failure to comply with this duty amounts to a criminal offence. If prosecuted, the employer could be liable to a maximum penalty of a £400 fine and/or three months in prison. There have been no prosecutions in Northern Ireland for a breach of this duty.

Unfair dismissal

A disabled person who has been dismissed from his/her employment because his/her employer thinks that his/her disability prevents him/her from doing their job properly may be able to claim that they have been unfairly dismissed. The ordinary conditions for claiming unfair dismissal are considered in chapter 17. In this context, a dismissal will be considered to be potentially fair if the reason for it is that the employee is not capable of doing the job for which he or she was employed (article 22(2) of the Industrial Relations (NI) Order 1976).

An employer who employs an employee having full knowledge of his or her disability cannot later seek to justify a dismissal on the grounds that the nature of the disability made him or her incapable of work or its subsequent demands. Moreover, in cases where the disability has developed or become more serious since the date of appointment, the employer must prove that the employee is no longer capable of the work. It is open to the employee to call evidence to contradict this.

Even where it has been shown that the employee is no longer capable of the work, the dismissal will still be considered to be unfair unless the employer can show that he or she acted reasonably in treating the incapacity as a sufficient reason to dismiss the employee (article 22(3)). In deciding whether the employer acted reasonably the tribunal will have regard to a number of factors. In this context, the most significant of these will be whether the employer took an informed view on the basis of proper medical information. (Note the right of access to medical reports compiled for employment purposes, mentioned in chapter 11). Also relevant will be whether the employer consulted with the employee before the dismissal and whether any attempts were made to find the employee alternative employment within the organisation.

If the employer fails to show that the reason for the dismissal was fair and that he or she acted reasonably in the circumstances as treating it as a sufficient reason to dismiss the employee, the dismissal will be considered to be unfair and the employee may be entitled to compensation, reinstatement or reengagement. For further details on the remedies available and the procedure involved in taking a case to an industrial tribunal see the chapter on employment rights.

Housing

In order to achieve independent living a disabled person must have access to housing suited to their specific needs. The object of this section is to look at the housing rights of disabled people in three areas: the public sector, the private sector and in relation to homelessness.

Public sector

In Northern Ireland public sector housing is provided and administered by the Northern Ireland Housing Executive ("the Executive"). The Executive attempts to meet the needs of disabled people in two ways.

Firstly, under the Chronically Sick and Disabled Persons (NI) Act 1978, section 3, the Executive, when proposing a new building scheme, is under a duty to have regard to the needs of the chronically sick or disabled and to distinguish which houses in the proposed scheme are suitable for their needs. This is a general duty only. The disabled person has no right to insist on the provision of public sector housing which is specially adapted to his or her needs.

Housing allocation

Secondly, all applications for public sector housing are subject to the Executive's Housing Selection Scheme (as approved by the Department of the Environment under article 22 of the Housing (NI) Order 1981). Applicants for housing are placed in order of priority on the basis of their particular needs. Top priority, *i.e.* A1 grouping, can be awarded where the applicant or a member of his or her family is in hospital or another institution from which they cannot be discharged due to lack of suitable housing for them to return to. Priority A2 grouping can be awarded where an applicant or a member of their family has special health or welfare needs and needs to be re-housed in more suitable accommodation, thus allowing them to remain in the community.

Private sector

The biggest obstacle to a disabled person wishing to either purchase or rent private property is that it will generally not be adapted to their special needs. The Executive facilitates some adaptation work in the private sector through Grant Aid. The Executive's system of grants was completely changed from October 1992 by the Housing (NI) Order 1992. In addition to the standard renovation grant, there are now two types of grants which make specific provision for disabled people.

Disabled facilities grant

By virtue of article 52(3) of the Housing (NI) Order 1992 a mandatory disabled facilities grant is available for work which will:
- provide access to, within or around the disabled person's dwelling,
- facilitate the preparation and cooking of food by the disabled occupant,
- improve or install a suitable heating system, and
- make it easier for the disabled occupant to use a source of power, light or heat.

A discretionary grant may also be available where the purpose of the work is to make the dwelling suitable for the accommodation, welfare or employment of disabled applicants (article 52(4)).

Grants will be awarded only where the work is necessary and appropriate to meet the needs of the disabled occupant and provided it is reasonable and practical to carry out the work, having regard to the age and condition of the dwelling or building (article 52(1)).

Applications can be made by either owner-occupiers or tenants. However, disabled facilities grants are means-tested. Depending upon his or her income, the applicant may be required to contribute to the cost of the adaptations. Moreover, multiple means tests will be applied if there is another person living in the dwelling who has an interest in it. This means that that person's income will also be taken into account in determining the amount of the grant.

Grants are available for the cost of both materials and labour but are subject to a maximum award of £50,000.

Minor works grant

Minor works grants are discretionary (article 69). They are available for the same type of adaptations as disabled facilities grants but are subject to a maximum award of £1,000. Applicants for minor works grants must be in receipt of income support, family credit, housing benefit or disability working allowance.

Persons who would like further details on these grants should contact:

- The Northern Ireland Housing Executive
  Home Improvement Service
  32-36 Victoria Street
  Belfast BT2 7BA
  tel: (0232) 317000

Homelessness

The provisions of the Housing (NI) Order 1988 are considered in full in chapter 18 on housing rights. It is worth noting that if the applicant is mentally or physically disabled or normally resides with someone in those categories, they will be defined as being in "priority need", one of the conditions for establishing A1 status under the Order.

Social services

The Chronically Sick and Disabled Persons (NI) Act 1978 places several duties on the Department of Health and Social Services (the DHSS)in relation to the disabled. Firstly, the Department is under a duty to inform itself as to the number and identity of disabled people living in Northern Ireland. Secondly, it is under a duty to arrange for them to be provided with practical assistance. And finally, it must supply them with information on the services available to them from the Department, other government departments, public bodies and voluntary organisations.

Section 2 of the 1978 Act outlines the forms of practical assistance which may be provided by the DHSS. These include: a home help, a radio, television, books or help in obtaining them, lectures, games and outings outside the home, help in taking advantage of educational opportunities, help with travelling to work or recreational facilities, adaptations to the home, help in taking holidays, meals at home and elsewhere, a telephone.

The DHSS, through the local Health and Social Services Boards, sets its own criteria in deciding whether the disabled person is in need of such assistance. However, once the Board has admitted that a need for the service exists, it is under a duty to meet it. The Board may decide to charge for the service but, if it does, the charge must be reasonable and no more than the disabled person can reasonably be expected to pay.

Further duties were placed on the DHSS by the Disabled Persons (NI) Act 1989. However, the most significant rights given to disabled people under the Act have not yet been brought into force. For instance, sections 1 and 2 give disabled people statutory rights to appoint an authorised representative or to have one appointed for them if they are unable to do so themselves. The intended function of the authorised representative was the representation of the views and interests of the disabled person in connection with the provision of personal social services. However, it seems unlikely that these provisions will become law in the forseeable future.

Further information on the services available can be obtained from local social services offices.

Access

A disabled person does not have the right to insist on physical access to any building. Although there is an increasing willingness to provide access to disabled persons, the legislation to reinforce this is limited.

The Chronically Sick and Disabled Persons (NI) Act 1978, sections 4 and 8 (as amended) place an obligation on anyone undertaking the provision of a building to which the public will have access or which is intended for use as a university, school, office or factory to make "appropriate provision" for the needs of persons with disabilities as regards means of access, parking and sanitary conveniences. "Appropriate provision" is defined in Part R of the Buildings Regulations (NI) 1990. These make general design recommendations regarding parking spaces, approach to the building, door widths and floor and wall surfaces.

The legislation is however, limited. Firstly, it only applies to the types of buildings specified above. Secondly, it only applies to new buildings or to existing buildings which are undergoing substantial structural changes. And thirdly, although the regulations are, in theory, legally binding, they are worded so generally as to be largely unenforceable in practice.

By virtue of article 6 of the Planning (NI) Order 1991, the Department of the Environment, when granting planning permission, is required to draw the attention of the applicant to the Buildings Regulations. However, planning permission will not be refused for failure to comply with the regulations and it is not a criminal offence to construct a building which contravenes the regulations.

Transport

Personal mobility is necessary for disabled persons to secure equality of access to employment and other social and recreational activities.

Private transport

There are various statutory provisions aimed specifically at the disabled user of private transport.

Driving licences

Disabled people receiving the mobility component of disability living allowance may apply for a provisional driving licence at 16 years of age, instead of the minimum age of 17 years specified for the able-bodied (Motor Vehicles (Driving Licences) Regulations (NI) 1989).

A person may not be granted a driving licence if he or she is suffering from a relevant disease or physical disability (article 6 of the Road Traffic (NI) Order 1981). Certain diseases and physical disabilities are specifically listed. These include:

- epilepsy
- liability to sudden attacks of disabling giddiness or fainting
- eyesight falling below a prescribed standard.

In addition to the prescribed diseases and disabilities, a licence will be refused if the applicant suffers from any disease or disability which would be likely to cause his or her driving to be a source of danger to the public.

If a person is aware that they are suffering from a relevant disease or disability, they must notify the Department of the Environment of their condition in writing. Failure to do so amounts to a criminal offence.

If a person suffers from a relevant disease or disability which is not prescribed, he or she is entitled to ask for a driving test to establish if his or her driving would be a source of danger to the public (article 6(2)(b) of the Road Traffic (NI) Order 1981). If the applicant passes the test, and is not otherwise disqualified, he or she may not be refused a licence solely on health grounds. However, if the test proves his or her fitness to drive vehicles of a particular construction or design only, any licence granted must be limited to such vehicles.

A person who suffers from epilepsy will not be refused a licence if he or she can satisfy certain conditions which establish that his or her condition is appropriately controlled (article 6(2)(d) of the Road Traffic (NI) Order 1981).

The Orange Badge Scheme

The Department of the Environment issues badges to be displayed on motor vehicles used by disabled people (Chronically Sick and Disabled Persons (NI) Act 1978, section 14). The conditions of entitlement to an orange badge are set down in the Disabled Persons (Badges for Motor

Vehicles) Regulations (NI) 1979. In order to qualify for an orange badge, the disabled person must be a person who:

- uses a motor vehicle supplied by the DHSS or is getting a grant towards the running of a car;
- uses a motor vehicle which is exempt from vehicle excise duty;
- is registered blind;
- is dependent upon the use of a wheelchair outside the home;
- has an amputation or absence of a limb which causes considerable difficulty in walking;
- suffers from defects of the spine or of the central nervous system or other motor defect which makes control of the lower limbs difficult; or
- has some other permanent and substantial disability which causes considerable difficulty in walking.

The advantage of having an orange badge is that badge holders are exempt from certain parking restrictions. The Scheme allows a vehicle displaying an orange badge and driven by a disabled person, or in which a disabled person is a passenger, to park:

- without charge or time limit at parking meters;
- without time limit where waiting is allowed for only limited periods;
- for a maximum of two hours where parking restrictions indicated by yellow lines are in force.

It is a criminal offence for a person to display an orange badge if he or she has no entitlement to it. It is also an offence for a person not entitled to a badge to use a parking space reserved for a disabled person's vehicle.

Badges can be obtained from the Road Service Division of the Department of the Environment.

Vehicle excise duty

All vehicles on the road are liable to vehicle excise duty, better known as road tax. However, by virtue of section 4(1)(g) of the Vehicle Excise Act (NI) 1972, disabled people can in certain circumstances claim exemption from vehicle excise duty for one car. In order to qualify for exemption, the disabled person must satisfy one of the following conditions:

- he or she must be in receipt of the care component of disability living allowance at either the middle or higher rate; or
- he or she must be in receipt of constant attendance allowance or attendance allowance at either rate; or
- he or she must be in receipt of the mobility component of disability living allowance at the higher rate; or
- he or she must be in possession of an invalid tricycle or a small car issued by the DHSS.

In addition, the car must be used solely by or for the purposes of the disabled person. For details about the allowances mentioned above, see chapter 19. Application forms for an exemption certificate can be obtained from:

- The Regional Disablement Service
  Musgrave Park Hospital
  Stockman's Lane
  Belfast BT9 7JB
  tel: (0232) 382255

The certificate can be used as proof of exemption when applying for a tax exemption disc from the vehicle licensing centre in Coleraine.

Rate relief

Applications for exemption from rates on property used by disabled people can be made under the Rates Amendment (NI) Order 1979, article 5. This provides for relief on garages or parking spaces which accommodate a vehicle used by and required for meeting the needs of a disabled person. Application forms for rate relief can be obtained from any local Rates Office.

Public transport

The rights of disabled persons in relation to public transport in Northern Ireland are limited. In spite of pressure from the European Community to introduce legislation on this issue, disabled people have no right to insist on access to public transport. Instead, section 75A of the Transport Act (NI) 1967 gives the Department of the Environment the power to provide grants towards expenditure incurred in providing vehicles and equipment to facilitate public transport for the disabled. Although such grants are available, access to both regular bus and train services in Northern Ireland remains poor.

Concessionary fares are similarly limited. Concessions are available to children, pensioners and to those registered blind. A "Blind Person's Pass" can be obtained from any Ulsterbus Office. The pass is free and entitles the holder to free travel within Northern Ireland on regular Ulsterbus, Citybus and NIR services.

Specific provisions for the mentally disabled

Many of the provisions detailed in previous sections of this chapter apply to both the physically and the mentally disabled, *e.g.* social services help and sheltered employment. However, due to the nature of their disability, the mentally disabled may have additional need for legislative protection. In Northern Ireland this is largely contained in the Mental Health (NI) Order 1986. This Order applies to people who are suffering from a "mental disorder" which is defined to include mental illness, mental handicap and any other disorder or disability of the mind.

The Order makes provision in six major areas. They are as follows.

- Articles 4 - 11 of the Order specify the circumstances in which a person may be compulsorily admitted to hospital for an assessment of his or her mental health.

- Articles 12 - 15 specify the circumstances in whch a person may be detained in hospital for treatment.

- Articles 18 - 26 provide for the appointment of a guardian.

- Part III of the Order makes provision for the remand, trial and detention of people suffering from a mental disorder who are involved in criminal proceedings or who are under sentence for a criminal offence.

- Part IV specifies the circumstances in which a person suffering from a mental disorder may or may not be treated without his or her consent.

- Part VIII provides for the management of the property and affairs of mental patients.

Any law which confers the power compulsorily to admit people to hospital, to detain them for medical treatment which they have not consented to, and to assume responsibility for the management of their affairs, must necessarily have serious civil liberties implications. The legislation is, not surprisingly, extensive and at times complex. A Code of Practice for use by doctors and administrators involved with mentally disordered people has been issued by the Department of Health and Social Services. Persons seeking information on the rights of the mentally disabled under the Mental Health Order should contact a solicitor or the Association for Mental Health:

*   Association for Mental Health
    Information Unit
    80 University Street
    Belfast BT7 1HE
    tel: (0232) 328474

Conclusions

The United Nations Declaration of the Rights of Disabled Persons asserts the right of disabled people to be self reliant, to live as they choose and to participate in the social, creative and recreational activities of their communities. Legislative provision in Northern Ireland falls short of enabling them to achieve these objectives. Government Departments, employers, builders, and the providers of public services etc, are placed under various general duties to consider and provide for the needs of disabled people, but these duties are usually not specifically enforceable. The disabled person is not given an individual right to insist on performance of these duties. The key to independent living lies in a comprehensive system of legally enforceable rights - not in a rag-bag mixture of general duties and discretionary powers.

Further information on the rights of disabled people can be obtained from the following organisations:

*   Disability Action
    Communications Unit
    2 Annadale Avenue
    Belfast BT7 3JR
    tel: (0232) 491011

- PHAB (Physically Handicapped and Able Bodied)
  25 Alexandra Gardens
  Belfast BT15 3LJ
  Phabline: tel: (0232) 322690 (Belfast)
       (0504) 371030 (Derry)
       (0622) 245954 (Omagh)

Chapter 15

Family and Sexual Matters

Brice Dickson and Madge Davison

The law governing the breakdown of marriages offers two remedies, "separation" and "divorce". Most of the rules on separation are to be found in the Domestic Proceedings (NI) Order 1980, while those on divorce are in the Matrimonial Causes (NI) Order 1978. A separation case will be dealt with in a summary way in a magistrates' court but a divorce must be heard either in a county court or the High Court. The High Court must be used if the case is a defended one.

Separation

In rare situations a spouse wishes to obtain an official decree of "judicial" separation rather than a decree of divorce. But what most people refer to as separation is a less formal status, namely that the spouses are living apart, often with one of them (usually the husband) paying money at regular intervals to the other. The wife obtains the *right* to such payments by applying to a magistrates' court for a "financial provision order", which might be for a lump sum or for periodical payments (known as "maintenance"). The law does not compel the spouses in such situations to live apart and indeed the legislation specifically allows for a case to be adjourned if, even though the spouses are already living apart, there is a reasonable possibility of a reconciliation. But if a financial provision order is granted and the parties then live together for a period exceeding six months, the order ceases to have effect.

The grounds for a financial provision order

There are two ways in which a financial provision order may be obtained. The first is by the agreement of both spouses. The second is by satisfying a court that one of the five grounds mentioned in the Domestic Proceedings (NI) Order 1980 has been fulfilled. These are:

- that the other spouse has failed to provide reasonable maintenance for the applicant;
- that the other spouse has failed to provide reasonable maintenance for any child of the family;
- that the other spouse has committed adultery;
- that the other spouse has behaved in such a way that the applicant cannot reasonably be expected to live with him or her;
- that the other spouse has deserted the applicant.

An application must be brought to the court within a year. The ground of unreasonable behaviour can include the following: practising sexual perversions, continually "nagging" or using obscene language, being a manic depressive, alcoholic or addicted to drugs, casting doubt on the paternity of children, doing DIY alterations which cause prolonged inconvenience, being convicted of criminal offences relevant to the family relationship, using violence on the spouse or children, and being hypercritical of the other spouse.

Other factors taken into account

A resident magistrate has to consider the following points before making an order:

- the income, earning capacity, property and other financial resources of the parties now and in the foreseeable future;
- the financial needs, obligations and responsibilities of the parties;
- the standard of living enjoyed by the parties;
- the age of each party and the duration of the marriage;
- any physical or mental disability of the parties;

- the contribution made by each of the parties to the welfare of the family, including whether one of the parties looked after the home and cared for the family;
- any other relevant matter, including the conduct of each of the parties.

If a case has been adjourned for a lengthy period, say for welfare reports on the children, it is possible to seek an interim order for maintenance in order to provide temporary financial relief.

Either party can apply to a magistrates' court for a variation of the original order on the ground that the party's means or circumstances have changed. An appeal against a decision can be made to a county court and from there to the High Court, but only on a difficult point of law.

Divorce

The Matrimonial Causes (NI) Order 1978 provides only one ground for divorce, namely "irretrievable breakdown of marriage". The spouse who asks for a divorce is called the "petitioner"; the other spouse is called the "respondent". In order to show that irretrievable breakdown has occurred, a petitioner must prove one or more of the following:

- that the respondent has committed adultery;
- that the respondent has behaved in such a way that the petitioner cannot reasonably be expected to live with him or her;
- that the respondent has deserted the petitioner for a continuous period of at least two years;
- that the parties have lived apart for a continuous period of at least two years and that the respondent consents to a decree being granted;
- that the parties have lived apart for a continuous period of at least five years.

Regarding adultery, it is only in rare cases that evidence is available, so a spouse's admission can be used in evidence. In cases of divorce by consent after two years of separation, it is necessary to satisfy the court that true consent exists: there must be no deceit or mistake as to any of the relevant information.

A person may not petition the court for divorce until the marriage has lasted for at least two years. A "decree *nisi*" is granted on the day of the hearing, with a "decree absolute" being granted six weeks later if there are no difficulties. Usually a petitioner for divorce will have to go into the witness box in court to give oral testimony. However, under article 13 of the proposed Family Law (NI) Order 1993 this will no longer be necessary if the divorce petition is based on two years' separation (with consent) or five years' separation (with or without consent).

Financial provision and divorce

Once a petition for divorce has been lodged, a court can make a variety of orders in relation to financial provision.

- Maintenance pending suit: the court can order either party to make periodical payments to the other in order to cover reasonable expenses arising between the beginning of the case and the time when the divorce is finally granted.
- Financial provision after a decree: the court can order a lump sum and/or periodical payments to be given to the spouse and/or the children of the family.
- Property order after a decree: the court can make an order regarding property belonging to the parties and this can include ordering a transfer of the matrimonial home.

Custody of, and access to, children

The law on this matter is due to be reformed by a Children (NI) Order, modelled on the Children Act 1989 for England and Wales. Amongst other changes the Order will replace custody and access orders with residence and contact orders. As no draft of the proposed Order had been published when this book went to press, the following account is based only on the existing law.

When a court hears an application for financial provision by one spouse against the other, it must consider whether to exercise its powers in respect of children (*i.e.* those under 18) before deciding what to do about the application. This means that the courts almost always award custody of the children to one party and access to the other, though the parties can also be granted joint rights over the children. Grandparents and step-parents can apply for custody and access too. In every case involving a custody dispute the first and paramount consideration is the welfare of the child. Factors which will guide the court as to what would be best for the child include the following:

- it is undesirable to disrupt the existing arrangements made for the child;
- one party's lifestyle may not suit the child;
- very young children are, generally speaking, better off with their mother;
- it is desirable to keep the children of a family together in one unit;
- the child may be old enough to express his or her own wishes regarding custody;
- it is not necessarily the case that one party's greater affluence will be beneficial to the child.

Types of custody order

In an application for a financial provision order under the Domestic Proceedings (NI) Order 1980 (see page 236), the magistrate may grant custody to either party to the marriage or to a parent of the child. Custody is granted to one person but the court can also specify that some or all of the rights or duties of parenthood should be exercised jointly by both parents. This means that one parent may have day-to-day care of the child but both parents may have a say in how the child should be brought up. In an application under the Matrimonial Causes (NI) Order 1978 (see page 235), the divorce court may make whatever order it thinks fit for the custody of any child. This means that in general one of the three following types of order is made:

- an order giving custody to one person and access to another;
- an order giving joint custody to two persons;
- an order splitting custody between two persons, meaning that day-to-day care and control is given to one ("actual custody") while the right to take decisions about the child's upbringing (*e.g.* as regards education) is given to the other ("legal custody").

Types of access order

"Access" is the contact a person has with a child when that person does not have custody. But it represents the child's right to maintain an important relationship, not a parent's right to be with the child. Whether the application is made under the Domestic Proceedings (NI) Order 1980 or the Matrimonial Causes (NI) Order 1978, the court may grant such access as it thinks fit, though under the 1980 Order the person to whom it is granted must be a parent, grandparent or a party to the marriage.

Child support

From April 1993, under the Child Support (NI) Order 1991, the Child Support Agency is able to ask single parents in receipt of social welfare benefits for the name of the other parent of their child. The Agency will then seek to recover money from that other parent. In return that parent may well apply for greater access to the child. If the first parent does not disclose the identity of the other parent, his or her welfare benefits may be reduced by up to 20%.

Domestic violence

One of the most important features of the Domestic Proceedings (NI) Order 1980 is the power it gives to magistrates to order protection for a spouse and children from a violent partner to a marriage or, since 1984, from a cohabitee. Two types of order can be made.

Personal protection order

To obtain this an applicant must satisfy the magistrate that the respondent has used or threatened to use violence against the applicant or a child of the family, and that an order is necessary for the protection of the applicant or child. Once obtained, the order restrains a spouse or cohabitee from "molesting" the applicant or child and prohibits the spouse or cohabitee from inciting, procuring or assisting another person to molest the applicant. It can be granted even if the applicant and the spouse or cohabitee are still living together.

Exclusion order

Very often a personal protection order is coupled with an exclusion order, which operates in one or more of the following ways:
- it gives the applicant exclusive use of the joint home;
- it prohibits the respondent from entering the home;

- it requires the respondent to permit the applicant to enter the home and have peaceful use and enjoyment of it;
- it prevents the respondent from selling the home or surrendering a lease on it;
- it orders the respondent not to damage or interfere with any services in the home;
- it orders the respondent not to remove any goods from the home and not to sell, damage or destroy any goods in it.

If the respondent damages, destroys or disposes of any goods in the home, the court can order him or her to repair, replace or restore these or to pay a sum of money instead. An exclusion order can also exclude the respondent from the street where the home is situated, but it must not interfere with the reasonable conduct of the respondent's life. It can exclude the respondent from specified premises other than the matrimonial home (or from their vicinity) provided the applicant or a child is living there, *e.g.* the applicant's parents' home, or a Women's Aid Refuge. In one case a magistrate was prepared to exclude a violent husband from the area between the matrimonial home and the nearest public telephone - to ensure that the wife could reach help unmolested. An exclusion order may last for up to six months and may be extended for any period not exceeding six months.

The power of arrest

A power of arrest is attached to every personal protection and exclusion order. The clerk of the court notifies the divisional commander of the RUC in the area where the applicant resides and where the excluded premises or areas are situated. A constable has power to arrest anyone whom he or she reasonably suspects of having breached an order by molesting the applicant or child, or by being in or attempting to enter the matrimonial home or other area specified in the order, or by damaging or interfering with any services or goods so specified. A constable may carry out the arrest without a warrant, using such force as is reasonable in the circumstances, and may if necessary enter the matrimonial home or other premises by force. Following his or her arrest, the person or cohabitee may be conditionally released or detained in custody until being brought before a court.

This is only a power of arrest, not a duty to arrest, so very often the exercise of the power rests on the judgment of a police constable. If no action is taken by the police the applicant can complain to the court about the breach of the order. Breach is itself to be made a criminal offence by the proposed Family Law (NI) Order 1993.

"Emergency" orders

The Domestic Proceedings (NI) Order 1980 also contains provisions to cope with an emergency situation in relation to domestic violence. It is possible for an applicant to be before a magistrate within a few hours of an attack. A magistrate has power to order an interim personal protection or exclusion order if satisfied that there may be imminent danger of physical injury to the applicant or a child. The hearing of the application will be in private, but where a magistrate refuses to grant an interim order there is no appeal. Interim orders do not take effect until the violent spouse or cohabitee is served with notice, and their effect is temporary, usually lasting for a period of five weeks or until the hearing for a full order. It is, however, possible to renew the interim order if the full hearing cannot take place within five weeks.

Problems in practice

There is no doubt that the powers in the 1980 Order, especially regarding exclusion orders, are extremely penal provisions. Since their introduction there has been some resistance to them, not least among the magistracy. Whilst most magistrates view applicants fairly and sympathetically, often assisting them by ordering that service of the orders on the spouse or cohabitee be carried out by the RUC, there are a few whose decisions are not always in keeping with the spirit of the law. Among the difficulties experienced in practice are the following:

- a belief that "professional" men should not be excluded from their homes;
- an attitude against granting these orders if the parties are living in the same home;
- demanding medical evidence of the assaults;
- refusing the orders unless the spouse or cohabitee has been violent to the children as well as to the applicant;

- refusing the orders if the violent spouse or cohabitee has nowhere else to live;
- refusing the orders if the magistrate considers there is the slightest chance of a reconciliation.

If magistrates voice any such reasons for refusing the orders there is nothing to stop the applicant in a suitable case from applying to the High Court for judicial review to have the magistrate's decision quashed (see chapter 2). A magistrate sitting in these cases often hears evidence of criminal offences ranging from common assault to grievous bodily harm. At the moment, regrettably, he or she does not automatically have to refer the case to the Director of Public Prosecutions for criminal proceedings to be considered.

Abortion

The law on abortion in Northern Ireland is much more restrictive than in the rest of the United Kingdom. It stems both from statute law and from the law laid down by judges. The Abortion Act 1967 does not apply here. The main Act which does apply is the Offences Against the Person Act 1861, which makes it an offence for a woman unlawfully to procure a miscarriage on herself by using "noxious poisons", "things" or "instruments". The maximum penalty is life imprisonment. This is also the penalty if someone else performs an operation on a woman so as unlawfully to procure a miscarriage.

The use of the word "unlawfully" shows that some abortions are lawful. It has always been accepted that they are lawful in cases where they are necessary in order to save the life of the mother. In *R. v Bourne* (1939) a gynaecologist in England was acquitted of carrying out an unlawful abortion on a 14-year-old girl who had been the victim of a multiple rape by soldiers. The judge said this was because the doctor had been of the opinion on reasonable grounds and with adequate knowledge that the probable consequences of continuing the pregnancy would have been to make the woman a physical or mental wreck. Although this view was queried by Lord Diplock in a 1981 case, it remains the law in Northern Ireland. Moreover, section 25 of the Criminal Justice Act (NI) 1945 specifically provides a defence to an abortionist if he or she acts in good faith for the purpose of preserving the life of the mother.

The law in practice

Naturally the medical profession in Northern Ireland is not happy that the law in this area is so unclear. Doctors receive no guidance from the Department of Health and Social Services and the medical teaching profession has had to draw up its own guidelines on the interpretation of the law for the benefit of medical students. The practice appears to be that abortions are performed in Northern Ireland only where there is a serious risk to health or life. More than half the women seeking abortions here are refused and abortions are performed only in the first three to five months of pregnancy. It remains uncertain whether there is any specific policy in relation to performing abortions on handicapped foetuses. There is also no guarantee that an abortion would be performed if a woman became pregnant as a result of rape. If the medical profession refuses to perform an abortion on a woman in Northern Ireland, and she does not want to give birth, she is effectively faced with the choice of a trip to England or recourse to a back-street abortion here. If she does choose to give birth there are agencies to counsel and help her.

Sexual offences

Although the overall crime rate in Northern Ireland is lower than that in England and Wales, one category of crime which is committed at a higher rate in Northern Ireland is that of sexual offences.

In England and Wales the main legislation governing these offences is the Sexual Offences Act 1956, which was updated by the Sexual Offences (Amendment) Acts 1976 and 1992. In Northern Ireland the main legislation is still Victorian in origin, being chiefly the Offences Against the Person Act 1861, the Criminal Law Amendment Act 1885 and the Vagrancy Act 1898. More recent laws include the Children and Young Persons Act (NI) 1968, the Sexual Offences (NI) Order 1978 and the Homosexual Offences (NI) Order 1982. There are really three main types of sexual offence: rape, buggery and indecent assault. After discussing these, special consideration will be given to crimes involving incest, prostitution and indecency.

Advice on some of the matters covered in this section can be obtained from either:

- Rape Crisis Centre (Belfast)
  PO Box 46,
  Belfast BT2 7AR
  tel: (0232) 249696

- Nexus,
  PO Box 220,
  Belfast BT1 7HP
  tel: (0232) 326803 or (0504) 260566 (Derry).

Rape

By article 3(1) of the Sexual Offences (NI) Order 1978, a man commits rape if he has unlawful sexual intercourse with a woman who at the time of the intercourse does not consent to it and at that time he knows that she does not consent to the intercourse or he is reckless as to whether she consents to it.

"Sexual intercourse" here requires penetration of the woman's vagina by the man's penis, but nothing more. As regards the woman's consent, apparent consent is not real consent. Rape is therefore committed whenever the woman's "consent" is obtained by threats of personal violence, by fraud, or whenever the woman is so mentally vulnerable, or young, or drunk, that her knowledge and understanding are such that she is not in a position to decide whether to consent or to resist. The man is guilty of rape if he obtains the woman's consent by impersonating her husband (hardly a likely occurrence), but not if he merely pretends to be some other person. If a man's defence to a charge of rape is that he believed that the woman was consenting to sexual intercourse, the jury must consider whether there were reasonable grounds for such a belief. The test is therefore objective, not subjective.

In 1991 the judges changed the ancient rule that a wife is always presumed to have consented to intercourse with her husband (*R. v R.*). A man can now be guilty of raping his wife, even if they are otherwise "happily" married.

The maximum penalty for the crime of rape is life imprisonment (section 48 of the Offences Against the Person Act 1861), while that for attempt to commit rape, or for assault with intent, is seven years' imprisonment (sections 1 and 2 of the Attempted Rape, etc Act (NI) 1960). The Northern Ireland Court of Appeal has said that the starting point for rape in a contested case should be seven years' imprisonment (*Attorney-General's Reference No. 1*, 1989)

There is a rule laid down by the judges (though it may soon be changed by a Private Members' Bill in Parliament) that a boy younger than 14 is incapable of committing rape or assault with intent to commit rape. But he can be convicted of aiding and abetting a rape or of indecent assault, as indeed can a woman. A woman cannot otherwise be convicted of raping a man.

In the case of females under 17, there can be no consent in law to sexual intercourse. The girl herself does not commit any offence by having intercourse (and may, *e.g.*, be prescribed contraceptives) but the male does, even if he has reasonable cause to believe that the girl is 17 or over. If the girl is over 14 and under 17 the man is liable to be sent to prison for up to two years, but the prosecution must be begun within 12 months of the commission of the offence. If the girl is under 14 the man can be sent to prison for life if intercourse takes place, or for up to two years if there was an attempt at intercourse (Criminal Law Amendment Act 1885, sections 4 and 5).

A rape victim can take out a civil action against the rapist, though obviously this is worth doing only if he has assets out of which he can pay compensation to the victim. The action has to be begun within three years of the incident (or of the victim turning 18, if that is later). In addition, a rape victim who becomes pregnant as a result of the attack, and who decides to give birth to the child and keep it, is now entitled to £5,000 compensation from the state (article 9 of the Criminal Injuries (Compensation) (NI) Order 1988).

Identification in rape cases

On account of the sensitive nature of trials alleging rape, special provisions have been introduced to protect both the alleged victim and the alleged rapist:

- by article 6 of the Sexual Offences (NI) Order 1978, after a person has been officially accused of a rape offence nothing which is likely to lead members of the public to identify a particular woman as the complainant can be published or broadcast in Northern Ireland;

- the only exceptions to this are where a judge directs that the restriction should be lifted in the public interest or in order to induce persons who are vital to the accused's defence to come forward;

- anyone who publishes information in breach of article 6 is liable to be fined up to £500.

It should be noted that anonymity attaches to the complainant only after a person has been officially accused. Until then, even though the matter may still be under investigation, the alleged victim's name (if she has not yet officially complained) may be revealed to the public. If the case does go to trial, however, every alleged rape victim has a right not to have to confront any question or evidence put forward by the defence about her sexual experience with someone other than the accused. This right can be overridden by the magistrate or judge only if he or she is satisfied that it would be unfair to the accused to refuse to allow the evidence to be submitted or the question to be asked. The woman, however, is not entitled to have her own legal representative in court.

The anonymity of the accused man is also protected (see article 8 of the 1978 Order), though he can waive this protection if he so wishes and a judge can lift the reporting restriction in the public interest. If he is eventually acquitted of the rape charge, the accused's name must still not be linked to the charge, even though he may have been convicted of some related offence such as indecent assault. If the accused is convicted of rape, his identity can then be revealed.

Buggery

Anal intercourse, whether between men or between a man and a woman, cannot amount to the crime of rape. In Northern Irish law the relevant provision is still section 61 of the Offences Against the Person Act 1861, which says that :

> *"whosoever shall be convicted of the abominable crime of buggery, committed either with mankind, or with any animal, shall be liable to imprisonment for life."*

By section 62 any attempt to commit buggery, or any assault with intent to commit it, is an offence carrying a sentence of up to 10 years' imprisonment.

Consent is not a defence to a charge of buggery, so a husband can be convicted of committing the offence on his wife, or a cohabitee on his willing partner. Following the 1981 decision in *Dudgeon v UK*, where the European Court of Human Rights held that the law in Northern Ireland making all male homosexual acts an offence was in violation of Article 8 of the European Convention on Human Rights, the government introduced the Homosexual Offences (NI) Order 1982. As explained below, this legalised certain categories of homosexual acts.

Indecent assault

Indecent assault is an assault or "battery" (*i.e.*, threatened or actual physical contact) accompanied by circumstances of indecency. Merely touching somebody without his or her consent and in circumstances of indecency can constitute the offence. Even if consent has supposedly been given, this is no defence if the assault was of a kind to cause harm interfering with the victim's health or comfort, or if it was obtained by fraud. Most importantly, a female who is younger than 17 (in England the age-limit is 16) cannot give a valid consent. Nor, depending on the circumstances, may a person who is mentally vulnerable. The House of Lords has recently held that persons who indulge in sado-masochistic practices can still be guilty of indecent assault, even though the participants fully consent to what is done to them (*R.* v *Brown*, 1992).

Behaviour constituting indecent assault can range from a tap on the bottom to forced oral sex. Indeed, because the current legal definition of rape is so limited, many very serious acts can be prosecuted only as indecent assaults. Penetration of a woman's vagina by anything other than a penis is such an act. The definition of rape is so limited for historical reasons: what was originally being protected was simply a woman's right not to be made pregnant unwillingly. Today the maximum penalty for indecent assault, whether committed against a man or a woman, is 10 years' imprisonment.

Closely allied to the crime of indecent assault is the offence of indecent conduct towards a child. This is governed by section 22 of the Children and Young Persons Act (NI) 1968, which provides that a person who commits an act of gross indecency with or towards a child under 14, or who incites a child under 14 to such an act with the accused or with another, is liable to be sent to prison for up to two years.

In England and Wales, by the Sexual Offences (Amendment) Act 1992, provisions on anonymity have been extended to cover not just rape cases but most other sexual offences too. As yet there has been no comparable extension of the Sexual Offences (NI) Order 1978.

Incest

Incest is still governed in Northern Ireland by the Punishment of Incest Act 1908. It can be committed by both males and females. Under section 1(1) of the 1908 Act a male is guilty of incest if he has sexual intercourse with a female who is, to his knowledge, his mother, sister, daughter or granddaughter. If the female is under 14 the maximum penalty is life imprisonment, otherwise the maximum is seven years' imprisonment. Attempts to commit incest carry a maximum sentence of two years' imprisonment. In all cases the consent of the female is immaterial.

Under section 2 of the 1908 Act a female commits incest if she is over 16 and consents to have sexual intercourse with someone whom she knows to be her son, brother, father or grandfather. The maximum penalty is seven years' imprisonment, whatever the age of the male involved. A girl under 16 who willingly has incestuous intercourse commits no offence.

For the purposes of the crime of incest, the terms "brother" and "sister" include half-brother and half-sister and it does not matter whether the child or grandchild involved is born in lawful wedlock. All prosecutions require the consent of the Attorney-General for Northern Ireland and must be held in private.

As regards the measures that can be taken to protect children from sexual abuse, the relevant legal provisions in Northern Ireland are primarily sections 31-32 of the Children and Young Persons Act (NI) 1968. Any person reasonably suspected of committing a sexual offence against a child can be arrested by the police without warrant (section 31). The child can be removed by the police to a place of safety if a Justice of the Peace issues a warrant authorising this (section 32). The JP must first be satisfied that there is reasonable cause to suspect that the child or young person has been or is being assaulted, ill-treated or neglected in a manner likely to cause unnecessary suffering or injury to health.

Prostitution

It is not an offence for a woman or a man to "sell" his or her body for sex, but it is an offence to solicit custom, to assist in the management of a brothel or to live off the earnings of a prostitute. Prostitution, for this purpose, need not entail actual sexual intercourse; it is enough, in the words of one judge, if a woman "offers her body for purposes amounting to common lewdness for payment in return" (Darling J in *R v de Munck*, 1918).

In all towns in Northern Ireland it is an offence for a prostitute to loiter and importune "passengers" for the purpose of prostitution: see section 167 of the Belfast Improvement Act 1845, section 28 of the Town Police Clauses Act 1847 (for Belfast and Derry) and section 72 of the Towns Improvement (Ireland) Act 1854 (for other towns). By section 1(1) of the Vagrancy Act 1898 - extended to what is now Northern Ireland in 1912 - it is an offence punishable by up to six months' imprisonment if a man:

- knowingly lives wholly or in part on the earnings of prostitution; or
- persistently in any public place solicits for immoral purposes; the judges have said that this offence cannot be committed by a man who kerb-crawls; the law was changed in England in 1985 but in Northern Ireland kerb-crawling remains, strictly speaking, a legal activity.

If a man is proved to be living with, or to be habitually in the company of, a prostitute, or is proved to have exercised control, direction or influence over the movements of a prostitute in such a manner as to show that he is aiding, abetting or compelling her prostitution, the burden of proof is then on him to show that he was not knowingly living on the earnings of prostitution (section 1(3) of the 1898 Act). The Criminal Law Amendment Act 1912 extended the scope of the earlier Act by permitting females to be convicted of aiding, abetting or compelling another woman's prostitution. Article 8 of the Homosexual Offences (NI) Order 1982 specifically criminalises men or women who live on the earnings of male prostitution, allowing a maximum penalty of seven years' imprisonment to be imposed.

The Criminal Law Amendment Act 1885 creates further offences in this area:

- section 2 makes it an offence to procure or attempt to procure any female to become a common prostitute and by section 3 the use of intimidation, fraud or drugs for these purposes is specifically criminalised;

- section 6 prohibits any person who is the owner, occupier or manager of premises from permitting defilement of girls under 17 on those premises;
- section 7 outlaws the abduction of women under 18 with the purpose of enabling them to have unlawful sexual intercourse with any man;
- section 8 makes it an offence for a person to detain any woman against her will in any premises so that she can have unlawful sexual intercourse with any man.

All of these offences under the 1885 Act carry a maximum prison sentence of two years. The offence under section 2 is one for which the police can arrest without a warrant.

Two more provisions affecting children should be noted here:

- Section 21 of the Children and Young Persons Act (NI) 1968, according to which it is an offence for any person who has the custody or care of a female under 17 to cause or encourage the commission of unlawful sexual intercourse with her or the commission of an indecent assault upon her. It can be enough if the accused person (who may be a man or a woman) has knowingly allowed the girl to consort with any person of known immoral character. The maximum penalty is two years' imprisonment.
- Section 23 of the 1968 Act makes it a crime punishable with six months' imprisonment and an unlimited fine to allow any child of at least four years of age to reside in or to frequent a brothel.

Indecency

There are some offences relating to sex which are designed to protect not particular victims but the general public. According to a leading legal textbook, under the ordinary common law (*i.e.*, the law laid down by judges), "in general all open lewdness, grossly scandalous behaviour, and whatever openly outrages decency or is offensive and disgusting, or is injurious to public morals by tending to corrupt the mind and destroy the love of decency, morality and good order, is an offence indictable at common law" (Archbold, 44th ed, 1992, page 2295). It seems that the offence can be committed only in a public place (so that at least one other person may see it). In theory, there is no limit to the penalty that can be imposed but it must obviously be proportionate to the outrageousness of the act. Merely leaving notes in public places for young boys is not by itself indecent (*R. v Rowley*, 1991), but exhibiting in a commercial art gallery earrings made out of human foetuses is (*R v Gibson*, 1990).

The judges have not yet confirmed that two or more persons can be convicted of conspiring to outrage public decency but they have said that there is an offence known as conspiracy to corrupt public morals (see *Knuller v DPP*, 1972). Another common law offence is that of exposing one's naked body in public. Very few prosecutions are brought these days for such a crime, though in theory "streaking", sun-bathing in the nude and "mooning" would qualify. A more common type of proceeding is the one brought under section 4(d) of the Vagrancy Act 1824 - extended to what is now Northern Ireland in 1871. This says that every man who wilfully, openly, lewdly and obscenely exposes his penis with intent to insult any female (*i.e.* a "flasher") is to be deemed "a rogue and vagabond". He can be sent to prison by a magistrate for up to three months.

District councils in Northern Ireland may make bylaws regulating certain acts of indecency and, except in Derry and Belfast, section 72 of the Towns Improvement (Ireland) Act 1854 provides that every person who commits any act contrary to public decency shall be liable to a fine not exceeding £20. More generally, it is an offence under section 9(1) of the Criminal Justice (Miscellaneous Provisions) Act (NI) 1968 - as amended by the Public Order (NI) Order 1987 - to behave indecently in any street, road, highway, other public place, any place to which the public have access, or any premises where intoxicating liquor is sold.

Homosexuality

Prior to the introduction of the Homosexual Offences (NI) Order 1982, acts of male homosexuality were illegal in Northern Ireland. Even the distribution of literature about homosexuality, or the provision of counselling, were criminalised through being labelled incitement or aiding and abetting. Although the law in England and Wales was altered by the Sexual Offences Act 1967, it was only after a judgment of the European Court of Human Rights in 1981 that the government changed the law for Northern Ireland. Article 3 of the 1982 Order provides that it shall not be an offence for a man to commit buggery or gross indecency with another man provided that the act is done in private, that the two men consent and that they are each at least 21 years of age. But this law does not alter some well-established principles - such as that a person under 14 cannot be convicted of buggery, and that homosexuality between members of the armed forces, or between merchant seamen, is unlawful.

It remains an offence for a man to procure another man to commit a homosexual act with a third man, but it is not an offence for a man to procure the commission with himself by another man of such an act. Persistent public solicitation, however, is still outlawed by the Vagrancy Act 1898 - unless a magistrate or a jury were to hold that homosexuality is not an "immoral purpose", which in Northern Ireland is unlikely. A judge or jury is also entitled to hold that homosexual advances by one man on another are good grounds for the defence of provocation if the latter loses his self-control and kills the first man (the so-called "Portsmouth" defence).

The 1982 Order (as later amended) also revised the maximum sentences which may be imposed for illegal homosexual acts. If the intercourse is with a boy under 16, the maximum penalty is life imprisonment. If with a man over 16, but who did not consent, it is 10 years. If with a man over 16 but under 21 who consented (and presuming the accused is over 21), it is five years. For other situations the maximum is two years' imprisonment.

There is no law which specifically prohibits lesbianism, certainly not if it is carried out by consenting adults. But the offence of indecent assault may be committed if one of the women involved has not properly given her consent.

The age of consent

It has already been pointed out that, as far as the right to consent to sexual intercourse is concerned, the age limit for females in Northern Ireland is 17, whereas in England it is 16. There is no age limit for males, but a male under 21 cannot lawfully consent to any homosexual act. Once a person has reached the age of 16, he or she can consent to any surgical, medical or dental treatment without needing to obtain the agreement of his or her parents or guardian. It appears, moreover, that even a child who is under 16 can consent to such treatment if it is clear that he or she fully understands the nature of the treatment being proposed. This means that it is possible for girls under 16 to be prescribed contraceptive treatment, even though it is unlawful for a male to have sexual intercourse with a girl who is under 17 (see the *Gillick* case, 1985).

A person can get married at the age of 16 if the consent of his or her parents or guardians is obtained, though even when such consent is absent the marriage will still usually be valid in the eyes of the law. Once a person reaches 18, no consents at all are required.

As regards responsibility under the criminal law, a boy under 14 cannot be convicted of rape or of assault with intent to commit rape. No child who is over 9 and under 14 can be charged with any crime unless the prosecution can prove that he or she knew that what was being done was wrong. In law, a "child" is a person who is aged 13 or less and a "young person" is someone aged 14 to 16; special rules have been laid down for processing such youngsters through the criminal courts, with "juvenile courts" being set up to deal with most minor offences. There is a conclusive presumption in law that no child under the age of 10 can be guilty of any criminal offence (Children and Young Persons Act (NI) 1968, section 69).

Chapter 16

Education Rights

Chris Moffat

T his chapter describes some of the rights which parents and their children have while the children are of compulsory school age. The main current legislation concerning education in Northern Ireland is the Education and Libraries (NI) Order 1986 (abbreviated here to the 1986 Order or the principal Order) as amended by the Education (NI) Order 1987 and the Education (Corporal Punishment) (NI) Order 1987. The Education Reform (NI) Order 1989, abbreviated to the 1989 Order, amends rather than replaces the 1986 Order.

The right to education

The United Nations' Convention on the Rights of the Child, in Article 28, recognises the right of every child to education, including:

- free primary education;
- access to different forms of secondary education, including general and vocational education, provided free or with financial assistance in the case of need; and
- access to higher education for all on the basis of capacity.

In Article 29 the Convention defines education as, amongst other things:

- the development of the child's personality, talents and mental and physical abilities to their fullest potential;
- the development of respect for human rights and fundamental freedoms;
- the development of respect for the child's parents, his or her own cultural identity, language and values, for the national values of the country in which the child is living and the country from which he or she may originate, and for civilisations different from his or her own;
- the preparation of the child for responsible life in a free society, in the spirit of understanding, peace, tolerance, equality of sexes, friendship among all peoples, ethnic, national or religious groups and persons of indigenous origins and respect for the natural environment.

Rights and duties of parents

The 1986 Order provides that pupils should be educated according to the wishes of their parents, so long as this is "compatible with the provision of efficient instruction and training and the avoidance of unreasonable public expenditure" (article 44). However, this general right is severely limited by the absence of practical options for many parents, the lack of agreed criteria concerning "unreasonable public expenditure" and the reluctance of the courts to intervene.

Parents have a duty to make sure that their children of compulsory school age (4-16 years) receive sufficient full-time education suitable to their age, ability and aptitude, and any special educational needs, either by regular attendance at school or in some other way (article 45). "Parent" includes a guardian and every person who has actual custody of a child or young person.

Children are of compulsory school age between the ages of 4 and 16 years. The relevant date for determining the lower and upper age limits of compulsory school age is now 1st July:

- children with fourth birthdays occurring before 1st July are of compulsory school age from the following September;
- children with 16th birthdays occurring before 1st July reach the upper limit of compulsory school age at the end of their current school year (1989 Order, article 156).

School attendance

If they wish, parents can send their children to a school which is not provided by an Area Board or other grant-maintained body, or they can educate their children at home, but the arrangements must be approved by the Department of Education for Northern Ireland, and the Area Board must be satisfied that they are suitable for the children's needs and that the children attend regularly.

If a Board thinks that parents are failing to provide for a child's education it must serve a notice giving them 14 days to explain what alternative arrangements they are making. If it is still not satisfied it must serve notice of its intention to make an attendance order specifying which school or suitable alternative schools the child will have to attend. Parents have a right to choose between the schools named on the notice or to propose an alternative (provided the school is willing to accept the child), but this must meet the criteria of suitability mentioned in article 45. In the last resort, if parents think a Board is acting unreasonably they may appeal to the Department of Education (1986 Order, article 101, as amended by the Order 1989, article 158).

The education service

Under the 1989 Order the Department of Education has the duty to promote the education of the people of Northern Ireland (article 2(b)). Each Area Education Board must ensure that there are available in its area sufficient schools for providing primary and secondary education. By "sufficient" is meant:

> *"sufficient in number, character and equipment to afford all pupils opportunity for education offering such variety of instruction and training as may be desirable in view of their different ages, abilities and aptitudes, and of the different periods for which they may be expected to remain at school, including practical instruction and training appropriate to their respective needs".*

In addition, each Board must have particular regard to:

> *(a) the need for securing that special educational provision is made for pupils having special educational needs;*

(b) the expediency of securing the provision of boarding accommodation, for pupils whose parents and the Board consider it desirable. (1986 Order, article 6)

Each Board must also secure the provision in its area of adequate facilities for further education, and may (but need not) provide nursery schools or nursery classes.

Educational provision

Attendance at different types of school can affect pupils' rights. The existence of two separate and effectively denominational sectors under different forms of management and funding has made it easier for sectarian and other non-educational factors to affect pupils' lives and careers. In addition, the fact that in most areas, secondary education is selective and pupils are divided between grammar or secondary schools at 11 years of age, has helped to perpetuate social inequalities. Recent changes, such as the introduction of new funding procedures, may eventually remove some of these disparities. However, lack of choice is likely to continue to be the experience of a significant number of pupils.

Types of schools

• *Controlled schools*

Controlled schools are schools which are provided and managed by the Area Boards. They include nursery, primary, secondary, grammar and special schools. Although controlled schools are meant to be non-denominational "state" schools, in practice they are seen as Protestant and the majority of pupils are Protestant.

• *Catholic maintained schools*

Catholic maintained schools are provided "voluntarily" by Catholic diocesan authorities. They include nursery, primary and secondary schools. Their running costs are met by Area Boards and 85% of approved capital costs are grant aided by the Department. Legally no pupil may be refused admission on religious grounds, but the schools are intended for Catholic pupils and are seen as Catholic schools.

- *Voluntary schools*

Voluntary grammar schools run by various trusts, denominational foundations and religious orders constitute the majority of voluntary schools. Those known as Category A have an have an agreement with the Department of Education or a Board, under which they receive 100% of running costs and 85% of their capital funding. They are permitted to charge certain fees, including an annual capital fee. Pupils in the prep departments and other "excepted" pupils in secondary departments, *e.g.* non-EC nationals and those in other voluntary (Category B) grammar schools, may be charged tuition and other fees.

- *Grant maintained integrated and controlled integrated schools*

Integrated schools are schools which are planned to be equally acceptable to both the Catholic and Protestant traditions within Northern Ireland. They aim to maintain a balance of numbers between the two main denominational traditions amongst pupils, teaching staff and governors and to provide a curriculum which meets the cultural needs of each community.

The 1989 Order provides for a voluntary category of such schools, known as grant maintained integrated schools. It is required that "the management and ethos of the school are such as are likely to attract reasonable numbers of both Protestant and Roman Catholic pupils" (article 66 (2)).

Integrated schools which have been set up independently with capital raised voluntarily (usually by parents) can apply for grant maintained integrated status. Once recognised, such schools may have their running costs funded 100% by the Department and are theoretically entitled to receive 100% capital funding.

Existing schools may also seek and be recognised as grant maintained integrated or controlled integrated if it appears to the department that "the school would be likely to be attended by reasonable numbers of both Protestant and Roman Catholic pupils" (1989 Order, articles 71(9) and 92(6)). Controlled integrated schools are subject to the same recognition procedures as grant maintained integrated schools but are under the management of an Area Board.

- *Grant maintained status*

Legislation to be brought forward in 1993 will provide for the creation of a general category of grant maintained schools which will open up the possibility of full funding (100% recurrent and capital) to any voluntary (including Catholic maintained) independent or new voluntary school, (apart from nursery or special schools) which wishes to opt for it. No single interest group will have majority representation on the board of governors. Such schools will be entitled to retain their existing, including denominational, character.

- *Independent schools*

Independent schools are not grant-aided. They do not have to comply with any other statutory rules of management or curriculum organisation, but they must be inspected and registered by the Department and must meet certain minimum requirements as to premises, accommodation and efficient and suitable instruction. They include a small number of nursery and preparatory schools, as well as schools founded by parents and others from cultural, linguistic or religious minorities. In some cases these schools wish to retain complete control of their schools, in others they have not been able to secure public funding.

- *Special schools*

"Special" schools are schools for disabled children and others with special needs. As far as possible such children should be provided with special education in "ordinary schools". There are a number of special educational units within ordinary schools. However, there are over 20 special schools in Northern Ireland, as well as a small number of hospital schools for children with particular types of disability which may create severe learning difficulties.

Educational access

Open enrolment

The 1989 Order is intended to provide for open enrolment. It gives parents the right to apply for admission to any grant-aided school, other than a nursery or special school, in any Board area in which they wish education to be provided for their child and that school will have a duty to admit the child unless:

- admission of the child would cause the school to exceed its "admissions number" for that school year; and
- it would "prejudice the provision of efficient education or the efficient use of resources"; or
- the preferred school is a grammar school and admission would be "detrimental to the educational interests of the child concerned" (1989 Order, article 36).

The 1989 Order gives the Department of Education the power to determine admissions numbers for all schools and to direct a board of governors to vary the admissions number for any particular year. Each school is required to draw up criteria to be applied in selecting pupils for admission to the school and must apply the criteria correctly. Schools may not exceed their enrolment and admissions numbers without the specific approval of the Department of Education, except to admit a child for whom an Area Board is maintaining a statement of special educational needs or who is the subject of school attendance order.

Nursery schools

Area Boards are not obliged to provide nursery education (for children from three to the lower limit of compulsory school age) and it is widely recognised that nursery provision in Northern Ireland is substantially below that in the rest of the United Kingdom. Around one-sixth of Northern Ireland's three and four-year-olds are catered for in nursery schools or nursery departments of primary schools. Three quarters of this provision is within the controlled sector.

Primary schools

There are around 970 primary schools in Northern Ireland, including 14 integrated primary schools, providing free education, as well as 26 fee-paying prep departments of voluntary grammar schools. In theory there are no restrictions on choice of primary school, although in practice the application of capacity-based enrolment and admissions numbers may threaten the viability of many primary schools. The Department of Education determines primary school enrolment and admissions numbers by taking into account the accommodation available for use by pupils. It must be satisfied that the school can "provide the educational experiences necessary for the common curriculum".

Primary school admissions

Application to primary schools is by means of standardised application forms. Area Boards must publish details of arrangements for parents to express their choice of primary school, arrangements for the admission of pupils to each school and details of each primary school's admissions criteria. There is no legal requirement that parents should limit their choice to one school. Primary schools' admission criteria must:

- give the order of priority in which pupils shall be admitted if the school is over-subscribed;
- give priority to children who will have obtained compulsory school age at the time of the proposed admission;
- not select pupils by reference to ability or aptitude, or performance in a test or examination held by, or on behalf of, the board of governors;
- apply admission criteria to pupils of both compulsory and below compulsory school age and to those who are already enrolled in an "approved" nursery class at the school.

Parents may appeal to an Appeals Tribunal against a decision to refuse admission to a school if they think the school did not apply, or did not correctly apply, its admissions criteria (see page 264).

Secondary schools

In most areas of Northern Ireland secondary schooling is selective. Theoretically between 25% and 45% of all school places are in grammar schools, which are the only schools legally permitted to select pupils by reference to "ability or aptitude". Variations in the proportion of places arise from differences in local provision, the match between the religious denomination of pupils and school providers, the willingness or ability of pupils to travel or board, the physical capacity of the school and the pre-disposition of the Department to amend admissions numbers of schools which are oversubscribed.

A small number of areas operate a non-selective or delayed-selection systems and have "comprehensive" or bi-lateral secondary schools, but there is no statutory definition of a "comprehensive" school. Pupils in these areas curently have to "opt in" to the selection procedure or transfer arrangements.

Selection tests

The Department conducts an examination (1986 Order, article 110) to determine pupils' suitability for grammar schools (or other schools approved by the Department). At the time of writing pupils were graded in terms of academic ability on the basis of "verbal reasoning-type" tests. Future arrangements for determining pupils' suitability for grammar school places may include assessment outcomes in the Northern Ireland Curriculum, but they are likely to be more difficult and expensive to administer and will not necessarily produce a single measure of "academic ability".

Unless parents notify the Department through their principal on the appropriate form, their child will be regarded as participating in any selection test. Under the present arrangements under-age pupils certified to the Department by their principal are permitted to take the selection tests. Over-age pupils will be permitted to take the tests in some circumstances, with the Department's prior approval. Pupils for whom Area Boards maintain statements of special educational need are not intended to take part in the transfer procedure tests.

Problems with the selection test

If a child's availability for, or performance in, a test is adversely affected by illness or other factors, parents must ensure that the principal notifies the Department immediately and sends any supporting evidence, *e.g.* a doctor's certificate or test supervisor's report, within a specified time limit. No allowance is made for illness in marking test papers, but an opportunity is provided for a child to take a supplementary test.

Parents should get in touch with the principal of the secondary school(s) they have nominated if their child's performance has been affected. They should provide whatever supporting evidence is available. The school must take into account medical or other problems which may have affected performance in any tests in admissions decisions. If parents are not successful they may appeal to an Appeals Tribunal (see page 265).

Parents who are dissatisfied with decisions taken on the basis of any transfer tests can complain. However, the Department maintains that there is no provision for changing a grade once awarded and parents must deal directly with secondary schools which have ultimate responsibility for admissions decisions.

Transfer arrangements

Arrangements for transfer to secondary school are administered by the Area Boards. They must publish information to enable parents to express a preference for the secondary school(s) they would like their child to attend, details of each school's enrolment and admissions number, the criteria each school will use to select pupils if over-subscribed, and the functions of the governors and principal in relation to admissions.

At least six weeks before parents are required to express preferences, schools must publish prospectuses containing details of curriculum, public examination results, school leavers' destinations and attendance rates.

Admissions criteria

Schools draw up their own admissions criteria subject to the Secondary Schools (Admission Criteria) Regulations (NI) 1990, as amended in 1992 and subsequently. They must:

- include the order of priority for the admission of pupils where a school is over-subscribed;
- include a reference to ability or aptitude only in the case of a grammar school;
- where a grammar school uses the results in the transfer procedure tests as one of its criteria, admit day pupils with grade 1 before pupils with any other grade, and those with grade 2 before those with grades 3 or 4; this need not apply to boarding pupils, so long as their number does

not exceed the number of boarders in 1990; these rules apply *irrespective* of the order in which parents have expressed preferences for schools and are subject to the requirement that boards of governors take into account medical or other problems which may have affected a child's test performance, where this is supported by a medical certificate or other appropriate documentary evidence;

• not include reference to performance in pilot assessments in Key Stage 2 in 1992-3;

• not include performance of a pupil in any test or examination held by or on behalf of the board of governors other than an assessment made by an Area Board at the request of a grammar school.

Other criteria

Schools may apply any other reasonable criteria for deciding which pupils should be admitted, and should consider any representations made by the Area Board in the case of a controlled school and the Council for Catholic Maintained Schools in the case of Catholic maintained schools. It is not clear what constitute "reasonable" criteria other than that they should be published and applied correctly.

Appeals Tribunals

Parents who are dissatisfied with the refusal of a school to admit their child may appeal to an Appeals Tribunal constituted by the Area Board (Schools Admissions (Appeals Tribunals) Regulations (NI) 1991, as amended). They may appeal only on the grounds that the board of governors of the school did not apply, or incorrectly applied, its admissions criteria *and* that the child would otherwise have been admitted to the school.

Appeals must be made in writing to the Tribunal. Parents must be given an opportunity to make written representations and to appear and make oral representations on their own behalf. The board of governors of the school in question must also be given a similar opportunity.

Appeals are normally held in private, although an Area Board representative may be permitted to attend where the school is a controlled one. The decision of the Tribunal may be by agreement or by simple majority vote. If it finds in favour of the appeal, it must direct the board of governors of the school to admit the child even if that means the school will exceed its admissions and enrolment number.

Problems with the appeal procedure

The majority of appeals are not upheld. It is not always possible for parents to make a reasonable assessment about whether a school applied its criteria correctly. They cannot insist that schools submit documentary evidence.

Parents who are dissatisfied with the decision of an Appeal Tribunal, or who believe that a school's admissions criteria are not in accordance with the Regulations, may seek a judicial review in the High Court (see chapter 2). Generally this can reverse a decision of a Tribunal only if it can be shown that the Tribunal considered inappropriate (or did not consider appropriate) evidence and/or that no reasonable authority could have made the decision in question. Even if a judicial review finds in favour of a complainant it may reverse an Appeal Tribunal decision only if a proper application of the criteria would actually have resulted in admission.

Discrimination and access

Under Article 2 of Protocol One to the European Convention on Human Rights parents have the right to "ensure education and teaching is in conformity with their own religious and philosophical convictions". The 1986 Order states that, subject to certain conditions, "the Department and Boards shall have regard to the general principle that...pupils shall be educated in accordance with their parents' wishes."

The government and Area Boards are prohibited, however, from operating or assisting any form of religious discrimination. They may not fund any school which discriminates on grounds of religion in its admissions (Northern Ireland Consititution Act 1973, section 19). Under the Fair Employment Acts schools are exempt with regard to the employment of teachers, but they may not discriminate in other ways (see chapter 12).

Religious discrimination

The continuing high unemployment experienced by Catholics has caused concern about possible discrimination in access to education. In its 17th Annual Report in 1992 the Standing Advisory Commission on Human Rights highlighted disparities of access for qualified pupils from Catholic maintained primary schools to places in Catholic grammar schools compared with access for Protestant pupils. It also queried the quality of provision in Catholic voluntary and maintained schools compared with controlled secondary and Protestant grammar schools. It called for immediate action to increase grammar school provision for Catholic pupils, to which the Department agreed. It also called for a review of long term discrepancies in the recurrent funding of maintained Catholic and controlled schools, and of the requirement for maintained and voluntary schools to make a voluntary contribution to 15% of their own capital funding.

The government responded in 1992 with plans to increase the number of Catholic managed grammar schools by providing 1,470 additional places in two new Catholic grammar schools and by promising new legislation to enable Catholic maintained and other voluntary schools to opt for 100% funding without having to lose their distinctive denominational ethos (see the Education and Libraries (NI) Order 1993).

Integrated education

The concept of integrated education arose out of efforts by parents from Catholic and Protestant backgrounds and those with other philosophical beliefs to work together voluntarily to establish a new type of planned, integrated school, which respected both religious traditions equally and which was open and accessible to pupils from both major communities. A number of such schools, initially independent, have been established and have received varying levels of public funding.

The 1989 Order made provision, subject to sufficient parental demand, for the development of integrated schools and imposed a duty on the Department of Education to "encourage and facilitate the development of integrated education" (article 64 (1)). It made possible the recognition of integrated schools as grant-aided schools (grant maintained integrated or controlled integrated) and amended provisions for the creation of controlled integrated schools.

Existing schools may seek to acquire either grant maintained integrated or controlled integrated status after securing approval of the majority of parents in a parental ballot, following either two "resolutions" of the board of governors or the written request of 20% of parents.

Parents who want the option of integrated schooling for their children still face significant hurdles. If there is no integrated school available in their locality the only test of parental demand which the Department currently accepts is that parents must first build their school, incurring major financial burdens. If there is an integrated school available, there is no satisfactory legal safeguard which can preserve its integrated character, such as a provision for such schools to maintain a balance of both Catholic and Protestant pupils in their enrolments. The Department can withhold recognition where it appears that a school would be unlikely to be attended by reasonable numbers of both Protestant and Roman Catholic pupils (article 71 (8)). Integrated secondary schools are "all ability" but are not permitted to select any pupils by reference to ability. Consequently existing integrated provision discriminates against "qualified" pupils transferring from integrated primary schools.

Parents who want the option of integrated education for their children should seek the advice of the Northern Ireland Council for Integrated Education, 16 Mount Charles, Belfast BT7 1NZ; tel: (0232) 236200

Irish medium education

There is no guarantee of education through Irish for parents who want it for their children. They must first set up an independent school and run it privately in order to demonstrate a given level of parental demand before the school can become eligible for public funding. Several private Irish language nursery schools have been established. In 1984 the Department recognised and funded the first Irish language primary school in Belfast but refused recognition and funding to a second. Two Irish language schools operate without public funding. Irish language education may in future benefit if the Council of Europe's Minority Language Convention is implemented. But for the moment there is little protection for the status of the Irish language within education in Northern Ireland. Those who want further information should contact the Ultach Trust, Room 202, Fountain House, 19 Donegall Place, Belfast BT1 5AB.

Sex discrimination

It is unlawful for educational authorities or bodies responsible for schools to discriminate between boys and girls as regards admission to schools or in the provision of educational facilities or benefits except in terms of admission to single sex schools or boarding accommodation (Sex Discrimination (NI) Order 1976, articles 24-29 and 66; see also chapter 13).

A large proportion of secondary level schools in Northern Ireland are single sex, and many girls' schools still have inadequate science, maths and CDT teaching facilities compared with boys schools, as noted by the 17th Annual Report of the Standing Commission on Human Rights. In other schools, including some co-educational schools, the curriculum may still be biased towards preparing girls for arts based, and boys for science based careers.

If parents or pupils want advice on how to avoid or combat discrimination, or if they have a serious complaint, they should contact the Equal Opportunities Commission (see chapter 13). A complaint concerning a grant-aided school or Board should, in the first instance, be notified to the Department of Education, which must investigate the complaint and deal with it under its powers in the 1986 Order (article 101). If the Department has not dealt with the matter after two months, a complaint can be taken to the county court.

The curriculum

The 1989 Order lays down a legally required curriculum for every registered pupil of compulsory school age in every grant aided primary and secondary school. Boards of governors and principals of every school have a duty to provide:

"a balanced and broadly based curriculum which (a) promotes the spiritual, moral, cultural, intellectual and physical development of pupils, and thereby (b) prepares them for the opportunities, responsibilities and experiences of adult life" (article 4(2)).

The curriculum must include provision for religious education and for "areas of study" made up of "contributory subjects" (listed in Schedule 2) some of which are compulsorily assessed (article 5). The areas of study must include the following:

- English
- mathematics
- science and technology

- the environment and society
- language studies (in relation to schools which are Irish speaking and the third and fourth key stages in other schools); every grant aided secondary school must afford all pupils the opportunity to be taught one of the following languages: French, German, Italian or Spanish; Irish may also be offered for compulsory study and assessment, but schools are not required to offer it.

The curriculum of every grant aided school must cover, with respect to each listed contributory subject taught at the school, the "attainment targets" (what pupils are expected to know) and the "programmes of study" (what is required to be taught) (article 5(4)). Each pupil must be assessed in accordance with such arrangements as are specified for assessing pupils at each of four key stages laid down by the Department of Education (articles 6 and 7).

The Department cannot prescribe any particular periods or timetable allocations for specific compulsory subjects but it has other general powers (1986 Order, article 17A) to make regulations concerning the curriculum, timetable and suitability of any study materials or resources used in a school.

Schools are required to promote "wholly or mainly through the teaching of contributory subjects and religious education, the attainment of objectives (specified by order of the Department) of the following educational themes: Information Technology; Education for Mutual Understanding; Cultural Heritage; Health Education; Economic Awareness and Careers Education (secondary schools only)" (article 8).

Courses leading to external qualifications (*e.g.* business certificates) are permitted only if approved by the Department of Education (article 9).

Pupils with special circumstances

In certain circumstances parents may ask, or the principal of a school may require, that the provisions of the curriculum be modified or not applied to individual pupils. This may include pupils with a special educational needs statement (see page 274). In such cases a principal may direct that for an "operative period" (not more than six months) articles 5 6 and 8 (curriculum, assessment procedures and educational themes) shall:

- apply with specified modifications, or

- not apply, or
- be revoked or varied but not extended beyond the operative period.

The principal must tell the governors and the pupil's parents:
- what has been done, its effect and the reason for doing it;
- what provision is being made for the pupil's education during the operative period of the direction; and
- either the manner in which he or she proposes to secure the full application after the end of that period of provisions for teaching the curriculum, assessments and educational themes, or

his or her opinion that the pupil has, or probably has, special educational needs by virtue of which the Board would be required to determine the special educational provision that should be made under article 31 of the 1986 Order (article 17 (4)).

Where parents are not satisfied that the principal has acted within the regulations, or are otherwise concerned about the situation, they may appeal to the board of governors of the school. The Board confirm the principal's action or direct the principal to take such action as it considers appropriate and notify the parents in writing. If parents are still not satisfied they may appeal to a Complaints Tribunal (see page 272).

Information about the curriculum and pupil achievement

Department of Education policy is to make as much information as possible available about each school on the grounds that it can encourage greater parental involvement and freedom of choice. Boards of governors of all grant aided schools must ensure that the requirements of the curriculum are being met by their school and must:

"a) determine and keep under review its policy in relation to the curriculum of the school and
b) make and keep up to date a written statement of that policy" (article 10(1))

All grant aided schools must make available "either generally or to prescribed persons" information relating (amongst other things) to:
- the curriculum of the school;

- educational provision for pupils and syllabuses followed;
- the educational achievements of pupils (including the results of any assessments of those pupils for the purposes of ascertaining those achievements); and
- the school's curriculum policy.

An individual pupil's assessment must not be made available to any person or bodies other than the parents of the pupil concerned and the Department, except in certain precisely specified circumstances. For instance, it may be made available to the board of governors of the school in the case of any pupil excepted from the curriculum, or to the Area Board in the case of a pupil at a special school (1989 Order, article 31) .

Problems with the curriculum

If parents are not satisfied with the arrangements for teaching or assessment they should first seek an interview with the principal of the school. If they are still not satisfied and think that the arrangements do not meet the requirements of the Northern Ireland Curriculum they should complain to the board of governors of the school. If they are still not satisfied parents can complain to a Complaints Tribunal established and administered by each Area Board, except with regard to any complaint about the teaching of religious education (1989 Order, article 33).

Religious education

According to the 1986 Order all schools must provide for both religious education and collective worship. This must be so arranged that:

> *"(a) the school shall be open to pupils of all religious denominations for instruction other than religious education, and*
> *(b) no pupil shall be excluded directly or indirectly from the other advantages which the school affords."* (1986 Order, article 21 (4))

Ministers of religion of any denomination must be given reasonable access to pupils in all grant aided schools in order to give religious education, provided parents do not object. In controlled schools (other than controlled integrated schools) religious education must be un-denominational:

- it must be "based upon the Holy Scriptures according to some authoritative version thereof but excluding instruction as to any tenet distinctive of any particular religious denomination",
- collective worship must "not be distinctive of any particular religious denomination" (1986 Order, article 21 (2)), and
- shall include religious education in accordance with any core syllabus specified under article 13(1) of the 1989 Order.

In voluntary schools (*i.e.* maintained and voluntary grammar schools, or grant maintained or controlled integrated schools) religious education must be "in accordance with any core syllabus specified by the Department of Education" but the boards of governors may otherwise determine provision for religious education and collective worship.

The "core syllabus" which all grant maintained schools are required to include in their religious education is one:

- "prepared, published and, if necessary, after representations, revised, by a group of persons ("drafting group") appearing to the Department of Education to be persons having an interest in the teaching of religious education in grant aided schools" (1986 Order, article 34, as amended by 1989 Order, article 13 (4)).

If parents do not want their child to receive religious instruction at school, or wish some other form of religious instruction to be given, they may ask that the child be excused from any religion education classes and collective worship and if necessary withdrawn from school for reasonable periods (1986 Order, article 21(5)).

If the parents of at least 20% of pupils at a school "address a complaint in writing to the Department alleging that all of any of the obligations" of a grant aided school concerning religious education or collective worship are not being carried out in good faith, the Department can investigate and instruct the board of governors as to the manner in which such obligations must be carried out (1986 Order, article 23).

Children with special educational needs

The 1986 Order requires Area Boards to assess the special educational needs of any child over two and under 19 years of age when they are told that the child may have special educational needs (article 29). For children under two they must also do this but they must first obtain the parents' consent.

A child has "special educational needs" if he or she:

"(a) has a significantly greater difficulty in learning than the majority of children of his or her age; or
(b) has a disability which prevents or hinders him or her from making use of educational facilities of a kind generally provided at ordinary schools for children of his or her age; or
(c) is under the age of five and would be likely to fall within sub-paragraph (a) or (b) when over that age. "(1986 Order, article 33)

An Area Board must make special educational provision for pupils who have special educational needs. Parents have a right to be fully involved in the process of determining those needs (article 31). Education for such children should be in ordinary schools alongside other children, no matter how severe the child's disability may be. However, account must be taken of the views of the parents, and a Board must be sure that education in an ordinary school is compatible with:

"(a) the child's receiving the special educational provision that he or she requires;
(b) the provision of efficient education for the children with whom he or she will be educated; and,
(c) the efficient use of resources ".(article 32 (2)

Where a child with special educational needs attends an ordinary school, the child must be allowed to take part in the activities of the school together with the other children provided that the above three conditions are met, and that it is "reasonably practicable" (article 32 (3)).

Assessment and statements

Assessment must be done in the proper way. Parents can make a formal request that the child be assessed and a Board cannot refuse if the request is reasonable. Parents then have the right to be consulted at all stages in the assessment procedure. An Area Board must also seek advice and opinions from a doctor, an educational psychologist and the child's school principal or another teacher.

After assessment is completed, a Board may decide to make a "statement". This is a legally binding document which sets out what special educational needs a child has and what provision a Board intends to make to meet those needs. Parents can comment on a preliminary draft and must be shown all the formal advice and evidence used to reach a decision. If a Board decides not to issue such a statement, or if parents are dissatisfied with the statement, there can be an appeal to the Department of Education.

Once a statement has been made, it is the responsibility of the Area Board to ensure that the board of governors of any school in which a child with special educational needs is placed makes the necessary special educational provision. Statements must be reviewed within every 12 months and children with a statement must be re-assessed between the ages of 13½ and 14½ years so that plans can be made for their future beyond compulsory school age. Detailed guidance for parents can be found in "Children with Special Educational Needs", published by:

- Disability Action, 2 Annadale Avenue, Belfast BT7 3JR (tel: 0232-491011)

Financial considerations

In theory, state schooling is free between the ages of four and 16, but only grant aided primary, secondary and special schools are specifically prohibited from charging fees. Under the 1989 Order it is unlawful for any grant aided schools to require parents to pay for or supply any materials, books, instruments, equipment or transport used for the national curriculum or required by any syllabus for an approved public examination. Where the provision is with parental consent, grant aided schools are, however, entitled to charge for:

- education and transport in connection with "optional extras", *i.e.*, subjects such as additional music, sports and even specialist academic subjects which are not required components of the national curriculum;
- entry fees for non-required public examinations;
- board and lodging for all residential field trips (but for parents on family credit or income support costs can be remitted in full) (article 130).

All grant aided schools are entitled to ask for voluntary contributions from parents to school funds provided it is clear that there is no obligation on parents to contribute and that pupils will not be treated differently according to whether or not their parents have done so.

Voluntary grammar schools are entitled to charge all pupils specified "capital fees". Unqualified secondary school pupils who obtained a fee-paying place at a voluntary grammar school prior to the implementation of the 1989 Order, and certain other excepted pupils (such as non-EC residents), may be liable for the full economic cost of their education.

Transport

An Area Board must make the arrangements it considers necessary for the provision of transport to facilitate the attendance of pupils at a grant aided school, and such transport should be provided free of charge (1986 Order, article 52). It may also, but does not have to, pay the whole or part of the reasonable travelling expenses of all pupils attending such schools. Government policy on open enrolment has meant that Boards generally pay travelling expenses in full, through the provision of free bus passes or petrol allowances for parents who drive their children to school.

Area Boards have been guided by another part of the 1986 Order (dealing with the duty of parents to secure regular attendance of their children at school) when deciding suitable school transport arrangements. Thus, if a primary school child lives more than two miles from the nearest "suitable" school, or if a secondary school child lives more than three miles from the secondary or grammar school from which an offer of a place has been received, Boards are required to provide free transport from the child's home to that school. "Suitable" is interpreted to allow for religious conscience and, under the 1989 Order, for a preference for integrated education.

Means-tested benefits

School uniforms and P.E. kit grants

Many schools in Northern Ireland require pupils to wear school uniform. In the case of post-primary school pupils an Area Board must give assistance towards the cost of their school uniform and P.E. kit if parents are on income support. Students in further education are eligible only for the P.E. kit grant. A separate application has to be made for each child each year, if possible before the school year starts, on an application form obtained from the Area Board offices. Boards generally issue vouchers rather than cash, but may reimburse expenditure on production of the appropriate sales receipts.

Education maintenance allowance

The educational maintenance allowance in Northern Ireland is a mandatory means-tested scheme. It is paid to assist with the costs of remaining at school beyond the minimum compulsory school-leaving age (16 years). However, its real value in relation to the cost of living has not been increased in the last few years. The amount of grant varies according to the income of the pupil's parents. A separate application must be made for each child each year. Once a grant has been approved, it is paid in arrears, in two half-yearly instalments, at the end of February and the end of August, subject to satisfactory school attendance.

School meals

Area Boards (and in the case of voluntary grammar schools, trustees or boards of governors) must provide:

"milk, meals or other refreshment for pupils of such description as the Department may determine, in attendance at grant aided schools.....and must make such charge and remit the whole or part of such charge in such cases and such circumstances as the Department may determine." (1986 Order, article 58)

Departmental policy on meals and milk is now subject to the Social Security Act 1986 and Area Boards can provide free meals and milk only for children whose parents are on income support. Children of parents in receipt of family credit are no longer entitled to free school meals and receive instead a cash payment, but this does not generally cover the equivalent daily meals charge.

Grants towards boarding fees

A Board can make a grant towards the cost of boarding where it is satisfied that:

> *"education suitable to [the pupil's] age, ability and aptitude and any special educational needs [he or she] may have cannot be provided for [him or her] otherwise than by the provision of board and lodging at a particular grant-aided school."* (1989 Order, article 135)

Under the 1989 Order the amount of the grant towards boarding fees is means-tested. Parents should apply to their Area Board for details of its boarding grants scheme.

Treatment at school

Absence from school

All schools must keep a register of pupils attending and must inform the Area Board if any registered pupil does not attend regularly and has no reasonable excuse (1986 Order, article 48). Non-attendance is regarded as reasonable in the following circumstances:

- sickness or other unavoidable cause (medical certificate required);
- if there are no arrangements for transporting the child to school and he or she is under 11 years of age and lives more than two miles away, or over 11 years and lives more than three miles away;
- if the child is employed on work experience; or
- if the parent can prove that he or she is engaged in a trade or business which requires him or her to travel and the child has attended school as regularly as the trade or business permitted and for at least 100 days during the last 12 months.

If a Board thinks that parents have failed to ensure regular attendance it may send an education welfare officer to the child's home to investigate. If there is no reasonable excuse for the absence, parents can be prosecuted. Parents in this situation should:

- seek legal advice from a solicitor;
- get in touch with their local Citizens' Advice Bureau; or

- contact the Parents' Advice Centre, Bryson House, 28 Bedford Street, Belfast BT2 7FE (tel: 0232-238800).

Truancy

It is increasingly being recognised that truancy is just as likely to be an indication of shortcomings in the school or in the home as of delinquency on the part of a child. However, in serious cases Boards may take a pupil to a juvenile court for non-attendance.

Discipline

The 1989 Order provides, in article 134, that the scheme of management for each grant aided school must include a written statement of measures for promoting discipline.

Corporal punishment

Teachers have the same obligations towards school-children in their charge as any careful parent would have. However, although this means they have the power to administer any punishment which is reasonable in the circumstances, they do not have the right to inflict corporal punishment. This is because Northern Ireland, like the rest of the United Kingdom, has to comply with the European Convention on Human Rights, under which corporal punishment is deemed to be inhuman treatment (see the Education (Corporal Punishment) (NI) Order 1987).

If parents feel that their child has been unjustly or unreasonably punished, they should get in touch with the principal of the school immediately. They have a right to be told of the reason for any punishment. If they are not satisfied, they should write to the chief education officer of the Area Board (or in the case of a maintained, voluntary or grant maintained integrated school, the chairman of the governors) setting out their complaint in writing.

Suspension and expulsion

Each Area Board, the governors of voluntary and integrated schools and the Council for Catholic Maintained Schools must prepare a scheme specifying the procedure to be followed in relation to the suspension or expulsion of pupils from schools under their management (1986 Order, article 49 and 1989 Order, article 146(3)). The final responsibility for providing education for a pupil in any area lies with the Area Board. Where a pupil is expelled from a voluntary school and no other provision is made, the Area Board must make arrangements for the pupil's education.

Normally a pupil should be suspended or expelled only if he or she has done something very wrong. A few schools have special withdrawal units for disruptive pupils but these are not always very effective. Suspension and expulsion, or the threat of these, may be used as a last resort. Suspension is meant to be an extreme measure and the period of the suspension is intended to provide time for the school and educational authorities to consider what alternative course of action should be taken. Expulsion is meant to be a measure of last resort and to involve all parties, including parents, in consultation over the most appropriate alternative educational provision for the pupil.

If a child has been withdrawn from classes, suspended or expelled, parents should be notified immediately of what has occurred and why. They should then see the principal to discuss the matter at the earliest possible time, but not before having discussed it with the child. If parents are asked to give undertakings about their child's future conduct, these should be put in writing to avoid any misunderstanding. If parents are still not satisfied they can ask for the matter to be reviewed. In the case of a controlled school, they should write to the chief education officer of the Area Board, and in the case of a maintained or voluntary school, to the chairman of the board of governors. In the last resort, if the suspension or expulsion is felt to be unreasonable, or no adequate alternative arrangements have been made, parents can appeal to the Department of Education. In this case they should get help from their local advice centre.

School records and reports

Schools keep records on their pupils and use some of this information when sending reports out to parents or others. The records usually contain information about academic progress and behaviour in school, but may also include details about pupils' attitudes, family and friends as well as behaviour outside school.

Generally parents and pupils over 16 years have a right to see any curricular record ("formal record of a pupil's academic achievements, his or her other skills and abilities and his or her educational progress") after a request in writing to the school (1986 Order, article 17A (2)(g) and Education (Pupil Records) Regulations (NI) 1990). If a parent or pupil regards the curricular record as inaccurate and gives notice in writing to the holder of the record, he or she may amend or correct it, or, if not satisfied that it is inaccurate, must append the written notice of complaint to the record and subsequently treat it as part of the record.

Similar arrangements must be made for any other records, including nursery school educational records and those for primary pupils below compulsory school age, and kept as part of a pupil's curricular record. Parents or pupils can appeal to the board of governors against a refusal to disclose or amend records.

In certain circumstances other people may be given access to pupils' records. If a pupil moves to another school or is under consideration for admission to another school, the curricular records and any notices attached must be transferred, or made available as appropriate, to the new school. Reports based on records may also be requested by an educational welfare officer, social worker or probation officer if a pupil has been in trouble and by a prospective employer or college. However, schools are advised that there is no requirement that they must disclose to other people any of the following information regarding a pupil:

- details about home circumstances or religious denomination;
- the results of an individual pupil's attainment assessments;
- reports for the purposes of juvenile or magistrates' courts;
- statements of special educational needs;
- educational records covered by the Data Protection Act (see chapter 11);
- information which in the opinion of "holders" would harm the physical, mental or emotional condition of the pupil or any other person to whom it relates;
- the contents of references to potential employers, universities or colleges or other national bodies concerned with student admissions.

If parents or pupils feel that school or curricular records or reports might contain biased, inaccurate or harmful information, they should write to the principal with a request for an interview. If this fails, or they want advice, they should get in touch with a Citizen's Advice Bureau or other advice centre.

Who runs education?

The government has published a parents' charter of rights and responsibilities and has said that it wants parents to play an active part in education. Parents concerned about the overall quality and range of educational provision, however, have only a limited number of ways of influencing how decisions are taken.

Parents and boards of governors

Parents have to be represented on the boards of all grant aided schools. governors must hold an annual parents meeting where parents may put forward their views on the school and elect parent governors (1989 Order, article 126). However, in many cases parents represent significantly less than one quarter of the membership and only a proportion of those may be elected rather than nominated by another body.

Only the boards of controlled integrated schools and grant maintained integrated schools have a reasonable balance of religious traditions and of elected parents and teachers. On controlled school boards, transferors' nominees, usually church representatives, form just under one half of the membership and on Catholic maintained and voluntary grammar school boards, trustees' nominees form just under two thirds of the membership. The balance is made up by nominees of Area Boards or the Department of Education (1986 Order, Schedules 4-7; 1989 Order, article 89 and Schedule 5). The overall size of Boards may vary according to the size of the school. This does not, however, significantly affect the proportion of different group interests represented. Boards of governors are composed as follows:

Reps. nominated by:	Cont. primary/ sec.	Cont. grammar nursery	Maint. primary/ sec.	New GM vol. status	Vol. grammar (Cat. A)	GM integ. status
Transferors or trustees	4/9	-	6/10 [1]	4/9 [1]	6/10 [1]	-
Foundation governors	-	-	-	-	-	3/8 [2]
Area Boards	2/9	3/8	2/10	2/9 [3]	-	-
Dept. of Education	-	2/8	-	1/9 [3]	2/10	2/8
Elected by:						
Parents	2/9	2/8	1/10	1/9	1/10	2/8
Teachers	1/9	1/8	1/10	1/9	1/10	1/8

Notes to table:

(1) One nominee to be a parent of a pupil at the school.

(2) One third of foundation governors to be parents of pupils at the school

(3) For new grant maintained, formerly maintained voluntary, schools DENI nominees may be shared with Area Boards. New grant maintained grammar, formerly voluntary grammar, schools have three DENI nominees only.

Responsibilities of school Boards

The 1989 Order considerably expanded the responsibilities of boards of governors of all grant aided schools. Apart from the specific duties already discussed, they are responsible for financial management, as well as the employment of teaching and other staff and the provision and publication of required information, including a prospectus and an annual report. An interesting insight into the range of their new communal obligations is the legal requirement that in their annual report they must give information concerning curriculum and educational provision under article 31(2)(a) and a detailed account of the steps:

"taken by the board of governors to develop or strengthen the school's links with the community and, in particular, to promote the attainment of the objectives of the educational theme called Education for Mutual Understanding". (1989 Order, article 125)

However neither parents on school boards, nor many schools themselves, have much opportunity to influence educational policy in a way which might make this duty more realistic. Nothing in the Education Orders, for instance, makes provision for schools in areas of significant social deprivation or social conflict, or those with educational disadvantage and parental apathy, to receive additional financial support for contributing to community regeneration or reconciliation.

Area Boards

The five Area Education and Library Boards in Northern Ireland consist of members nominated from amongst the councillors of the district councils in the Board's area (40%) and members nominated to represent the interests of controlled and maintained schools and libraries in the area.

Area Boards have an administrative role in deciding what education to provide in their area. However, the Department of Education has overall power to approve education capital expenditure, and to authorise, modify or reject, any proposed changes in educational provision. In theory, parents and local communities can comment on proposals which Area Boards must submit, or are directed to submit, to the Department, where the Board or a person other than the Board proposes to:

- establish a new controlled (or voluntary) school
- have an existing school recognised as grant aided
- discontinue a controlled (or voluntary) school
- make a significant change in the character or size of a controlled (or voluntary) school which would have a significant effect on another grant aided school (1986 Order, article 14)

However, there is little evidence that parents' views or interests are taken into account.

Management and maintenance of schools

Area Boards are responsible for the management and maintenance of all controlled schools in their area and for the maintenance of all other schools, where requested by the managers and trustees. Maintenance includes preparing financial schemes for the allocation and delegation of "budget shares" (articles 47, 49 and 50), organising admissions arrangements and co-ordinating a range of services including special education, school meals and transport etc. Voluntary grammar and grant maintained (including integrated) schools are funded directly by the Department, which is required to have "regard to the allocation formulae for the time being included in schemes in accordance with article 49" (*i.e.* Boards' allocation formulae).

The Standing Advisory Commission on Human Rights in its 17th Annual Report criticised the operation of previous financial schemes for the maintenance of schools on the ground that they had resulted in long term discrepancies in recurrent school funding, to the detriment of Catholic maintained compared with controlled schools. The Department of Education has accepted the recommendation that in future it should monitor all schools' recurrent and capital funding and make its findings known.

The Department of Education

The 1989 Order gives the Department of Education total control over the education service. It has the power "to secure under the Department's control and direction, the effective execution by Boards and other bodies on which, or persons on whom, powers are conferred or duties imposed under the Education Orders of the Department's policy in relation to the provision of the education service" (1989 Order, article 2(b)). It may "give directions as to the exercise of any power conferred or the performance of any duty imposed on that authority by the Education Orders" (1986, article 101, as amended by 1989 Order, article 158).

The Department's most significant social responsibility under the 1989 Order, (article 64) is:

"(1) to encourage and facilitate the development of integrated education, that is to say the education together at school of Protestant and Roman Catholic pupils;
(2)...pay grants to any body appearing to the Department to have as its object the encouragement or promotion of integrated education."

Educational funding and human rights

Apart from specific powers under the Education Orders already discussed, the Department determines educational policy largely through its control of educational expenditure and its administrative relationship

(backed by power to give directions) with the Area Boards, the trustees and governors of voluntary schools and other statutory bodies such as the Northern Ireland Curriculum Council and the Council for Catholic Maintained Schools.

The way in which it has exercised this control has been criticised by the Standing Advisory Commission on Human Rights and others. In 1990 the Northern Ireland Catholic bishops unsuccessfully challenged, under the Northern Ireland Constitution Act 1973, the Department's right to provide 100% capital funding for grant maintained integrated schools as compared with the 85% capital funding received by voluntary Catholic schools. The 17th Annual Report of the Standing Advisory Commission criticised apparent disparities of access to grammar school places between the Catholic and Protestant community and called for a review of the effect of the 15% voluntary contribution to capital funding on Catholic maintained schools. The Commission also highlighted the Department's failure to give equality of treatment with respect to capital funding to integrated schools. Some of its other recommendations were for more rigorous and widely-published assessments of the impact of educational policy on Protestant, Catholic and integrated schools' action to remedy the imbalances in science attainment by girls compared with boys and efforts to address poor attainment levels.

The Department's response to these criticisms has been patchy and piecemeal. Many of the issues of discrimination arise out of major inequalities in Northern Ireland education. Dealing with discrimination in isolation from issues of major structural inequality in education itself could be self-defeating.

The recommendations of the Standing Advisory Commission included two conclusions which have been largely ignored by the Department of Education. Not only do a majority of parents in Northern Ireland favour more integrated schools but a significant majority favour comprehensive education. The education legislation currently in place has ensured that these parents and many teachers who share their views will continue to be ignored because other more powerful interests are represented in the education service. A legal and democratic structure which obliged the Department to respond more readily to the expectations of ordinary parents might help to reduce, rather than increase, social inequalities and barriers in education.

Chapter 17

Employment Rights

Richard Steele

There has been extensive legal intervention in employment relations in Northern Ireland for many years. For convenience the resulting laws, whether made by Parliament or by judges, can be divided into two categories. This chapter covers both, though the main focus is on the first. For an account of employment law with particular reference to religious discrimination, women and the disabled, see chapters 12, 13 and 14 respectively.

- *Individual employment law* is concerned with the rights and obligations flowing from the terms of the contract between an employee and an employer. In recent years employees have been given the protection of a "floor" of employment rights, which can be improved upon by negotiation with an employer. To gain protection of most individual employment rights, qualifying periods of employment are required and generally the rights increase with length of service. In addition, many of the rights apply only to employees working full-time, *i.e.*, a person who works 16 hours or more a week for the same employer or who has worked eight hours or more a week for the same employer for more than five years.

- *Collective employment law* is primarily concerned with the regulation of the bargaining relationships between trade unions and employers or employers' associations.

Employment law and the legal system

The introduction of substantial employment rights for employees has also resulted in the creation of specialised judicial bodies:

- The *industrial tribunals* are established under the Industrial Training (NI) Order 1984. They comprise three persons: a legally qualified chairman and two lay representatives, one chosen from a panel nominated by the Confederation of British Industry (CBI), the other from a panel nominated by the Northern Ireland Committee of the Irish Congress of Trade Unions (NIC/ICTU). Industrial tribunals deal mainly with individual employment matters such as unfair dismissal, redundancy, trade union rights, maternity rights and sex discrimination. They are intended to provide cheap, quick and informal methods of hearing complaints but in many cases, due to the complexity of the legislation, the reality is different. Legal aid is not available for tribunal hearings but it is possible to utilise the "green form" scheme, whereby subsidised advice and assistance can be obtained from a solicitor in advance of a hearing. Appeals are available on a point of law to the Court of Appeal.

- The *Fair Employment Tribunal*, created by the Fair Employment (NI) Act 1989, hears complaints of discrimination on grounds of religious belief or political opinion (see chapter 12) and is constituted in the same way as industrial tribunals.

- The *Industrial Court* is established by the Industrial Relations (NI) Order 1992 and acts as an arbitration body. It is composed of a legally qualified President and two lay members, one chosen from a panel nominated by the CBI and the other from a panel nominated by NIC/ICTU. It also has statutory responsibilities in relation to recognition and disclosure of information for collective bargaining purposes.

The relevant government department responsible for employment legislation and manpower policy is the Department of Economic Development (DED), but responsibility for certain employment functions has been devolved to various statutory bodies:

- The *Labour Relations Agency* (LRA), now established by the Industrial Relations (NI) Order 1992, has the duty to promote the improvement of industrial relations and encourage collective bargaining machinery. It mainly provides advisory, conciliation and arbitration services.

- The *Health and Safety Agency* (HSA) was established by the Health and Safety at Work (NI) Order 1978. It reviews health, safety and welfare in connection with work and the control of dangerous substances and makes recommendations to the appropriate government departments. It is with those departments and the district councils that responsibility for enforcement of safety laws rests.
- The post of *Certification Officer* was established by the Industrial Relations (NI) Order 1992. The Certification Officer has duties in respect of trade unions and employers' associations.
- The *Commissioner for the Rights of Trade Union Members* was established by the Industrial Relations (NI) Order 1992. The Commissioner may give advice and assistance to a trade union member when taking certain legal proceedings against a trade union.
- The roles of two other statutory bodies - the Fair Employment Commission and the Equal Opportunities Commission - are described in chapters 12 and 13 respectively.

Contracts of employment

The great majority of employment rights which can be adjudicated upon by an industrial tribunal are limited to employees. An employee is defined by article 2 of the Industrial Relations (NI) Order 1992 as an individual who has entered into or works under a contract of employment.

The basis of an employment relationship is the law of contract. A contract is formed when an employer makes a job offer to a potential employee and that offer is accepted. The terms of the contract define the rights and duties of both parties. These terms are normally a mixture of express, implied, statutory and incorporated terms.

- *Express terms*, which may be written or oral, are those actually agreed by the employer and employee.
- *Incorporated terms* are those agreed by collective bargaining between a trade union and an employer and incorporated into the contracts of employment of each employee covered by the collective agreement.
- *Statutory terms* are those implied into a contract by an Act of Parliament, such as equal pay legislation.

- *Implied terms* may exist by the operation of custom and practice in an industry or as a result of a wages order (see page 291).

The courts have held that certain implied terms are basic to every contract of employment. The most important of these are:

- that an employee will obey all lawful and reasonable orders, take reasonable care in his or her work, not wilfully disrupt the employer's business and be honest; and
- that an employer will pay agreed wages, take reasonable care for the employee's safety and health, not require an employee to do illegal acts and not act in a manner likely to destroy the relationship of trust or confidence.

Written statements of terms

By section 4 of the Contracts of Employment and Redundancy Payments Act (NI) 1965 an employer must provide all full-time employees with a written statement of certain major terms of the contract of employment. This written statement is not itself the contract of employment but it may amount to much the same thing by being the only or best evidence of it, especially if the employee has signed a copy. The written statement must include the following:

- the identity of employer and employee;
- the date the employment began, and whether any previous employment counts as continuous employment with the present employer and, if so, when it began;
- the title of the job;
- the scale or rate of pay;
- the intervals at which wages are to be paid;
- the hours of work and normal working hours;
- entitlement to holidays, holiday pay and accrued holiday pay on termination of employment;
- terms and conditions relating to sickness, including sick pay;
- details of pensions and pension schemes, in particular whether the pension scheme (if any) is "contracted out" of the state scheme;
- the length of notice the employee is entitled to receive and obliged to give;

- details of disciplinary rules and the name of the person to whom an employee can apply if he or she is dissatisfied with a disciplinary decision;
- details of grievance procedures and the name of the person to whom an employee can refer a grievance.

Instead of setting out all the required information in the written statement, the employer can refer the employee to other documents, such as Works Rules or a collective agreement. If changes are made to the contract of employment, the employer must inform the employee within one month.

If an employee does not receive a written statement within 13 weeks, section 5 of the 1965 Act provides that an application can be made to an industrial tribunal for a decision as to which particulars should be given. Furthermore, either the employer or the employee can apply to an industrial tribunal for an interpretation of the terms contained in the written statement. An employee can complain to an industrial tribunal while still in employment or within three months of leaving the job. If the employer refuses to observe the terms of the contract of employment, the employee must at present sue in the courts for damages for breach of contract.

Monetary rights during employment

Wages councils

In Northern Ireland, rates of pay and conditions of employment for most employees are agreed by collective bargaining. In a number of low-paid industries, however, legally enforceable minimum wage levels are set by wages councils established by the Wages (NI) Order 1988. Article 15 empowers wages councils to make wages orders fixing a single minimum hourly rate for basic hours and a single minimum hourly overtime rate for time worked in excess of the basic hours.

A wages order applies to the workers within the scope of the wages council and covers both full-time and part-time workers. However, wages councils are specifically prevented from exercising their functions in relation to workers under the age of 21. An employer who fails to pay the statutory minimum remuneration is guilty of an offence and liable to a fine of up to £400. In addition, the court may order the employer to pay the worker the amount of underpayments occurring during the period of two years ending with the date of the offence. A worker may claim such underpayments by suing for breach of contract in the civil courts.

Employers are required to keep such records as are necessary to show that they have observed the statutory minimum rates and to retain these records for a period of three years. They must also post up current wages council rates. Contravention of these requirements is again an offence punishable by a fine not exceeding £400. The wages council system is enforced by the Wages Inspectorate of the Department of Economic Development. An inspector has power to require the production of wage-sheets and other records and to inspect, examine and copy them. Furthermore, an inspector is empowered to enter premises, interview workers, require the production of records and lists of homeworkers and may institute civil proceedings on behalf of a worker.

The government has announced that it intends to abolish wages councils in Northern Ireland, just as it is doing in Britain under the Trade Union Reform and Employment Rights Act 1993.

Deductions from wages

Article 3 of the Wages (NI) Order 1988 provides that an employer must not make any deduction from the wages of any worker, or receive payments from the worker, unless the deduction or payment is authorised by statute or by a relevant provision in the worker's contract, or agreed in writing in advance by the worker.

Article 4 provides that, subject to article 3, where an employer makes deductions from a retail worker's wages on a pay day on account of cash shortages or stock deficiencies, the total amount deducted must not exceed one-tenth of the gross wages payable on that pay day. If, however, the cash shortage or stock deficiency is sufficiently large, the deductions can be spread over a number of pay days. Article 6 provides that in relation to the final instalment of wages the one-tenth limit does not apply.

Articles 7 and 8 enable a worker to complain to an industrial tribunal about excessive wage deductions within three months of the deduction being made.

Itemised pay statements

Under articles 44-47 of the Industrial Relations (No 2) (NI) Order 1976, all full-time employees must be given an itemised pay statement every time they are paid. The statement must specify the gross and net wages payable, the amounts of any fixed or variable deductions and, where parts of the net wage are paid in different ways, the amount and method of each part payment. If there are several fixed deductions, an employer, instead of listing each separately, can give a standing statement of fixed deductions which must be renewed at least every 12 months.

If an employee does not get an itemised pay statement or disputes the content of the statement, he or she can complain to an industrial tribunal for a decision as to what should be included in the statement. If unnotified deductions have been made, the tribunal can order the employer to repay the amounts so deducted in the 13 weeks prior to the claim.

Guarantee payments

Articles 3-8 of the 1976 (No 2) Order provide that all full-time employees who have been employed for one month or more may be entitled to certain guarantee payments from their employer if they are laid off or put on short-time working. However, an employee will lose the right to payment if he or she refuses an offer of suitable alternative employment, if there is no work because of a trade dispute involving the employer or an associated employer, or if he or she does not comply with the reasonable requirement of the employer to be available for work. The right to guarantee payments is currently limited to a maximum of £14.10 a day and will be paid for up to five days in any three month period. An employee who does not receive the appropriate payment can apply to an industrial tribunal within three months.

Payment when suspended on medical grounds

There are certain types of employment in Northern Ireland, such as work with lead, paint and chemicals, which are covered by health and safety regulations allowing an employee to be suspended for medical reasons. A list of these regulations can be found in Schedule 1 to the 1976 (No 2) Order. Articles 9-13 of the 1976 (No 2) Order provide that an employee who has been suspended under these regulations and who has been continuously employed for one month or more is entitled to receive a normal week's pay for a maximum of 26 weeks. However, an employee will not be entitled to such payment if he or she is incapable of work due to illness or disablement, unreasonably refuses an offer from the employer of suitable alternative work, or does not comply with the reasonable requirements of the employer to be available for work.

Money owed on an employer's insolvency

An employee who is owed money by an insolvent employer can claim as a preferential creditor for unpaid wages up to a maximum of £800, for amounts owed in respect of a guarantee payment, payment during medical suspension, payment for time off work on union duties or to look for other work during redundancy notice, and for a "protective" award (see page 302). In addition, an employee can apply to the Department of Economic Development for payment out of the Northern Ireland Redundancy Fund of certain sums owed by the insolvent employer. Under articles 42-47 of the Industrial Relations (NI) Order 1976, the following can be claimed from the Department:

- arrears of pay up to a maximum of £205 per week for up to 8 weeks;
- holiday pay to which the employee became entitled during the previous 12 months, up to a maximum of £205 per week;
- statutory minimum notice pay up to a maximum of £205 per week;
- a basic award of compensation for unfair dismissal;
- repayment of apprenticeship fees.

When the Department makes such a payment to an employee, it can then seek to recover the debt from the insolvent employer. An employee who has applied to the Department can complain to an industrial tribunal within three months if the Department has not made the payment or if the payment is less than the amount entitled.

Trade union membership and activities

A certain degree of protection and some enforceable rights have been given to employees concerning trade union membership rights.

Dismissal

Article 22A of the Industrial Relations (NI) Order 1976 provides that an employee can complain of unfair dismissal if he or she is dismissed:

- for being, or proposing to become, a member of an independent trade union (*i.e.*, one which is not under the control of an employer or an employer's organisation);
- for taking part at "an appropriate time" in the activities of an independent trade union; an "appropriate time" means time which is either outside working hours or during working hours if the employer has given consent;
- for non-membership of a trade union.

The right not to be dismissed for trade union membership or activities applies to all employees and no period of continuous employment is required. In addition, a special interim procedure can be used to hear the case and there may be entitlement to a special award of compensation. An employee who has not been dismissed but has been otherwise victimised for trade union membership or activity or non-membership can also complain to an industrial tribunal within three months.

Time off work for trade union duties and activities

Under article 37 of the 1976 (No 2) Order an employee who is an official of an independent trade union recognised by the employer is entitled to reasonable time off work with normal pay to carry out duties concerned with industrial relations between the employer and the employees, or to attend industrial relations training courses which are relevant to those duties and approved by NIC/ICTU or by the employee's union. Guidance about time off for union duties is contained in a Code of Practice issued by the Labour Relations Agency. Article 37 also provides that an employee who is a member of an independent trade union recognised by the employer is entitled to reasonable time off work without pay to take part in trade union activities, though this does not extend to time off for activities involving industrial action.

Maternity rights

Ante-natal care

Article 41A of the 1976 (No 2) Order provides that an employee who is pregnant has the right not to be unreasonably refused time off work with pay to enable her to receive ante-natal care.

Maternity leave and pay

A woman who has been employed in a job for at least two years by the eleventh week before the expected birth of her child is entitled to take up to 40 weeks' maternity leave and this is extendable by four weeks if the woman is ill. During that period she can claim statutory maternity pay for 18 weeks, six of which will be at the higher of the two stipulated rates (*i.e.* 90% of average earnings), though the woman's contract with her employer may entitle her to greater rights. Some changes will be made to the law on this area when the Trade Union Reform and Employment Rights Act 1993 is extended to Northern Ireland (probably by an Industrial Relations (NI) Order 1993).

Dismissal

Article 14 specifies that if a female full-time employee is dismissed because she is pregnant or because of any other reason connected with her pregnancy she can complain to an industrial tribunal of unfair dismissal if she has been continuously employed by the employer for two years or more. Dismissal in such circumstances will on the face of it be unfair. However, the employer may be able to prove that the dismissal was fair if at the effective date of termination the employee was or would have become, because of her pregnancy, incapable of adequately doing the job which she was employed to do, or if, because of her pregnancy, she could not do her work without contravention of a statutory duty or restriction. Nevertheless, even if the employer shows that the dismissal was for one of the above reasons, the employee will still be unfairly dismissed if there was a suitable vacant alternative job which was not offered to her. This is a rapidly developing area of law. Dismissal of an employee on grounds of pregnancy may also constitute sex discrimination (see chapter 13).

Right to return to work

Under article 15, a female full-time employee who takes leave because of pregnancy has the right to return to her job within 29 weeks of the date of confinement and on terms and conditions as favourable as if she had not been absent. To have this automatic right to return she must have been employed for two years by the beginning of the eleventh week before confinement and must have notified her employer in writing at least three weeks before she stopped work that she intended to return to work.

The mother may be required to furnish written confirmation of her intention to return at any time after seven weeks following confinement. When she is able to resume her job she must give her employer three weeks' notice. An employer can delay the employee's return by up to four weeks if reasons are given. The employee can delay her return by up to four weeks if she is ill and produces a medical certificate, or, if there is an interruption of work (*e.g.* due to industrial action), she can postpone the date of her return until two weeks after work resumes.

Even if the above notification procedures are followed, the right to return is subject to two exclusions:

- if it is not reasonably practicable to allow her to return to her original job, she may be offered alternative employment;
- if the firm employs less than six people, she need not be re- employed at all.

If the employee is not permitted by the employer to return to work she can apply within three months to an industrial tribunal under the unfair dismissal provisions. Alternatively, if due to redundancy her job no longer exists and her employer cannot offer her a suitable alternative job, she is entitled to a redundancy payment and can apply to an industrial tribunal within six months. In both cases she will be considered to have been employed up to the date on which she intended to return to work.

Time off for public duties

Article 39 of the 1976 (No 2) Order entitles an employee to reasonable time off work without pay to perform certain public duties, *e.g.*, if the employee is a Justice of the Peace or a member of a district council, a Health and Social Services Board or an Education and Library Board.

Health and safety at work

Health and safety standards in employment are regulated by both the judge-made common law and by a wide range of legislation. Under the common law, employers have a general duty to take reasonable care for the safety and health of their employees. As regards legislation, in addition to specific health and safety provisions giving protection in, *e.g.*, factories and offices, employees receive health and safety protection under the Health and Safety at Work (NI) Order 1978.

General duties of employers

Article 4 of the 1978 Order specifies that it is the duty of every employer to ensure, so far as is reasonably practicable, the health, safety and welfare at work of all employees. This means, amongst other things, and as far as is reasonably practicable:

- providing plant and systems of work that are safe and without risks to health;
- ensuring safety in connection with the use, handling, storage and transport of articles and substances;
- providing such information, instruction, training and supervision as is necessary to ensure the health and safety at work of the employees.

An employer must prepare, and when appropriate revise, a written statement of general policy with respect to the health and safety at work of the employees and bring it and any revisions to the notice of the employees (unless there are fewer than six). The Health and Safety Agency has issued a guidance note entitled "Employers' policy statements for health and safety at work".

Safety representatives

The Safety Representatives and Safety Committee Regulations (NI) 1979 require employers to recognise safety representatives appointed by recognised trade unions and to consult with them. An employer must establish a safety committee within three months if two or more safety representatives request it. The powers and duties of a safety representative are set out in the 1979 Regulations and are elaborated upon in two accompanying codes of practice. He or she can investigate potential hazards and dangerous occurrences at the work place, investigate complaints and make representations to the employer. To enable them to carry out their functions, safety representatives are entitled to such time off work with pay as is necessary.

Other duties

In addition to the general duties owed by an employer to the employees, the 1978 Order stipulates the duties of employers and the self-employed to non-employees, the duties of persons concerned with premises to persons other than their employees, and the duties of manufacturers as regards articles and substances for use at work. It is also the duty of every employee to take reasonable care for the health and safety of anyone who may be affected by the employee's acts or omissions at work. More recently the health and safety legislation has placed additional duties on employees. In particular, the Management of Health and Safety at Work Regulations (NI) 1992 require employers to make a suitable and sufficient assessment of the risks to health and safety to which their employees are exposed. Where there are five or more employees the findings of the assessment must be recorded as well as any group of employees found to be especially at risk. Employers must provide employees with appropriate health surveillance having regard to the risks identified by the assessment. Employers must also make arrangements for the effective planning, organisation, control, monitoring and review of preventive and protective measures. To assist them undertake such measures employers must appoint competent persons with sufficient time and resources to fulfil their functions. They are required, in addition, to establish appropriate procedures to be followed in the event of serious and imminent danger to persons at work. Finally, employers must provide employees with comprehensible and relevant information on risks to their health, preventive and protective measures, procedures, the identity of competent persons who will implement the procedures and any risks notified to the employer by another employer who shares the work place.

Enforcement

Enforcement of the health and safety legislation is the responsibility of various government departments and the district councils. The main enforcing body is the Health and Safety Inspectorate of the Department of

Economic Development. This Agency advises government bodies on the making of health and safety regulations and prepares and issues codes of practice on health and safety and approves codes made by others.

Failure of an employer to comply with safety legislation is normally a criminal offence. On conviction in a magistrates' court, penalties are by way of fines only. On conviction in the Crown Court, the penalty can be up to two years' imprisonment and an unlimited fine. In addition to their power to prosecute, enforcement officers have been given the right by articles 23-27 of the 1978 Order to:

- issue improvement notices requiring specified improvements to be carried out;
- issue prohibition notices forbidding employers from continuing specified activities if there is a risk of serious personal injury;
- seize, and render harmless, any substance or article believed to be a cause of imminent danger or serious personal injury.

An employer can appeal to an industrial tribunal against the issuing of either an improvement notice or a prohibition notice.

Termination of employment

An employment relationship can end in a number of ways. It may end by the mutual agreement of the parties, by the expiry of a fixed term contract or as a result of the employer's insolvency. Alternatively, it can be terminated at the request of either the employer or the employee. The law has given a degree of protection to employees on termination.

Minimum notice requirements

Section 1 of the Contracts of Employment and Redundancy Payments Act (NI) 1965 lays down the following minimum periods of notice for every full-time employee who has been employed for at least one month (the periods can be extended by agreement):

- after one month, but less than two years: one week's notice
- after two years: two weeks' notice
- one additional week for each year's work up to a maximum of 12 weeks' notice.

Written statements of reasons for dismissal

A dismissed employee who has been continuously employed for six months or more prior to the date of dismissal is entitled by article 48 of the Industrial Relations (NI) Order 1976 to ask the employer for a written statement setting out the reasons for the dismissal. If the employer does not provide a statement, or if the particulars given are inadequate, the dismissed employee can apply to an industrial tribunal within three months. The tribunal can order the employer to pay the dismissed employee two weeks' wages, up to a maximum of £410.

Redundancy

The law takes two approaches to redundancy:

* it requires employers to inform trade unions before redundancies are implemented;
* it provides for compensation to be paid to employees made redundant.

Consultation on redundancies with trade unions

Articles 49-57 of the 1976 Order provide that if an employer proposes to make an employee redundant and recognises an independent trade union for the work group to which the employee belongs, the employer must consult representatives of the trade union before any dismissal takes place. Consultation must begin at the earliest opportunity and at least within the following timescale. If more than 100 employees are to be made redundant within 90 days, consultations must take place at least 90 days before the first dismissal. If 10 or more employees are to be made redundant within 30 days, consultations must take place at least 30 days before the first dismissal.

The employer must disclose the following information in writing to trade union representatives:

* the reasons for the proposed dismissals;
* the numbers and descriptions of workers affected;
* the total number of employees of such description employed;
* the proposed method of selecting employees for dismissal; and
* the proposed method of carrying out the dismissals.

The employer must consider any proposals from the union representatives and if these are rejected reasons must be given.

If an employer does not consult union officials within the consultation period requirements, the appropriate trade union(s) can complain to an industrial tribunal before any dismissal takes place or within three months of the first dismissal. If the tribunal upholds the complaint it may partly safeguard an employee's wages by making a "protective" award. This orders the employer to pay wages to redundant or potentially redundant employees for a specified period.

Individual redundancy payments

The intention of the Contracts of Employment and Redundancy Payments Act (NI) 1965 is to give a minimum level of compensation to employees dismissed for redundancy. The level of payment depends on the employee's age, pay and length of service. Compensation is for loss already suffered, not for any future loss. The provisions apply to full-time employees who, since becoming 18, have at least two years' continuous employment with an employer or associated employer. If the facts are disputed, the employee must prove that he or she was dismissed and the employer must then show that the dismissal was not for redundancy.

By section 11, redundancy occurs where an employer ceases business or where there is surplus labour. Section 13 provides that dismissal occurs where the employer terminates the contract of employment with or without notice, or where a fixed term contract expires without being renewed, or where an employee terminates the contract because of the employer's conduct - "constructive dismissal". If it is shown that the employee was not dismissed, there will be no entitlement to a redundancy payment.

Employees who have received notice of redundancy and who have worked continuously for two years or more are entitled under the provisions of article 41 of the Industrial Relations (No 2) (NI) Order 1976 to reasonable time off work to look for new employment or to make arrangements for training for future employment. During this period employees are entitled to be paid the appropriate hourly rate, up to a maximum of two days' pay.

The redundancy award

The size of the redundancy payment is dependent upon three factors: the amount of basic weekly pay (to a maximum of £205), the number of years' continuous employment (to a maximum of 20 years) and the age of the redundant person. A redundant employee is entitled to:

- half a week's pay for each year of employment between the ages of 18-21;
- one week's pay for each year of employment between the ages of 22-40;
- one and a half week's pay for each year of employment between the age of 41 and normal retirement age.

However, for each month that an employee's age exceeds 64 the redundancy payment will be reduced by one-twelfth. The maximum entitlement is £205 x 20 (number of years) x 1½, *i.e.* £6,150.

Unfair dismissal

To bring an unfair dismissal claim an employee must normally be in full-time employment and have been continuously employed for two years before the termination of employment. But if an employee is dismissed for trade union membership or activity there is no qualifying period of continuous employment. Also, if a full-time employee is dismissed instead of being suspended on medical grounds, the qualification is reduced from two years to one month. A complaint of unfair dismissal must be made to a tribunal within three months of the termination of employment.

Dismissal

Article 21 of the Industrial Relations (No 2) (NI) Order 1976 provides that dismissal takes place where the contract of employment is terminated by the employer with or without notice, where a fixed-term contract expires without being renewed, or where the employee terminates the contract of employment because of the conduct of the employer. For there to be a "constructive" dismissal arising from an employee's resignation, the employer must have been guilty of a fundamental breach of the employment contract. If the employer contends that no dismissal took place, it is for the employee to satisfy an industrial tribunal that this is not the case.

Fair or unfair dismissal

Article 22 provides that some dismissals are automatically fair while others are automatically unfair. It is for the employer to show that there was a fair reason for dismissal. When deciding whether this is so, an industrial tribunal will take no account of any pressure, such as industrial action, put on an employer to dismiss an employee. There will be a *fair dismissal* if:

- the employee is not capable of doing the job for which he or she was employed;
- the employee has not the qualifications necessary for the job;
- the employee's conduct warrants dismissal;
- the employee is redundant;
- the continued employment of the employee would contravene a duty or restriction imposed by law; or
- there is some other substantial reason to justify dismissal.

There will be an *unfair dismissal* if:

- it is related to an employee's membership or activity in an independent trade union or non-membership of a trade union;
- the employee is selected for redundancy in contravention of an agreed procedure or agreement; or
- there has been a contravention of the Transfer of Undertakings (Protection of Employment) Regulations 1981.

The employer's reasonableness

It is for the tribunal to decide whether the employer acted reasonably or unreasonably. There may have been a fair reason for dismissing an employee but the employer may still have acted unreasonably. The standard applied by the tribunal is that of the reasonable employer. Tribunals have recognised that there exists a broad band of reasonable responses within which one employer might decide to dismiss while another might decide to impose a lesser penalty, such as a final written warning. The effect has been to make it more difficult for an employee to be successful in an unfair dismissal claim.

A decision on whether an employer acted reasonably is a question of fact for an industrial tribunal to decide. Only if it can be shown that no reasonable tribunal could have reached the same decision can a tribunal decision be successfully challenged on appeal.

When considering the reasonableness of a dismissal tribunals take into account the Code of Practice issued by the Labour Relations Agency on "Disciplinary Practice and Procedures in Employment". This specifies certain features which should be an essential part of any disciplinary procedure, in particular that employees should know of complaints against them, be given an adequate opportunity to state their case and have the right to be accompanied by a trade union official or fellow employee at any disciplinary hearing. In addition, disciplinary action should not be taken until the complaint has been investigated carefully and an internal appeals procedure should be provided.

Remedies for unfair dismissal

Although the legislation lays primary emphasis on securing the reinstatement or re-engagement of the dismissed employee, there is no legal right for an employee to get his or her job back and in practice few awards of reinstatement or re-engagement are made. In the last analysis, if an employer sacks an employee and refuses re-employment, the only remedy available is monetary compensation.

Reinstatement takes effect as if an applicant has never been dismissed. This involves full restoration of pay and other benefits, including seniority and pension rights. *Re-engagement* occurs where the tribunal thinks that reinstatement is not practicable. It allows the employer to offer the employee another suitable job.

An *interim relief procedure* applies to an employee who is dismissed for trade union activity or for non-union membership. The employee must apply to an industrial tribunal within seven days of the dismissal. If the tribunal considers that the unfair dismissal application is likely to succeed, it may order reinstatement, re-engagement or the continuation of the contract of employment so that the employee can remain on full pay until the tribunal makes its final decision.

As regards *compensation*, two types of award can be made, although in certain cases an additional or special award is available. Compensation will be reduced if a tribunal decides that an employee contributed to the dismissal. An employee is also under a duty to make efforts to reduce the loss suffered.

- A "basic" award compensates the employee for the loss of the job and is calculated in the same way as a redundancy award (see page 303). The basic award is subject to a maxium of £205 x 20 x 1^1/$_2$, *i.e.* £6,150.

- A "compensatory" award is made to compensate the employee for the actual loss suffered from the date of dismissal, up to a maximum of £11,000. The amount will be such as the tribunal considers just and equitable in all the circumstances. In practice, the calculation involves loss of earnings from the date of dismissal to the date of the tribunal hearing and future loss of earnings from the date of the tribunal hearing.

- An "additional" award is made in two circumstances where an employer has failed to comply with a reinstatement or re-engagement order. Firstly, in the case of a normal dismissal, an award of between 13 and 26 weeks' pay can be made. Secondly, where an employee has been dismissed for discrimination as defined by the Sex Discrimination (NI) Order 1976 or the Fair Employment (NI) Acts 1976-89, an award of between 26 and 52 weeks' pay can be made. The maximum weekly pay that can be taken into account in both situations is again £205.

- The legislation provides for a "special" award of increased compensation to employees dismissed for trade union membership or activities, for non-membership of a trade union or for unfair selection for redundancy on such grounds. The minimum basic award is calculated in the normal way, but subject to a minimum of £2,700. On top of the basic and normal compensatory awards, a special award may also be made where the employee requests but does not obtain re-engagement or reinstatement. The award is 104 weeks' pay, subject to a minimum of £13,400 and a maximum of £26,800. If, however, a tribunal makes an award of re-engagement or reinstatement which is not complied with, then, unless the employer can show that it was not reasonably practicable to comply with the award, the special award is 156 weeks' pay, subject to a minimum of £20,100 but with no limit on the maximum.

Trade union law

A trade union is defined by article 2 of the Industrial Relations (NI) Order 1992 as an organisation which consists:

- of workers of one or more description and has as its principal purpose the regulation of relations between workers and employers or employers' associations; or
- wholly or mainly of an affiliated or constituent group of such organisations or their representatives.

The basis of a trade union's right to exist is the Industrial Relations (NI) Order 1992, and by article 3 of this Order they can sue and be sued in their own name. Even though a trade union is in law an "unincorporated association", any judgment, order or award may be enforced against it as if it were a public company.

The 1992 Order distinguishes between independent unions and others. A union is independent if it is not under the control of an employer or a group of employers and is not liable to interference arising out of the provision of financial or other support which tends towards such control. Only independent trade unions are accorded statutory rights concerning union recognition, disclosure of information and consultation. Their members are given further rights concerning unfair dismissal and redundancy.

Trade union recognition

There is no general legal obligation requiring an employer to recognise a trade union. The decision to recognise and the extent to which recognition is afforded is a decision for an employer.

Collective bargaining and legal rights for unions

The normal method of negotiation between trade unions and employers or employers' associations is by way of collective bargaining. By article 26 of the 1992 Order collective agreements are conclusively presumed not to have been intended by the parties to be legally enforceable unless the agreement is in writing and contains a provision which states that the parties intended the agreement to be a legally enforceable contract. In practice, collective agreements are not enforceable. But certain terms of collective agreements, such as wage rates and holiday entitlement, are incorporated into an individual's contract of employment and can be agreed with an individual employee and the employer.

The 1992 Order says it is the duty of every employer to disclose information about his or her undertaking to the representatives of any trade union for the purposes of collective bargaining. A complaint of failure to disclose information can be referred to the LRA, which will attempt conciliation. If this fails, the matter may then be referred by the LRA to the Industrial Court, which may make a declaration stipulating a period within which disclosure is to be made. If the information is still not forthcoming, a further complaint may be made *via* the LRA to the Industrial Court, which may then order that the contracts of the employees specified in the claim should include the specified terms and conditions.

If an employer proposes to make an employee redundant and recognises an independent trade union for the work group to which the employee belongs, the employer must consult representatives of the trade union before any dismissal takes place (see page 301).

The Health and Safety at Work (NI) Order 1978 requires an employer to consult with safety representatives appointed by independent trade unions. The Transfer of Undertakings (Protection of Employment) Regulations (NI) 1981 require an employer to inform and consult trade unions in advance of certain business transfers. Enforcement is by way of complaint to an industrial tribunal by the relevant union. The maximum compensation is two weeks' pay for each employee affected.

Rights of trade union members

A person expelled or excluded from a trade union may have a right to sue under the common law, but the Industrial Relations (NI) Order 1992 provides an additional remedy. By article 6, where there is a union membership agreement (UMA) in force whereby an employee must belong to a specified trade union or one of a number of specified unions, every person who is in employment or is seeking employment has the right not to have a union membership application unreasonably refused, and not to be unreasonably expelled from a specified trade union.

A person can complain to an industrial tribunal that an application for membership has been unreasonably refused, or that he or she has been unreasonably expelled, within six months of the refusal or expulsion. The complaint is not to be determined solely on the basis of whether or not the union acted in accordance with the rule book. If a person is awarded a declaration by the tribunal, he or she can then apply to an industrial tribunal for compensation. This must not exceed £16,150 if the person has been (re)admitted to membership. If the person has not been (re)admitted, the compensation will be such as the tribunal considers just and equitable in all the circumstances, but not exceeding £26,810. In both cases there will be a minimum level of compensation of £2,700. As in unfair dismissal cases, the applicant is under a duty to "mitigate" (*i.e.* reduce) the loss suffered and any award may be lessened because of contributory fault.

The Industrial Relations (NI) Order 1992 establishes a right for a trade union member not to be unjustifiably disciplined by his or her union. Types of conduct for which discipline is unjustifiable include:

- failure to participate in, or conduct indicating opposition to, industrial action;
- alleging that a union official has acted contrary to union rules or unlawfully;
- seeking assistance or advice from the Certification Officer or the Commissioner for the Rights of Trade Union Members (see page 289).

A union member who is unjustifiably disciplined may complain to an industrial tribunal for redress. Compensation is calculated in the same way as an award arising from unreasonable exclusion or expulsion from a trade union.

The 1992 Order establishes other rights for trade union members. In particular, a member can apply for an injunction to stop industrial action taking place where a ballot has not been held. In every contract of membership there is an implied right to terminate membership on giving reasonable notice. Where a union member's grievance with a union is not resolved within six months, the union member may then take legal action. Finally, an employee may require an employer to cease the deduction of the union dues from wages. Where this is not done the employee may complain to an industrial tribunal.

Trade union ballots

Article 102 of the 1992 Order enables the Department of Economic Development to provide public funding for trade union ballots. There will be no compulsion on a union to hold a ballot or to accept funding for one.

Independent trade unions will be able to apply for reimbursement of costs incurred in:

- ascertaining the views of members as to strike action;
- carrying out an election;
- amending the union rules;
- obtaining a decision on an amalgamation or transfer;
- obtaining a decision as to the acceptance or rejection of a proposal made by an employee in relation to terms and conditions of employment;
- any other purposes the Department may specify.

Payments will be made only in cases where, so far as is reasonably practicable, the voting is by way of secret ballot.

Industrial action

Trade unions are themselves subject to the same immunities as those enjoyed by, *e.g.*, members and officials under article 15 of the 1992 Order. In consequence, unions are immune from certain civil suits if the action taken was in contemplation or furtherance of a trade dispute. These so-called "economic" wrongs for which unions, their members and officials receive immunity are inducement to break a contract, interference with the performance of a contract, intimidation and conspiracy.

A trade dispute is defined in article 2 of the 1992 Order as a dispute between workers and their employer which relates wholly or mainly to one or more of the following:

- terms and conditions of employment;
- engagement or non-engagement, or termination or suspension of employment;
- allocation of work;
- matters of discipline;
- membership or non-membership of a trade union;
- facilities for officials of trade unions;
- machinery for negotiation or consultation.

Secondary action

Article 17 of the Industrial Relations (NI) Order 1982 restricts the amount of lawful secondary action that may take place. It defines secondary action as occurring in all situations where a person induces a breach of, or threatens to interfere with, contracts of employment with an employer who is not a party to a dispute. The existing immunities from being sued do not apply to interference with commercial contracts by remote secondary action, but the article specifies several situations where secondary action is not remote and for which immunity will remain. These situations are:

- where the principal purpose of the action is directly to prevent or disrupt the supply of goods or services during the dispute and it is likely to achieve that purpose, and

- where the action interferes with the contracts of employment of an associated employer or of its customer or supplier, the purpose is directly to disrupt the supply of goods or services between any person and the associated employer, it is likely to achieve that purpose, and the goods are substitutes for goods or services which would have been supplied to or by the employer in dispute.

Balloting requirements

The Industrial Relations (NI) Order 1992 provides that immunity from tort action will be lost where a trade union fails to hold a secret ballot before authorising or endorsing industrial action. Articles 44-46 of the 1992 Order specify the conditions which must be satisfied in respect of such secret ballots. For example, entitlement to vote must be given to those members who will be called upon to take industrial action and the voting paper must contain a question which requires the person answering it to say by answering "Yes" or "No" whether he or she is prepared to take part in a strike and/or a question of whether he or she is prepared to take part in action short of a strike. In addition the following statement must appear, *without qualification*, on every voting paper:

"If you take part in a strike or other industrial action, you may be in breach of your contract of employment".

Liability to pay compensation

A union may be held responsible for the actions of its officials (so-called "vicarious" liability). It is for the courts to decide whether a union is liable for the acts of its members or officials in respect of wrongs such as negligence or nuisance. In respect of the economic wrongs mentioned above, a union will be vicariously liable only for specified unlawful actions which are authorised or endorsed by a "responsible person", defined by article 21 of the Industrial Relations (NI) Order 1992 as:

- the principal executive committee;
- a person with the power to authorise such acts;
- the president or general secretary;
- any other employed official; or
- any committee of the union to which an employed official regularly reports.

However, the union will not be liable for acts authorised by the last two above if the rules of the union prevent that person or committee from authorising industrial action. Nor will the union be liable if the act has been repudiated by the first two above.

Where a union is found liable in court proceedings, the amount of damages which may be awarded is subject to certain upper limits specified by article 22 of the 1992 Order. These limits apply to all proceedings except those for negligence, nuisance or breach of duty relating to the use of property or resulting in personal injury. The limit on damages is dependent upon the membership of the union, ranging from £10,000 for membership up to 5,000 to £250,000 for membership above 100,000.

For the purposes of calculating the number of members which a trade union has, members outside Northern Ireland are included. Damages may not be recovered from protected property such as political and provident funds belonging to a union or to an employers' association.

Picketing

There is no general right to picket. As with trade disputes, an immunity is conferred, this time by article 16 of the 1992 Order, which provides that it shall be lawful for a person to picket:

- at or near his or her own place of work, or
- if he or she is an official of a trade union, at or near the place of work of a member of that union whom he or she is accompanying and representing.

The picketing must be for the purpose of peacefully obtaining or communicating information, or peacefully persuading any person to work or abstain from working. In addition, if a person works at more than one place, or at a place where it is impracticable to picket, he or she is entitled to picket any premises of the employer from which he or she works or from which his or her work is administered.

Pickets can easily fall foul of both the criminal and civil law. For instance, they may be liable to criminal charges for obstruction of the highway or of the police, intimidation or contravening the Public Order (NI) Order 1987 in respect of meetings and marches (see chapter 9). They may also be liable to a civil action for trespass or nuisance.

Chapter 18

Housing Rights

John Coyle and Angela Hegarty

One of the major areas of contention in the past in Northern Ireland has been housing. Since the establishment of the Northern Ireland Housing Executive in 1972 much of the controversy over housing allocation has subsided, but some problems remain, largely in relation to repairs and public funding. There are also problems in relation to the law, which whilst it guarantees a number of rights fails to protect individuals in some respects, most notably when they are homeless. For an explanation of specific housing rights enjoyed by disabled persons, see chapter 14. For an explanation of housing benefit, see chapter 19 on social security rights.

The law distinguishes between different types of housing in Northern Ireland - the public rented sector, the private rented sector, and home owners. An occupant's rights and obligations are defined both by statute law and, if the occupant is a tenant, by the tenancy agreement or "lease."

A lease is essentially a contract between the landlord and the tenant agreeing, for example, how much rent the tenant pays, who is responsible for repairs and so on. It does not have to be formally written down, but it is obviously easier to decide what the conditions of a written lease are if there is a dispute. In addition to whatever is agreed in the lease the law lays down certain conditions, *e.g.* that the tenant is allowed "quiet and peaceful enjoyment" of the property and is given a minimum period of notice to quit.

Generally in public sector housing a tenant will be given a written lease. In the private rented sector it is more common for leases to be verbal.

Public rented sector housing

The main provider of public sector housing in Northern Ireland is the Northern Ireland Housing Executive (NIHE), which generally speaking performs the same functions as local authorities in Great Britain. It was set up and carries out its tasks under statute, which means that many of its decisions are judicially reviewable in the courts.

NIHE and registered housing association tenants enjoy certain special rights which are not necessarily enjoyed by private sector tenants. These relate, for example, to security of tenure, the right to buy and rights to take in lodgers and sub-let.

Allocation

NIHE allocates accommodation according to priority. When a person one applies to NIHE for accommodation he or she will be placed either on the Group A priority waiting list or on the Group B general waiting list. Within these groups an application will also be prioritised, *e.g.* a person for example one may be classed as "emergency AI status". On the general waiting list (Group B) a person must have been resident in Northern Ireland for seven years and will be allocated points depending upon his or her current accommodation and family circumstances.

Tenancy agreements

Each NIHE tenant is given a standard form tenancy agreement which is a legal document setting out the terms and conditions of the occupation of the premises. A tenant is entitled to a copy of the tenancy agreement and a straightforward explanation of its terms (article 38(3) of the Housing (NI) Order 1983). The most important terms of the agreement relate to payment of rent and rights and obligations in respect of repairs.

Rent

The tenancy agreement stipulates that the tenant agrees to pay all the rent owing. Any failure to do so results in NIHE trying to recover the amount as a debt or, in extreme cases, attempting to recover possession with a court order. Unlike privately rented accommodation there is no legal compulsion on NIHE to provide a tenant with a rent book, although in practice a giro book is usually supplied.

The obligation to pay rent is usually only imposed upon the tenant, *i.e.* the individual whose name appears on the tenancy agreement, and not his or her family. Where there is a joint tenancy the duty to pay is imposed on all the tenants. Arrears of rent occur generally for the following reasons:

- Where there has been a mistake: if there is a mistake by the tenant, he or she is responsible for arrears in full and will have to come to an arrangement to pay. If there is a mistake by NIHE any overcharging should in general be recoverable by the tenant while any undercharging cannot generally be recovered by NIHE.

- Where the tenant is unable or unwilling to pay: a tenant who cannot pay because of too little money or an emergency is best advised to start paying again at the first available opportunity, even if it is only part of the rent. One should seek advice on any extra benefit entitlement, *e.g.* housing benefit or family credit. This can sometimes be backdated, for up to 52 weeks, if good cause for a late claim can be shown (*e.g.* serious physical or mental illness). If possible a voluntary arrangement to pay off arrears should be entered into if any extra cash from benefit occurs. If the tenant cannot come to such an arrangement, NIHE will use the following methods of recovery.

Recovery of arrears of rent

NIHE will first try to get a voluntary agreement with a tenant to repay the arrears, either by instalments or by a lump sum. If the tenant does not take up this option, NIHE may apply informal pressures such as refusing to grant a transfer or failing to carry out improvements. If these also fail to have an effect, NIHE may turn to recovery through redirecting other financial sources such as grants, compensation benefits etc.

Since the repeal of the Payments for Debt (Emergency Provisions) Act (NI) 1971 in 1991 the method for recovering arrears of rent from state benefits is as follows. There is a limit of £1.50 on deductions but this must be paid if a tenant is six weeks or more in arrears. If a benefit office agrees, deductions may be made after only four weeks, as this may be in the best interests of the claimant and his or her family. A tenant who gets income support, family credit or housing benefit can apply on grounds of hardship to NIHE's district manager to have no deductions made from redecoration or self-help repair allowances, but these are the only types of payment which qualify. NIHE may also deduct up to £1.75 per week from student grants. Where a tenant owing arrears is successful in a claim against NIHE, arrears can be deducted by NIHE before the money from the claim is handed over.

NIHE can also pursue debtors through the courts. Where the amount outstanding is less than £500 NIHE can apply to the small claims court. More common however is the issue of a "process" in the local magistrates' court. Neither of these court actions can, however, lead to the repossession of the dwelling. In order to do this NIHE must apply to a county court for the grant of an "ejectment civil bill". If the amount outstanding is more than £5,000 NIHE must apply to the High Court.

Levels of NIHE rents

NIHE fixes the level of its rents by totting up a points score for each dwelling based on its size, age and facilities and then multiplying the total by a figure set by the Department of the Environment every year. When the rent is increased NIHE notifies the tenant.

Where a tenant believes that an assessment is wrong he or she should write to the local district office of NIHE. If this is unsuccessful a further approach can be made to the Ombudsman, an application can be made to the High Court for judicial review of the rent or the tenant can wait to defend an action for arrears. In the latter two cases legal or other expert advice should be sought.

Repairs

The tenancy agreement in summary lays down that NIHE agrees to keep in repair the structure and exterior, to maintain anything in the dwelling which is its responsibility and to decorate the exterior every seven years. Anything which the tenant can remove is not NIHE's responsibility.

NIHE argues that its duty to repair arises only when its district manager has received written and specific notice from or on behalf of a tenant and after a reasonable period of time has elapsed. NIHE has indicated that it will respond to telephone calls in emergencies but believes that it is not legally obliged to do so. Local offices will prioritise repairs according to their urgency and set time limits within which the repair will be done. The standard of repair should be consistent with the age, character and prospective life of the house. In other words expensive major restoration work to property due for redevelopment is unlikely, while minor holding repairs may be carried out.

If a property is damaged by flood, fire or other disaster, NIHE is not obliged to repair or restore it, but will normally do so unless the cost would be unreasonably high. NIHE is entitled to enter the building to do repairs but will only do so between 9am and 6pm after giving 24 hours' notice except in emergencies.

Security of tenure

If a tenant occupies a dwelling as his or her "only home" and the landlord is the NIHE or a registered housing association, the tenancy will, except in certain special circumstances, be a "secure tenancy". A secure tenant generally has the right to remain for as long as he or she wants in the dwelling. Exceptions to this are set out in the Housing (NI) Order 1983. As well as having the right not to be evicted except by due process of law and after a valid notice to quit giving four week's notice has been served, the tenant can lose possession of the property only if the landlord body gets a court order (article 27). Such an order for possession will be made only if one or more of 11 situations exist.

In the first six situations the court must think that an order for possession is reasonable, in the seventh there must be alternative accommodation available for the tenant, and in the remaining four both of these conditions must be present. The grounds for possession are as follows (see article 29):

- non-payment of rent or the breach of another obligation in the tenancy agreement;
- causing an annoyance to neighbours or using the premises for an illegal or immoral purpose;
- damaging or destroying any furniture provided, or failing to remove a lodger responsible for such damage or destruction;

- inducing the landlord to grant the tenancy by knowingly or recklessly making a false statement;
- failing to give up the premises while works are being carried out, even though the tenant knew this would be required;
- where a secure tenant has paid a fee in respect of an exchange of homes;
- where the landlord needs to do works of demolition or construction, all of which cannot be carried out in a reasonable time and for which possession is needed;
- where a house designed for a disabled person is now occupied by someone who is not disabled and is required again for a disabled person;
- where a registered housing association dwelling is usually let to a person who finds it difficult to have his or her housing needs met (other than for financial reasons) and the current occupant is not such a person;
- where the accommodation is for a person with special needs and the current occupant is a person who does not have those needs;
- where there is under-occupation of a house of which the tenancy was obtained through "statutory succession" by a member of the previous tenant's family (other than the spouse).

"Statutory succession" by a relative to a secure tenancy

If a secure tenant dies, the law provides for one succession by his or her nearest relative. Who this relative shall be is set out in article 26 of the Housing (NI) Order 1983. The right falls first to a husband or wife of the deceased, so long as he or she occupied the property as his or her principal home at the time of the tenant's death. For any other relatives, article 26 specifies residence for 12 months prior to the tenant's death and again the person must have lived in the property as his or her principal home. In practice the NIHE reduces the time requirement to six months.

There is only one succession allowed and, in cases of dispute, the NIHE may nominate who that person is to be. It must be an uncle, aunt, nephew, niece, child or "common law" husband or wife.

Transfer and exchange

NIHE allows a tenant to apply for a transfer. This is not a legal right but as it is provided for in the Executive's handbook it should be administered fairly and reasonably. Applications should be made to the Executive's local district office and will be considered for priority depending on whether the tenant has any rent arrears, though this barrier to transfer may be waived by the Executive if there are social and medical grounds and an arrangement is made to repay the arrears. The allocation of priority is on grounds similar to those discussed in connection with homelessness (see pages 322-324).

Exchanges of houses have been put on a statutory basis by article 32(A)(1) of the 1983 Order. This gives tenants the right to exchange, provided they have NIHE's written permission, which can be withheld only on very specific grounds.

The right to buy

The 1983 legislation on a tenant's right to buy has been repealed and replaced by provisions contained in the Housing (NI) Order 1992. The previous complicated home purchase scheme and NIHE's own voluntary purchase scheme are to be replaced by a new House Sales Scheme issued by NIHE under article 96 of the 1992 Order This scheme will operate in much the same way as the previous arrangements, *e.g.* tenants will generally have a right to buy after three years.

Squatting in Housing Executive property

"Squatting" is a term commonly used to refer to entering and remaining in property without the permission of the occupier. In fact there are two elements to the conduct, entry and occupation, and both are criminal offences.

When a squatter or his or her dependents first enter a house they are trespassers who may be summarily evicted without a court order. The Criminal Justice (NI) Order 1986 confirmed that it was a criminal offence to enter property without the permission of the owner and in addition made it an offence to remain on the property after being asked to leave by the person lawfully entitled to possession. A resident magistrate (RM) can grant a possession order for the premises once a squatter has been convicted of an offence under the Order. If the squatter has used force or threatened violence then an offence has been committed under the Protection of the Person and Property Act (NI) 1969 and is punishable by a fine or imprisonment. In addition it is an offence to force entry and create an actual or possible breach of the peace (*e.g.* through barricading a building). Convictions of this kind are, however, rare.

Whenever someone squats in NIHE property the following options are more likely to be used:

- A member of NIHE staff visits the property and encourages the squatters to leave. If they do not a warning letter will be sent, giving the squatters seven days to vacate the premises and threatening legal action if they remain beyond that time. If they still refuse to go the matter is referred to NIHE solicitors to initiate a criminal prosecution or civil action. It is highly unlikely that squatters could successfully defend such an action.

- An action in the civil courts for possession of the premises, eviction of the squatter and sometimes even compensation for the unauthorised occupation (money known as "mesne profits") is usually begun by the issue of an "ejectment civil bill" in a county court, but may also be begun by issuing an "originating summons" in the Chancery Division of the High Court if the value of the property is significant. Where the premises concerned belong to NIHE, a registered housing association, a district council or the Crown a possession order can be suspended for up to three months. Any judgment obtained can be enforced against the squatters by the Enforcement of Judgments Office.

Immediately after court proceedings NIHE will issue a "use and occupation" book with a covering letter making it clear that a tenancy is not being granted (*McCann v NIHE,* 1979). The squatters are then required to make periodic payments (as mesne profits, not rent, although in practice the two amounts are similar). The squatters remain trespassers and consequently have no right, for example, to have the property repaired. They do however have some rights, in limited circumstances, in relation to injuries incurred on the property as a result of disrepair (see Occupiers' Liability (NI) Order 1986).

NIHE officials are entitled to enter the property provided force is not used. A common tactic is to request that squatters come to the local NIHE office for an appointment. NIHE officials then enter the squat and secure it against the squatters' return, a course of action which is illegal if underhand.

Squatters are not protected by the illegal eviction and harassment provisions of the Rent (NI) Order 1978 (articles 54-56) but a squatter who has been evicted may apply to NIHE as a person who is homeless.

The Housing Executive's duties to the homeless

For homeless people, or those threatened with immediate homelessness, there are two routes by which they may acquire "emergency A1 status" from NIHE. One route is the administrative scheme devised by the Executive itself; the other is the legal right available to some homeless persons created by the Housing (NI) Order 1988 and in operation since April 1989.

NIHE's administrative scheme

Under the Executive's own Housing Selection Scheme, a homeless person will normally get emergency A1 status if he or she is homeless due to:

- fire, flood, or other circumstances beyond the applicant's control;
- marital breakdown;
- successful court action by a landlord for the possession of a dwelling which the landlord may want to use for himself or herself or for a member of his or her family;
- the ending of a "tied" tenancy, *i.e.,* a tenancy which is let by an employer as part of a contract of employment (such as a farm labourer's cottage);
- being a serviceman moving to civilian life without accommodation, or the widow of a recently deceased serviceman losing married quarters;
- an exceptional need to sell the dwelling currently occupied; or
- other circumstances regarded by NIHE as exceptional, including situations where a person, through no fault of his or her own, has to reside in emergency accommodation or persistently change address in order to have accommodation.

The first and last of the above criteria may be particulary applicable in Northern Ireland due to the civil disturbances here.

Homelessness under the 1988 Order

Establishing a legal right to A1 status under the Housing (NI) Order 1988 requires the applicant to prove three points.

- That he or she is *in fact* homeless, having no place to live in Northern Ireland by virtue of ownership, a tenancy or an express or implied licence (*i.e.* a permission to be on property), or is *deemed* to be homeless because he or she cannot occupy a property with members of his or her family due to its physical condition or cost, or the applicant not being physically able to get into it, or there being a risk of violence from someone else living in it, or there being a threat of homelessness within the next 28 days through a court order for eviction.

- That he or she is "in priority need", *e.g.* is pregnant, over 60 years old or mentally or physically disabled (or normally resides with someone who is in one of these categories). Priority need also covers a young person (aged 16-21) who is at risk of sexual or financial exploitation, someone who has dependent children, or who is subject to domestic violence or to violence from outside the home, and a person who has a home which is rendered uninhabitable due to fire, flood or other unexpected disaster including illegal eviction.

- That he or she is not responsible for losing "settled" accommodation, when it was reasonable for him or her to continue to occupy that accommodation. This is the condition known as "intentionality". It applies whether the settled accommodation is in Northern Ireland or elsewhere. Behaviour by the spouse, partner or child of an applicant will not count against his or her application.

In reality, the majority of homeless people are excluded from the categories of people who are "in priority need". This is because they are single people, with no dependent children, aged between 21 and retirement age, and without any mental or physical disability, whose homelessness has not been a result of natural disaster or violence.

NIHE's duties under the 1988 Order

Those people who are both homeless and in priority need are entitled, as a minimum, to be provided by NIHE with suitable temporary accommodation for a reasonable period (up to 28 days) and to be given advice and assistance. They are also entitled to have their belongings stored, pending rehousing (article 13). NIHE is allowed to make a reasonable charge for this accommodation and storage. Even if the Executive finally decides that the applicant is intentionally homeless, these services have to be provided for a reasonable period thereafter in order to allow the applicant to find other accommodation (article 10(3)). It is a criminal offence knowingly to make a false statement to the Executive intending to get accommodation as a result (article 17).

A fully qualifying applicant will be made two suitable offers of accommodation (article 12). If these are turned down, the applicant may be eventually housed from the ordinary housing waiting list, which is open only to persons who were born in Northern Ireland or who have resided here for the previous seven years. Someone coming directly from another EC country has no right to register on the list unless he or she also works in Northern Ireland.

Challenging NIHE's decision

If NIHE, through its district office, refuses to grant A1 status to an applicant under the 1988 Order, the applicant is entitled to be told the reasons for this in writing (article 9). The remedy for unsuccessful applicants is an appeal through NIHE's own appeals procedure, initially to the Regional Manager and then to the Director of Housing and Planning.

If NIHE makes a decision which is wrong in law, exceeds its powers or is unreasonable, perverse or absurd, the applicant may apply to the High Court for a judicial review of the decision, but NIHE has to have acted particularly badly for the High Court to grant a review. Even if successful the matter may simply be returned to the Executive for reconsideration according to proper procedures, and this may not lead to a different conclusion from that reached earlier. Applicants should, however, always seek legal advice if refused housing by the NIHE. If temporary or permanent rehousing is not suitable, the applicant can also challenge this in court.

Grants

A new grants scheme was set up under the Housing (NI) Order 1992. Briefly, the new system applies a means test to applicants and distinguishes between mandatory grants (*i.e.* where the applicant satisfies all the criteria the grant must be awarded) and discretionary grants (where NIHE may give financial assistance but is not required to). The new scheme recognises the following types of grants:

- renovation grants - aimed at making unfit properties fit;
- disabled facilities grants - for adaptation of fit properties for disabled residents;
- replacement grants - to replace unfit isolated rural dwellings where renovation grants are inappropriate;
- minor works assistance - for carrying out minor works for specified target groups;
- repair grants - to carry out works required to be done by a statutory notice;
- common parts grants - to carry out repairs or improvements to the common parts of a building which contains more than one flat;
- houses in multiple occupation grants - to bring unfit houses in multiple occupation up to the required standard.

NIHE have produced a series of leaflets on the new grants system and these and further information can be obtained from any local NIHE grants office.

Private rented sector

Private tenants are those whose landlords are not NIHE or a registered housing association. There are three types of private tenancies - restricted, regulated and unprotected. It is essential to find out which type of tenancy is in question to be able to discover a tenant's rights to repair or to security of tenure and how much rent will have to be paid.

Restricted and regulated tenancies are protected tenancies under the Rent (NI) Order 1978. Most privately rented accommodation in Northern Ireland is "unprotected" by the Order. Unprotected tenants have only a few legal rights outside those agreed with the landlord in any written or verbal tenancy agreement. Such agreements do not have to be in writing if they are for under one year or from year to year. They can be entirely oral or partly oral and partly written. Tenancies will be private but not protected if the landlord is the Crown, a government department or an Industrial or Provident Society. If the lease is for more than 99 years or a "fee farm grant" the agreement will again fall outside the protection of the Rent Order. A fee farm grant is a very long lease (*e.g.* 999 years) subject to a "ground" rent; it is almost equivalent to full ownership.

Protected tenancies

A tenancy will *not* be protected if any of the following apply:

- the Net Annual Value (NAV) is over £140; the NAV of any property can be checked at the local rates office;
- the property was built or converted after 6th November 1956;
- the landlord shares essential facilities with the tenant;
- the property has all reasonably necessary furniture, excluding cooking utensils, linen and crockery, unless a restricted rent certificate covers the dwelling or a public health notice has been served;
- the landlord provides food or servies which are a substantial part of the rent, unless a restricted rent certificate covers the dwelling or a public health notice has been served;
- the tenancy was not or cannot be presumed to have been rented out and controlled by the old Rent Restrictions Acts.

If the tenancy is protected the next step is to decide whether it is restricted or regulated. Telephoning the Rent Officer at Stormont (0232-520000) is a short cut to finding out. A tenancy is a regulated tenancy unless it is subject to a restricted rent certificate issued by a district council or unless, immediately before the commencement of the Rent (NI) Order 1978, the tenancy was controlled by the old Rent Restriction Acts and the NAV was under £60. A tenancy is also deemed to be restricted if a statutory nuisance notice has been issued by a district council. A landlord can apply to the council to convert a tenancy into a regulated tenancy if it comes up to a certain standard (set out in Schedule 3 of the 1978 Order).

Regulated tenancies are protected tenancies other than those which are restricted and they are obliged by law to meet certain standards. Since the introduction of the Housing (NI) Order 1992 the standards laid down in the Rent Order have been amended with the result that a dwelling will meet the regulated tenancy standards if it is fit for human habitation.

Private tenants' rents

The levels of rent are differently controlled for restricted, regulated and unprotected tenants.

Restricted tenancies

The rents in restricted tenancies are fixed at what they were when the Rent (NI) Order 1978 came into force. They are usually just a few pounds per week. Tenants will often pay the rates also and these may now be more than the rent. A restricted rent can be increased only if the landlord applies to his or her district council in order to convert the tenancy into a regulated tenancy. There can be no review of the rent by the rent assessment committee. Any excess of rent paid by a tenant can be recovered by withholding future instalments (article 23(2) of the Rent (NI) Order 1978).

Regulated tenancies

The rent of regulated tenants is supposed to be approximately equal to what NIHE would charge (article 27 (2)) and is regulated by the 1978 Order. The rent is fixed by applying to the Rent Office to have it registered and can be altered (apart from clerical errors) only by an order of the rent assessment committee or by the Department of Environment (article 33). If a tenant applies to have the rent registered at a regulated rent, anything paid in excess of that rent during the previous two years can be recovered from the landlord (article 23(2)).

Unprotected tenancies

The rent charged in these tenancies is generally the amount the market will stand for the property, given its location, size, repair and facilities, but the amount will be affected by two factors:
- NIHE is authorised to restrict the amount of rent which can be paid through housing benefit . This restriction can be appealed to an

independent housing benefit review board. A tenant has to pay any excess which NIHE will not pay.

- The level of subsidy to home owners through mortgage interest tax relief means that it can be cheaper to buy rather than rent at the level a landlord may need to charge in order to make a profit.

All private tenants are entitled to a rent book (article 38 of the 1978 Order) and failure to provide one by a landlord is a criminal offence.

Private tenants' rights to repairs

Restricted tenancies

Restricted tenants rarely have any repairing rights in their tenancy agreement. Usually the obligation to do repairs is on the tenant. Restricted tenants can normally only use the statutory nuisance and unfitness procedures described below. Withholding rent is not an option as the rent is so low.

Regulated tenancies

The landlord's duties to repair are laid down in articles 41 and 43-45 of the Rent (NI) Order 1978. He or she is responsible for the structure, the exterior (including paintwork), the supplies of electricity, gas and water and the interior, except for those obligations which article 42 imposes on the tenant. These latter include responsibility for fireplaces, tiles, all glass, tap washers and seals and any damage caused by the tenant or a lawful visitor. The tenant is also responsible for the interior decorative order.

If a landlord is in breach of his or her repairing duties by not carrying out the work after written or verbal notice has been given, a regulated tenant can do the following:

- Apply to the rent assessment committee to have the rent reduced (article 31, as amended).
- Apply to the Environmental Health Department of the local district council for an inspection of the property. If the landlord has broken his or her repairing duties, the council will issue a certificate of disrepair (COD), listing the works required. If the landlord does not

do the work, an order can be sought in a magistrates' court and ultimately a landlord may be fined. The council can also carry out the work itself if the landlord has not done it, and recover the cost from the landlord. If the council refuses to issue a COD, a tenant can appeal to a county court within 28 days (articles 47 and 48).

- Ask the Environmental Health Department to inspect the premises to see if the disrepair is prejudicial to health or a nuisance (section 110 of the Public Health (Ireland) Act 1878). The council may issue a notice forcing the landlord to bring the nuisance to an end. If the council does not issue a formal notice it may use an informal "seven day notice" procedure. In urgent cases where there is default by the landlord, a "nine day notice" will be issued if the ordinary procedure would lead to delay (article 65(1) of the Pollution Control and Local Government (NI) Order 1978). Again the council can carry out the work and recover the costs.

- Inform NIHE that the house is unfit for habitation. A new set of unfitness criteria was introduced by the Housing (NI) Order 1992 and they relate to the following: standard of repair, structural stability, freedom from damp, natural lighting, ventilation, water supply, drainage and sanitary facilities, food preparation facilities and disposal of waste water.

Procedures if a house is unfit

If a house, or part of it, is deficient in one or more of the matters just mentioned so as to make it unsuitable for occupation, it is unfit. NIHE will first decide if the house can be made fit at reasonable expense. If it can, NIHE will issue a repairs notice forcing the owner to do the work in a specified time. Reasonable expense is based on whether the work can be carried out at a cost equal to or below 34 times the NAV of the property. The owner has a right of appeal, within 21 days of the issue of the notice, to a county court. The owner may, however, offer an undertaking not to use the property for human habitation until it is made fit.

If the house cannot be made fit at reasonable expense, a "time and place meeting" is called by NIHE. This meeting will involve the Executive, the local council's Environmental Health Department, the owner, and any mortgagee (such as a bank or building society). The owner may offer an undertaking to make the house fit and not to use it for human habitation until it is made fit. If this is the outcome a tenant cannot appeal. If no undertaking is accepted NIHE must issue a *demolition order* unless this would affect adjacent buildings or the building is listed. If this is so, a *closing order* will be issued. The owner, or a tenant with more than one year to run on a lease, can appeal against a demolition order to a county court.

It is an offence to remain in the property beyond the date stipulated in a demolition order. Tenants should therefore try to make the best out of a bad situation by ensuring that they get "emergency A3 status" (which permits them to be rehoused by the Executive) and applying for compensation in respect of home-loss, disturbance and good maintenance.

It is not open to a regulated tenant to withhold rent to do repairs if there is no repairing duty on the landlord contained in the written tenancy agreement. A regulated tenant may, however, if taken to court for rent arrears, argue that any arrears should be set off against a failure by the landlord to do repairs. A tenant has no right simply to stop paying rent in protest at the lack of repair.

Unprotected tenancies

While unprotected tenants, like restricted tenants, cannot use the certificate of disrepair procedure and cannot apply to the rent assessment committee for a rent reduction, it may be possible for them to obtain assistance as follows. They should first of all look at the express terms of any written agreement, if one exists. This will set out, to some extent, the repairing rights and duties. In addition, the law generally implies the following terms into most agreements:

- that the tenant has the right to quiet enjoyment, *i.e.* not to be disturbed (section 41 of the Landlord and Tenant (Amendment) Act 1860);
- that a furnished property is fit for occupation at the beginning of the tenancy;
- that the landlord is responsible for any common parts of which he or she retains control, such as stairways and halls;
- if a property is rented out during the time it is being built, it should be built with proper materials and be fit for habitation on completion.

If the landlord knows or should know of disrepair, which is his or her obligation because of an express or implied term of the tenancy, and he or she has failed to carry out repair works, a tenant can take legal action for damages or a court order. Damages can include compensation for the reduction in value and enjoyment of the tenancy, inconvenience, annoyance, ill health and distress, and damage to the tenant's goods. If the amount of damages is under £500, it can be claimed in the small claims court. If the amount is over £500 the matter will normally be dealt with by a county court. Legal aid is available in this court but not in the small claims court, though the fees in the latter are very low.

An unprotected tenant may also withhold rent in order to cover the cost of doing the repairs, but should follow this specific procedure:

- the landlord should be twice notified of the disrepair by recorded letter, and given a reasonable time to deal with it; copies of the letters should be kept by the tenant;
- if the landlord does not comply, three estimates should be sought and the job given to the lowest tender;
- once the work has been done, an invoice should be forwarded to the landlord for payment;
- rent should be withheld to cover the cost if the landlord refuses to pay; if the cost is high, rent may be accumulated in advance and put in a separate bank, post office or credit union account.

Liability for defective premises

While only a tenant or a joint tenant can sue on the tenancy agreement, this limitation does not apply to claims for negligence, which can extend to friends, family and other guests. However, the basic rule is that a landlord is not liable for injuries arising from defects, whether visible or hidden, apart from any contractual obligations. But on to this principle are grafted the following exceptions:

- if a landlord was also the builder or designer he or she may be liable for a negligent act or omission causing forseeable injury or damage;
- if the injury was caused outside the tenanted property (*e.g.* on a staircase, walkway or lift), a landlord may be liable if the injury was forseeable;
- under the Defective Premises (NI) Order 1975, any person carrying out works to a building, including conversions, should do the work in a professional manner using proper materials, so that it is fit for habitation when completed; this duty is owed to all future purchasers of the building and the 1975 Order also removes the legal immunity

on a seller or landlord of property for any act or omission on the property before the sale or lease takes effect.

If a landlord tries to exclude liability for negligence from the tenancy agreement, this must be tested against the Unfair Contract Terms Act 1977, which requires the exemption clause to be reasonable (section 2(2)). Liability for death or personal injury can never be avoided, by whatever means (section 2(1)).

Private tenants' security of tenure

The following rights are enjoyed by all private tenants:

- a notice to quit, which need not be in writing, though it normally is, must be given at least four weeks in advance unless the tenancy agreement specifies a longer period (article 62 of the Rent (NI) Order 1978);
- the tenant must not be harassed by any person with the intention of forcing the tenant to give up his or her home, or any part of it, or the exercise or any right (*e.g.* a right of way) or remedy (*e.g.* rights to repair); such harassment could amount to the serious offence of intimidation and should be reported to the police;
- the landlord must not unlawfully deprive a tenant of his or her house, or any part of it; this is also a criminal offence unless it was reasonable to believe that the tenant did not live there any more (article 54(1) of the 1978 Order);
- evictions which do not follow the legal process of a notice to quit and proceedings in court are also unlawful (article 56);
- tenants who have a written agreement can sue for damages if they are legally evicted or harassed; if they do not have a promise by the landlord of quiet enjoyment, this will be implied into the agreement unless it is actually excluded (section 42 of the Landlord and Tenant (Amendment) Act 1860).

Protected tenancies

Both types of protected tenant enjoy the same security. They can be evicted only after a valid notice to quit has been served and a decree obtained in a county court. The owner is therefore substantially restricted from regaining possession so long as the tenant uses the dwelling as his or her main residence.

Schedule 3 of the Rent Order specifies the circumstances a landlord must show to the court (unless he or she proves that there is suitable alternative accommodation available for the tenant) in order to recover possession. The court must also believe that it is reasonable to make an order. In six situations the court may, but does not have to, grant possession:

- the duty to pay rent or some other tenancy obligation has been broken by the tenant;
- there has been a nuisance or annoyance to others or use of the premises for immoral or illegal purposes;
- the tenant has allowed the premises to deteriorate or has actually damaged them;
- the tenant or sub-tenant has damaged furniture;
- the tenant has served a valid notice to quit, as a result of which the landlord has entered into a contract to sell and the court believes he or she would be seriously prejudiced if the sale did not go ahead;
- the tenant has sub-let or given the property away by a formal transfer without the landlord's consent.

In eight further situations the court *must* grant possession:

- the tenancy is a service tenancy (let with a job) but the job has ended and the landlord wishes to rent the property to someone coming into his or her employment;
- the property is needed for the landlord's occupation or for a member of his or her close family, it was not bought after 1978, and great hardship would not be caused by granting possession rather than refusing it;
- the tenant has sub-let at a rent more than the maximum recoverable rent for restricted or regulated tenancies;
- the house is the main house on any agricultural land and the court believes the landlord intends to sell the land;
- the house was formerly occupied by the landlord and is required for his or her own use (provided the landlord informed the tenant before 1978 that the property might be recovered);

- the house has been bought for retirement, the owner has retired and died, and a family member who lived with him or her wishes to occupy it;
- the house is for a minister of religion, or a full-time lay missionary, and is the place from where he or she will perform his or her duties;
- a serviceman wishes to recover possession in order to live in the house and he or she was in the services when the house was bought and let out.

If a landlord misrepresents or conceals any facts to get back possession, the tenant may get compensation for resulting damage and loss (article 20 of the Rent (NI) Order 1978).

The only other ways in which protected tenants can lose possession are:

- if there is a closing or demolition order on the premises (article 45 of the Housing (NI) Order 1981); (if the house is only subject to an undertaking to make it fit, it can be reoccupied by a tenant again on the same terms and conditions as before);
- if the landlord applies under article 69 of the Rent (NI) Order 1978 to a county court on the basis that a tenancy was misclassified as protected; possession proceedings can begin immediately if the landlord is successful.

Protected tenants can pass on their tenancies twice, after their death, to successors (known as "statutory tenants by succession"; see also page 319). The first successor will be the tenant's spouse, if he or she is residing in the house. Other family members must be living with the tenant permanently for over six months prior to the death, and not living there as a nurse or caretaker. If there is a dispute as to who should succeed, the Rent Order provides a specific preference order (Schedule 1). There can be two or more joint statutory tenants, but the property will return to the landlord on the second statutory tenant's death.

A statutory tenant occupies property on exactly the same terms as the original tenant and the tenancy can be transferred during the lifetime of the statutory tenant so long as the landlord agrees and is a party to any agreement (article 17). The transfer must be voluntary and no money should change hands, except to pay for the statutory tenant's outgoings, or for any improvement he or she has made. If part of the premises are used for business purposes a sum can be paid for goodwill (article 18).

A court in matrimonial proceedings (separation, divorce, annulment or judicial separation) can transfer a protected or statutory tenancy (article 6). The court can also direct adjustments to cover any liabilities or obligations arising before the transfer.

Unprotected tenancies

These tenants generally have little security. An unprotected tenant can remain in the property for any agreed period, but if he or she breaks the agreement (perhaps by non-payment of rent) the landlord need serve only a four week notice to quit (article 62) and then may take court proceedings. If the NAV of the property is over £500, these proceedings will have to be in the High Court, otherwise they will be in the county court. A landlord does not have to show any of the circumstances listed above for protected tenancies, nor show that suitable alternative accommodation is available. A tenant can ask for a "stay" (*i.e.* a delay) on the operation of the court order for a few weeks or months. Legal aid is not available for court representation.

The rights of home owners

Home owners are responsible for doing all repairs and, subject to building control and planning permission, can carry out any improvements or extension work to the home. An owner can remain in the property for whatever period he or she wishes, provided that any lender's payments are up to date, that the property is not vested by a government body and that it has not become unfit for habitation.

Paying for the house

There are two main payments: rates, payable to the Department of the Environment, and, if the purchase price of the property involved a loan, mortgage repayments to a building society or other lender.

Rates

Rates are a form of tax for local services. They are calculated by taking the Net Annual Value (NAV) of the property and multiplying that by the annual rate struck by the district council. If the occupier disagrees with a valuation, the matter can be taken up with the district valuer, then with the Commissioner for Valuation and ultimately with the Lands Tribunal.

Where the levels of rates are not contested they are generally payable by the occupier. An occupier on benefit, low wages or other forms of very limited income may apply to NIHE for housing benefit to cover up to a maximum of 80% of the rates. In suitable cases benefit can be backdated for up to 52 weeks, but the claimant must show good cause for submitting a late claim (*e.g.* serious illness or family stress). If rates are unpaid, the Department will recover them by court action.

At present it seems unlikely that the new council tax in England and Wales will be introduced in Northern Ireland.

Mortgage repayments

These payments are the most important a home owner has to make. Failure to keep them up may result in the lender taking court proceedings to recover possession of the property. A mortgage is a legal device to allow a person to borrow money to buy property while using that property as security against any future failure by the borrower to repay. A failure to make repayment allows a lender to approach the High Court to ask for that security. The court, however, has a discretion as to what should happen.

If a borrower on a mortgage is in arrears, for whatever reason, he or she should immediately contact the lender to make arrangements for getting through the crisis. Advice can be sought from a Citizens' Advice Bureau, Belfast Housing Aid or other advice agency. The following are some ideas to put to the lender:

- the borrower could ask to move to "interest only" payments; this is immediately possible if the mortgage is of the straight repayment variety and if it has an endowment policy attached this can be cashed in and used to pay the accumulated arrears;
- if eligible, the borrower could claim income support from the DHSS to enable the interest to be paid; income support is payable three

months after the initial application, so the borrower should advise the lender of this gap and the reason for it;

- if the arrears are substantial, the borrower could suggest that the term of the mortgage should be lengthened (*e.g.* from 25 to 30 years), thereby slightly reducing the monthly repayments, or that the arrears should be "capitalised" (*i.e.* added to the sum originally borrowed);

- if the lender's branch office gives no satisfaction regarding proposals to reduce the arrears, the borrower could write to the head office.

If repossession proceedings are not defended, a court order will frequently be made giving the lender the right to immediate possession. Once the period allowed for appeal has passed (a few weeks), without the borrower leaving the premises, the lender can apply, after giving notice of intention to do so, to have the court order enforced by the Enforcement of Judgments Office. The lender might even at this stage respond to reasonable and realistic proposals for paying off the arrears, though the lender's legal costs will be added to the arrears then owing.

An owner who loses his or her home in this manner may be classified by NIHE as homeless (see pages 322-324), though may be considered "intentionally" so. A family member who has not participated or acquiesced in the failure to keep up payments (except a dependent child) may also apply as homeless and the intentionally homeless person can then be housed with him or her as a member of the family.

Repairing or improving the home

This is the owner's responsibility unless damage has occurred because of the negligence of another person, such as a neighbour or builder. Otherwise an owner will have to finance any work out of savings, by borrowing, by grants from NIHE or perhaps by grants or loans from the DHSS social fund (see chapter 19).

A bank or building society may lend money if the value of the property, less any existing loan (the "equity"), justifies it. It is always worth checking first whether the work would be covered by a grant. In certain cases these may pay for up to 90% of the work. Eligibility depends on the type of work and the value of the property.

The social fund administered by the DHSS can make grants of up to £400 for essential work to income support claimants who are also responsible for repairing their home. There is no strict entitlement to this, as the local office's funds may have run out and the Department has a wide discretion. It may instead offer a loan. Advice on the rate of repayments should then be taken. If the property is for some reason defective the following points should be remembered.

- If the property had grant-aided work carried out to it and the defect relates to this work, the NIHE's approval of the work when paying out the grant is no guarantee that the work was carried out properly. The Executive may in certain circumstances be guilty of maladministration sufficient to found a complaint to the Ombudsman, but it is not legally liable to present or future owners.

- A surveyor instructed by a lender cannot generally escape liability for any negligent failure to recognise what should have been apparent if he or she had used reasonable care and skill.

- A property built after 1975 should be built in a professional manner with proper materials and be fit for habitation upon completion. A builder will be liable to anyone subsequently buying the property: article 3 of the Defective Premises (NI) Order 1975. There is a time limit on liability, namely six years after the owner (or tenant) knew or should have known of the defect.

- If a property has been bought from NIHE or a registered housing association and the Department of the Environment decides that it is defective because of its design or construction, the owner may apply to NIHE to reinstate the dwelling or in serious cases to buy it back.

Owners who have great difficulty in selling their homes by reason only of the "troubles" may benefit from the "SPED" (Special Purchase of Evacuated Dwellings) Scheme. This allows public purchase of a house which cannot be sold because of its location and closeness to civil disturbances or in cases of verifiable intimidation. If a house falls into this category the owner should enquire from a Citizens' Advice Bureau, a solicitor or Belfast Housing Aid as to whether he or she is eligible for help.

Planning rights

Planning in Northern Ireland is largely governed by the Planning (NI) Order 1991, which substantially amended the previous planning legislation including the 1972 Order. Planning permission is required for any development of land and "development" is defined very widely in the legislation. Planning permission is also required for change of use, although only for "material" changes. Application for permission is made to the Department of the Environment for Northern Ireland (DOE) and must be in the prescribed form.

Vesting and compulsory purchase

The law governing vesting procedures is contained in the Planning (NI) Order 1991 and the Housing (NI) Order 1983, as amended.

Applications for vesting are usually made by NIHE in furtherance of its development powers, after an inspection, to the DOE, which also has the power to vest on its own behalf (article 87 of the 1991 Order). Such applications are made under the Local Government (Compulsory Acquisition of Land) Regulations (NI) 1975, as amended by the 1991 Order. Where NIHE proposes to compulsorily purchase it must apply for a vesting order. The DOE considers the application and any objections made to it and may be required to hold a public inquiry, *e.g.* when the vesting application is in pursuance of a development scheme or is an acquisition for planning purposes under the Planning Orders.

Conduct of public inquiries

The chairperson of a public inquiry will be appointed by the Planning Appeals Commission if the vesting application is made under the Planning Orders and by the DOE if the application is made under the Housing (NI) Order 1983. Any person with an interest in the land and any other person allowed by the chairperson can appear in person or be heard through a representative. Case law has established that the rules of natural justice must be adhered to in the proceedings, *i.e.* no person may be a judge in his or her own case, there is a right to a fair hearing and those in charge of the inquiry must act fairly. After the conclusion of the inquiry the DOE may make a vesting order, notice of which must be published and served. Anyone who wishes to challenge the vesting order has one month from its publication in which to apply to the High Court to have the order suspended or overturned. A vesting order may be challenged only on certain grounds and an application to challenge such an order may be made only by someone with sufficient "standing", *i.e.* he or she must show that they are sufficiently affected by the order.

Where no inquiry has been held the DOE must serve notice of its decision on the applicant and consider his or her representations. There is no appeal mechanism but it is possible to apply to the High Court to have the decision judicially reviewed (see chapter 2).

Compensation

Anyone who has an interest in the land vested has the right to be compensated for the loss of that interest, although the level of compensation will depend upon the kind of interest involved, *e.g.* a tenant will be entitled to less compensation than an owner. The rules relating to such compensation are contained in the Land Compensation (NI) Order 1982 and the Planning (NI) Order 1991. Furthermore, NIHE is obliged to rehouse persons displaced by a vesting order, as provided for by articles 40-41 of the Land Acquisition and Compensation (NI) Order 1973, as amended.

Planning Appeals

Appeals of routine planning decisions, *e.g.* refusals to grant planning permission, are heard by the Planning Appeals Commission. They are usually heard by one member of the Commission who makes a report to the full Commission and a decision is then taken. Details are available from:

- The Planning Appeals Commission
  107 Great Victoria Street
  Belfast BT2 7AG
  tel: (0232) 244710

Chapter 19

Social Security Rights

Eileen Evason

This chapter provides a very general guide to the rights of social security claimants in Northern Ireland. As a preliminary to the more descriptive material which follows, three important observations should be made.

- The word "rights" with regard to social security claimants must be used with caution. The fact of the matter is that the claimants have no more rights than those which the government is willing to permit at any point in time. In recent years, benefits to which people might have thought they had a right *e.g.* by virtue of past contributions, have been abolished, cut or modified. Hence contributions are in fact only a tax and any notion of something resembling a contractual relationship between the state and the individual is erroneous. It must also be noted that entitlement is often governed by the judgment of civil servants and professionals.

- Social security systems have a diversity of objectives which are often in conflict with each other. On the one hand there is a general objective of preventing financial hardship. On the other there are parallel objectives such as preserving the nuclear family and incentives to work. The result is a system which discriminates against the unemployed and most categories of single parents, with poverty being the result. In addition, it can be argued that the present Conservative government is deliberately restructuring the social security system so that it more clearly reflects the government's values and philosophy. The system is therefore not in any sense a neutral, value-free system of support for those in need.

- The law on social security matters is extremely complex. For reliable detailed advice you should go to a Citizens' Advice Bureau, a local advice centre or a Social Security Agency office.

The unemployed

Unemployment has long been a pressing problem in Northern Ireland. The rising tide of unemployment has not, however, resulted in more generous treatment of the unemployed by the benefits system. If anything the position has worsened.

The basic provision is unemployment benefit, for which there is no test of means and which is part of the national insurance scheme. To get this benefit it is not sufficient simply to be without work: a number of conditions govern receipt.

- Claimants must have paid Class 1 (*i.e.* employee) national insurance contributions, to the value of 25 times the lowest possible contributions, in either of the last two complete tax years preceding the benefit year. The benefit year is virtually the same as the calendar year and the tax year, of course, runs from April to April. Someone claiming benefit in September 1992 will therefore have to have paid the contributions in either the 1989/90 or 1990/91 tax years.

- Claimants must have paid or been credited with 50 times the lowest possible amount in the last two complete tax years.

Claimants who only partially fulfil these conditions have no entitlement at all. Those who do fulfil them can be disqualified from benefit for up to 26 weeks if they have left their previous employment voluntarily without good cause or were dismissed for misconduct. Such disqualifications can be appealed, but claimants will need sound advice so that they are aware of the room for debate concerning such matters as "good cause" for leaving a job.

Beyond this, receipt of benefit is also dependent on the claimant being judged available for work. This hinges on giving the "correct" answers on the relevant forms and at interviews. For instance, married women will need to be able to state the arrangements which could be made immediately for child care if they had the chance of employment. In addition, in general claimants can place restrictions on what employment they are prepared to accept only if they have a usual occupation and this exemption can last for only up to 13 weeks. Claimants must also be actively seeking employment and can be disqualified from benefit if it appears that they have failed to apply for or accept employment or training or failed to act on recommendations or attend interviews which are intended to assist in securing employment.

If claimants get through all of this, they are entitled at current rates to £44.65 per week plus £27.55 for an adult dependent. This lasts for a year only. The result is that many of the unemployed find it necessary to turn to the means-tested system of income support (see page 353), either immediately or when their entitlement to standard benefit is exhausted. Persons deemed voluntarily unemployed will, however, receive income support at a reduced rate, while those deemed not available for work or not actively seeking work are entitled to nothing.

In connection with means-tested support for the unemployed, two other points are worth noting.

• The old supplementary benefit scheme discriminated against the unemployed generally. Whereas pensioners (and other groups of claimants on benefit for more than one year) received the higher long-term rate of benefit, the unemployed, regardless of the length of time they had been on benefit, were kept on the lower ordinary rate. In 1988, income support replaced supplementary benefit, but within the new scheme the less eligible status of the unemployed has been preserved in that there are special additions, known as premia, topping up the basic rates for categories of claimants such as the elderly and disabled, but none for the unemployed.

• In recent years the benefit system has developed a distinction between young single persons and older claimants. Thus, with some exceptions, those under 18 are now excluded from income support altogether on the assumption that they should be in training schemes. A special lower rate of income support is paid to 18-25 year olds.

The sick and disabled

The needs of the sick and disabled can be said to fall under four main headings:

- replacement of earnings;
- compensation;
- assistance with additional costs;
- help for the carers.

The benefits system deals with all four areas but provision is scattered and often very limited. What is clearly required is an integrated comprehensive benefit for disabled persons and full recognition of the real costs incurred by carers.

Replacement of earnings

Here the benefit system distinguishes between the short-term and long-term sick and between those with and without adequate contribution records. This part of the system also reflects the current preference for off-loading responsibility from the state to another party, in this case the employer.

Statutory sick pay (SSP)

SSP is administered by employers, who deduct 80% of payments made from their total liability for national insurance contributions. Employees have a right to SSP unless, *e.g.*, they have a contract for less than three months or are over pensionable age. The rate of benefit depends on gross earnings, but at £52.50 per week (with no additions for dependents) the current maximum is hardly generous and it cannot be paid for more than 28 weeks. Disputes can be referred to Social Security Agency adjudication officers and claimants have a right to appeal to a social security appeals tribunal.

There remain a number of issues of concern.

- The rate of errors made by employers appears to be between 15% and 30%.
- Employees may be reluctant to question an employer's decision on entitlement.
- Where payments are delayed or inadequate SSP claimants may be less likely to receive their full entitlement because, unlike claimants to sickness benefit (see below), they are outside the welfare system and not always able to obtain relevant information.

Sickness Benefit

This is payable to persons who are not entitled to SSP, are incapable of work and satisfy the relevant contribution conditions. The current rate is £42.70 plus £26.40 for an adult dependent.

Invalidity pension

For long-term sickness and disability (*i.e.* more than 28 weeks), the principal non-means-tested benefits are invalidity pension and severe disablement allowance. Receipt of invalidity pension depends primarily upon prior entitlement to sickness benefit, SSP or maternity allowance, plus continued incapacity. The current rate is £56.10 per week, plus £33.70 for an adult dependent and £10.95 for each dependent child, which is paid on top of child benefit. In addition, invalidity allowance will be paid on top of invalidity pension with the amount depending on age at the onset of incapacity to work but reduced by any entitlement the claimant has under SERPS (see page 353).

From the claimant's point of view invalidity pension is in many respects one of the best buys in the social security system:

- the benefit is significantly higher than unemployment benefit;
- the earnings rule for spouses (£44.65 per week) is more generous than for unemployment or sickness benefit;
- whereas unemployment benefit is taxable, invalidity benefit is not.

Not surprisingly, therefore, the long-term sick are under close scrutiny - there are considerable savings to be made by deeming such claimants to be fit for work and hence transferable to unemployment benefit and/or income support. Thus, a claimant will normally, and perhaps repeatedly, be required to attend for examination by the medical services of the DHSS. If it is decided that the claimant is fit for work but the claimant's own doctor does not support this decision the DHSS may require a second examination by another doctor and if this is also un-favourable benefit will be stopped.

It is essential that claimants appeal if they have the support of their own doctor. Two points are worth remembering.

- If possible, a consultant's report should be obtained for the hearing.
- "Fit for work" does not necessarily mean fit for one's normal occupa-tion or indeed that work is available. It means that there is something

the claimant could do - even with the disability he or she has - regardless of whether opportunities for such work exist.

Severe disablement allowance

Persons who do not qualify for the above benefits may be entitled to severe disablement allowance (SDA), which has replaced non-contributory invalidity pension. Receipt is conditional upon three main elements:

- the claimant must have been incapable of work for 28 weeks;
- the claimant must have been incapable of work since his or her twentieth birthday or be 80% disabled;
- there are age and residence conditions.

The value of this benefit is, in fact, debatable. The current rate (£33.70 plus additions for dependents) is low and the "80% plus" requirement is very severe. The assessment scheme for this latter point is the same as for industrial injuries, though receipt of attendance or mobility allowance means that claimants will qualify automatically. SDA claimants are however now entitled to an age related addition similar to that payable with invalidity benefit.

Compensation

The issue of compensation arises chiefly in relation to people who have been disabled as a result of industrial accidents or disease. There are no contribution conditions for these benefits but any accident which has occurred must have arisen out of, and in the course of, employment. In the case of disease the claimant can claim only if his or her ailment is on a list of prescribed diseases and if he or she has worked in a specified employment which has caused the disease. The case-law on this is extensive and, perhaps for this more than any other part of the benefits system, claimants wishing to appeal should contact a reputable advice centre if their trade union cannot (as it normally can) assist.

For industrially injured claimants unable to work, SSP and invalidity benefits are payable in the normal way. Additional benefits available are payable 15 weeks after the accident or onset of the disease regardless of whether the claimant is at work or not. The basic provision, disablement benefit, depends on the degree of disablement. In the majority of cases nothing will be paid if the condition is assessed at less than 14%. Otherwise weekly disablement benefit varies from £18.32 to £91.60. In addition, claimants may receive constant attendance allowance if their disablement is assessed at 100%, if they require constant attendance and if they claim within three months. Persons getting this allowance may also qualify for exceptionally severe disablement allowance.

Additional costs

Apart from replacement of earnings and compensation there is the issue of the additional costs of disability. For this purpose two benefits are provided:
* attendance allowance;
* disability living allowance.

A full assessment of potential entitlement to these benefits should always be made, especially as they are disregarded under the income support scheme (*i.e.* claimants do not have their benefit reduced by the amounts received) so that, if secured, they constitute a real addition to resources, particularly for the elderly and poorest of the disabled. In addition, receipt of attendance allowance or the higher/middle rate of the care component of disability living allowance give rights to those who care for the claimant - notably in connection with the invalid care allowance and home responsibilities protection under SERPS (see page 353).

Attendance allowance - over 65's only

Attendance allowance is paid to those who are over 65 and so severely disabled (physically or mentally) that during the day they need frequent attention in connection with bodily functions or continued supervision in order to avoid danger to themselves or others, and/or during the night they require prolonged or repeated attention in connection with bodily functions or need someone else to be awake for prolonged periods. At current weekly rates, £44.90 is paid if care is needed day and night and £30.00 if the need is for the day or night.

There are also residence conditions to be satisfied and benefit cannot be paid until the need has lasted for six months (except in the case of the terminally ill). Persons in hospital or other publicly provided accommodation lose their entitlement after four weeks.

This benefit is the subject of some confusion and a number of difficulties:

- it is normally paid to the person who needs care, not to the carer, and receipt hinges on need, not the existence of specified persons caring;
- there are no contribution conditions and the means of the person are irrelevant;
- the six months provision can cause particular hardship where the need is evident.

Disability living allowance (DLA)

DLA is for persons under 65 and replaced attendance allowance and mobility allowance in 1992. Because it is slightly more generous than attendance allowance, which has been retained for the over 65's, provisions to assist the disabled now appear to be age discriminatory. Those previously on attendance or mobility allowance have been transferred to DLA.

DLA consists of two components (care and mobility) and claimants may qualify for either or both. The care component is payable at three rates. The highest rate (£44.90) is for persons requiring care or supervision both day and night. The middle rate (£30.00) is payable to those needing care or supervision day or night. The new, lower rate (£11.95) is payable to persons requiring care for a significant part of the day or unable to cook a main meal. Persons under 16 cannot qualify under the cooking condition.

The mobility component is payable at two rates to persons over age 5. The higher rate (£31.40) is for persons unable or virtually unable to walk, persons who are both deaf and blind, the severely mentally impaired and double amputees. The lower rate (£11.95) is for those able to walk but requiring guidance or supervision.

Invalid care allowance

Although it has been estimated that those people, normally women, who provide the care for the sick and disabled in our society save the state roughly £20 billion per year, invalid care allowance represents the only significant recognition of the costs they incur and the service they provide.

Benefit currently amounts to £33.70 a week plus additions for dependents. The main conditions governing receipt are as follows:

- claimants must be of working age and caring for someone in receipt of attendance allowance or the middle/higher rate of the DLA care component;
- the task must take up 35 hours a week;
- the claimant must not be gainfully employed (i.e. earning over £50 a week) or in full-time education.

Prior to 1986, married women were excluded from receipt of this benefit, a restriction found to be contrary to the European Community's Equal Treatment Directive. Whilst the removal of this discriminatory provision has helped some persons, the gains have not been as much as expected because of provisions governing the interaction between this and other benefits. Thus, invalid care allowance cannot be paid on top of another major benefit, such as widowed mother's allowance. Moreover, if the claimant is in receipt of means-tested income support, the latter will be reduced accordingly though the carers premium will be payable. In addition, invalid care allowance cannot be paid if the carer is a dependent of a person in receipt of any benefit which includes the appropriate addition for dependents. Thus, a woman caring for a relative whilst her own husband is on invalidity benefit and claiming for her as a dependent will not be entitled to invalid care allowance. As invalidity benefit is not taxable, any alteration in this arrangement would need to be considered carefully.

Single parents

No fewer than 19% of Northern Ireland families are now headed by single parents, the overwhelming majority of these being women. Two minor provisions for this group are one parent benefit and child special allowance. One parent benefit is a small addition, currently £6.05, to child benefit for the eldest child, but as it cannot be paid where certain other benefits (notably insurance benefits for widows) are being paid and, as it is counted as a resource for income support purposes, many single parents are no better off as a result of receiving it. A similar difficulty applies with regard to child special allowance, which can be paid to divorced or separated women on the death of a husband who has been maintaining the child if relevant contribution conditions are satisfied.

Beyond this, with regard to single parents generally, the benefit system distinguishes between men and women and deals differently with female single parents depending on the cause of single parenthood - the main division being between widows and the rest. Thus:

- there is no entitlement to any benefit in the insurance structure for men who are widowed; if they are unable to work their only option is means-tested support;

- with regard to female single parents, provision is made for widows under the insurance system but for all other female single parents the main state benefit is once again means-tested income support.

Provision for widows

Provision for widows now consists of three elements.

- Widow's payment of £1,000 is generally payable to women under 60 whose husbands have paid the requisite contributions, though this condition does not apply to those widowed through industrial accident or injury.

- Widows with dependent children will, if the husband's contribution record is satisfactory, receive the weekly widowed mother's allowance, currently £56.10 per week, plus £10.95 for each child in addition to child benefit. This is payable immediately and for as long as there are dependent children.

- Widow's pension is payable only to women over 45 and again there are contribution conditions. It can be paid immediately to a widow who has no dependent children and women receiving the widowed mother's allowance can, when they cease to be entitled to this, transfer to widow's pension. Less will be paid if the husband's contributions record is inadequate and women between the ages of 45 and 55 when they become entitled are awarded a proportion of the full basic rate.

Widows can still be seen as an advantaged sub-group within the general category of single parents and it can be noted that for those able to find employment a further bonus is that earnings do not affect entitlement, though cohabitation or remarriage does. By virtue of the lowness of these benefits and, of course, of women's wages, widows may still need to claim means-tested support.

Single parents other than widows

For single parents other than widows, the only options are means-tested benefits. Single parents not in employment (*i.e.*, working less than 16 hours per week) can claim income support if their resources are below the prescribed levels.

Single parents who are able to secure employment may also have their income increased through means-tested aid. The two main provisions are:

- family credit (which acts as a passport to various other benefits), and
- housing benefit.

These benefits are available generally to those on low pay and are discussed in more detail below. It can be noted here, however, that they are of particular importance to female single parents given the extent of low wages amongst women employees.

Major changes occurred in April 1993 for single parents when the Child Support Agency came into operation. The Child Support (NI) Order 1991 provided for the creation of the Agency which will take over responsibility for the assessment, collection and enforcement of maintenance. Claimants of income support and family credit will be required to use the Agency. The new arrangements have aroused concern for a number of reasons.

- First, a set formula will be applied in assessing maintenance due and this is such that hardship may be caused to husbands and second families.
- Second, any hardship experienced will not benefit single parents. Maintenance will be deducted pound for pound from the benefit of those on income support though there will be a £15 disregard for those on family credit. In general therefore the measure is about defraying costs rather than aiding single parents.
- Third, women who fail to use or cooperate with the Agency and do not, for example, provide details of a husband's whereabouts will incur financial penalties, *i.e.*, reduced benefit payments for a period.

- Fourth, rigorous pursuit of former spouses and higher payments may re-open matters of dispute such as access and put women at risk of harassment or abuse. Women in difficulty or doubt should contact:

- Gingerbread (NI),
  169 University Street,
  Belfast BT7 1HP
  (tel: 0232 234568)

Retired people

A central aim of the 1975 social security legislation was that everyone would be entitled to a basic pension plus an earnings-related pension either from their employer or from the state. Legislation in 1986, however, sought to reduce the commitment of the state and leave more to the private market by encouraging membership of company pension schemes and greater reliance on personal pensions. The logic of this approach is clearly open to question in the light of the Maxwell scandal, the growing evidence of the inadequacies of safeguards for those in company pension schemes and the difficulties produced where advice on personal pensions owes more to considerations of profit and commissions than to the needs of those advised.

The current position with regard to non-means-tested support is as follows.

- Provided contribution conditions are fulfilled, a category A pension is payable (current rate £56.10 per week).

- Category B pensions (£33.70) are paid to married women relying for their entitlement on their husband's contributions.

- Where the husband is dead, category B pensioners are paid at the category A rate.

- Non-contributory category pensions (£33.70) are payable to those who were, or whose husbands were, over retirement age in 1948.

- Category D pensions, (£33.70) are non-contributory and are paid to pensioners who are over 80 years of age and have no other pension or a pension below the category D level.

For a full pension, contributions for 90% of working life are required. Entitlement is no longer conditional upon retirement and earnings do not affect the benefit payable. Three other points should be noted.

- Persons on invalidity benefit may wish to defer transferring, as pensions are taxable whereas invalidity benefit is not. In such cases, however, invalidity benefit will be adjusted in line with retirement pension entitlement.

- With regard to divorced women, as soon as the decree absolute is obtained full contributions should be paid. Many women are unaware of this; one consequence of non-payment will be reduced pension rights. Another, of course, is that the DHSS can at a later date demand payment of the sum that should have been paid earlier.

The basic pensions are low but may be increased in various ways. Claimants may be entitled to graduated retirement benefit under the 1961-75 state scheme. Normally, however, the amounts involved are trifling. Secondly, those retiring after April 1979 may have entitlement under the state earnings related pensions scheme (SERPS) introduced in 1975 and sharply modified in 1986. The basic pension may also be increased if people defer making a claim.

All of these bits and pieces add up to less than might be expected, hence many pensioners have to rely on income support and housing benefit. Entitlement should always be checked in relation to these.

Income support

Because benefits available as of right are inadequate in many respects, income support, formerly called supplementary benefit, is of great importance. Income support is to assist those not in full-time (*i.e.* 16 hours plus) employment (and not married to someone in full-time employment) with capital of under £8,000. The benefit consists of the difference between the assessed resources of the claimant and the prescribed applicable amounts. The applicable amounts consist of three elements.

- A basic personal allowance which varies according to age and marital status.

- For certain categories of claimants set additions are made known as "premia".

- Help with some types of housing costs (notably mortgage interest payments). For help with rent and rates, income support claimants must make a separate claim for housing benefit.

The scheme has given rise to a number of difficulties. To begin with, the basic allowance for single people under 25 is very low (currently £34.80 a week) and certainly insufficient for such claimants to live independently in the community. In addition, there is now no provision for increasing the weekly benefit of claimants with special needs (*e.g.* the cost of a special diet or extra heating). The premia which have been substituted for these provisions are not always sufficient to cover such special needs. Moreover, many claimants who might previously have been able to claim help with such needs do not always happen to fall into a category attracting a premium. Moreover "single payments" (lump sums for exceptional items of expenditure) have been replaced by the social fund.

The social fund

The social fund came fully into operation in April 1988 and replaced not just single payments but also maternity and death grants. It provides two sets of assistance.

- Under the non-discretionary section of the scheme, persons on income support or family credit can claim a maternity expenses payment of £100 and the same groups, plus persons on housing benefit, may be able to claim help with funeral expenses. Small amounts known as severe weather payments are also payable.
- Under the discretionary part of the scheme, persons on income support can be awarded *budgeting loans, crisis loans* and *community care grants.*

Budgeting loans can be given for occasional, exceptional items of expenditure. Crisis loans may be obtained in cases of emergency or disaster. However all loans will be recovered by direct deductions, at source, from claimants' benefits. Moreover, claimants may be refused a loan if they are deemed to be too poor and indebted to be able to repay the loan. Also, because the system is cash limited, a social fund officer may refuse to assist because to do so would mean exceeding the budget. For such claimants there is now no statutory safety net and an application to a charitable organisation may be the only option open to them.

Community care grants are payable to persons moving out of institutionalised care and to vulnerable groups such as the elderly, the disabled and families under stress. The guidance and directions issued by the DHSS to social fund officers are very restrictive. Claimants have no right of appeal to independent social security appeal tribunals, but they can ask for the decision to be reviewed.

Family credit

Family credit is payable to employees and the self-employed in full-time work (16 hours or more per week) with dependent children, if their capital does not exceed £8,000 and their income falls below the prescribed level. While those with capital of more than £8,000 are totally excluded, claimants with between £3,000 and £8,000 are deemed to have a weekly income of £1 per week for each block of £250. Capital under £3,000 is completely ignored.

Determining whether or not income falls below the prescribed level is complicated.

- The first step is to calculate total income, *i.e.*, net wages plus benefits in payment - excluding child benefit, attendance allowance, disability living allowance and housing benefit.
- The next stage is to calculate maximum family credit (MFC), *i.e.* the most the claimant could receive. The MFC varies according to family size and the ages of children.
- Finally, income is compared with what is known as the threshold figure - £69.00 for all families. If income is below the threshold, benefit equals the full MFC. If income is above the threshold, benefit equals MFC less 70% of the difference between income and the threshold.

Two additional points can be made. Firstly, family credit has been presented as a more generous benefit than family income supplement, which it replaced in 1988. On paper this is indeed the case, but in practice, as family credit counts as income for housing benefit purposes, families may find that once account is taken of the reduction or loss of housing benefit the improvement is rather less than expected. Secondly, family credit does not give entitlement, as family income supplement did, to free school meals. Once again, therefore, the real gains are less than claimants may realise.

Housing benefit

Housing benefit is paid to all whose income is sufficiently low. For income support claimants benefit equals maximum housing benefit minus non-dependent contributions. For others the assessment of entitlement is again a tortuous process.

- The first stage is to calculate the maximum housing benefit (MHB), *i.e.*, the most that could be payable. MHB consists of rent and rates, less any deduction for non-dependents. In plainer English, this means that, if claimants have grown-up sons and daughters in the household, those persons are assumed to be contributing specified amounts towards housing costs regardless of whether or not they can or wish to do so.

- The second stage is to calculate the claimant's "applicable amounts" *i.e.*, his or her needs according, with some minor variations, to the income support scale rates. For example, a married couple would have an applicable amount of £69.00. If income is below the applicable amount, benefit equals the MHB. If income is above the applicable amount, a percentage of the difference between income and the applicable amount is deducted from the MHB and benefit equals whatever remains.

Two points can be made on this stage of the process. Firstly, the tapers, *i.e.*, the rate at which benefit is cut if income is above the applicable amount, are much harsher than prior to 1988. Persons on very low incomes can find that they are considered too affluent to receive housing benefit. Secondly, the use of the applicable amounts under the income support scheme means that persons discriminated against under this are similarly penalised as regards housing benefit. To take an obvious example, the applicable amount for single unemployed people under 25 in the income support scheme is £34.80. The notion that someone can live on this for a week is idiotic and to take this figure as the basis for the assessment of need for help with housing costs makes no sense at all.

Beyond this, taking housing benefit as a whole, there are a number of evident problems.

- Dissatisfied claimants can ask the housing authority to review its decision and then request a hearing by a housing benefit review board. There is no appeal beyond this and the only other option is judicial review (see chapter 2). Few claimants make use of these appeals provisions - probably as most find housing benefit incomprehensible.
- Housing benefit must be seen as part of the broader package that exists to assist people with housing costs. Within the package there are marked inequities. Most obviously, persons on comfortable wages may be receiving subsidies in the form of mortgage tax relief whilst persons on very much lower incomes in rented accommodation may be deemed too well off to require support from housing benefit. In addition, those in receipt of mortgage tax relief will not have the circumstances of non-dependent household members taken into account and their assistance reduced accordingly.

Conclusion

The social security system is constantly changing and this chapter has done no more than provide the broadest of outlines of the current position. More detailed information is available most readily from:

- The Child Poverty Action Group,
  4th floor,
  1-5 Bath Street,
  London EC1V 9PY
  (tel: 071-405-5942).

Further Reading

International protection of human rights

A.H. Robertson, *Human Rights in the World* (3rd ed, 1989, revised by J.G.Merrills); Manchester University Press;
Paul Sieghart, *The Lawful Rights of Mankind* (1986); Oxford University Press;
Scott Davison, *Human Rights* (1993); Open University Press, Buckingham.

Civil liberties and human rights in the United Kingdom

Malcolm Hurwitt and Peter Thornton, *Civil Liberty: The Liberty/NCCL Guide* (4th ed, 1989); Penguin Books, London;
K.D.Ewing and C.A. Gearty, *Freedom Under Thatcher: Civil Liberties in Modern Britain* (1990); Clarendon Press, Oxford;
Peter Thornton, *Decade of Decline: Civil Liberties in the Thatcher Years* (1989); Liberty/NCCL, London;
Geoffrey Robertson, *Freedom, the Individual and the Law* (6th ed, 1989); Penguin Books, London;
Paul Sieghart (ed), *Human Rights in the United Kingdom* (1988); Pinter Publishers Ltd, London;
S.L. Bailey, D.J. Harris and B.L. Jones, *Civil Liberties: Cases and Materials*, (3rd ed, 1991) Butterworths, London;
K.D. Ewing and W. Finnie, *Civil Liberties in Scotland: Cases and Materials* (1982); W. Green & Son Ltd, Edinburgh;
Claire Palley, *The United Kingdom and Human Rights* (1991); Stevens & Sons, London.

Civil liberties and human rights in Northern Ireland

Anthony Jennings (ed), *Justice Under Fire: The Abuse of Civil Liberties in Northern Ireland* (1988); Pluto Press, London;
Sydney D. Bailey (ed), *Human Rights and Responsibilities in Britain and Ireland: A Christian Perspective* (2nd ed, 1990); Macmillan Press, Basingstoke;

Colin Camphell (ed), *Do We Need a Bill of Rights?* (1980); Temple Smith Ltd, London;
Helsinki Watch, *Human Rights in Northern Ireland* (1991); Human Rights Watch, New York.

Law in Northern Ireland

Brice Dickson, *The Legal System of Northern Ireland* (2nd ed, 1989); SLS Legal Publications, Belfast;
Brice Dickson and Deborah McBride (eds), *The Digest of Northern Ireland Law* (looseleaf, 1988 and 1990); SLS Legal Publications, Belfast;
Brigid Hadfield, *The Constitution of Northern Ireland* (1989); SLS Legal Publications, Belfast;
Brigid Hadfield (ed), *Northern Ireland: Politics and the Constitution* (1992); Open University Press, Buckingham;
Angela Hegarty (ed), *The Rights Guide* (1990); NIACRO, Belfast.

Specific topics

Vaughan Bevan and Ken Lidstone, *The Investigation of Crime: A Guide to Police Powers* (1991); Butterworths, London;
David Bonner, *Emergency Powers in Peacetime* (1985); Sweet and Maxwell Ltd, London;
Clive Walker, *The Prevention of Terrorism in British Law* (1986); Manchester University Press;
Sean Doran, *Criminal Procedure in Northern Ireland* (1988); ch.5 of *The Digest of Northern Ireland Law*; SLS Legal Publications, Belfast;
James Wood and Adam Crawford, *The Right of Silence: The Case for Retention* (1989); Civil Liberties Trust, London;
Andrew J. Goldsmith (ed), *Complaints Against the Police: The Trend to External Review* (1991); Clarendon Press, Oxford;

Nigel Rodley, *The Treatment of Prisoners under International Law* (1987); Clarendon Press, Oxford;
A. Reynaud, *Human Rights in Prisons* (1986); Council of Europe, Strasbourg;
Peter Thornton, *Public Order Law* (1987); Financial Training Publications Ltd, London;
Eric Barendt, *Freedom of Speech* (1987); Clarendon Press, Oxford;

Justice, *Freedom of Expression and the Law* (1990); Justice, London;
Article 19, *No Comment: Censorship, Secrecy and the Irish Troubles* (1989); Article 19, London;
Patrick Birkinshaw, *Freedom of Information* (1988); Weidenfeld and Nicolson, London;
David J. Smith and Gerald Chambers, *Inequality in Northern Ireland* (1991); Clarendon Press, Oxford;

Christopher McCrudden (ed), *Fair Employment Handbook* (1990); Industrial Relations Services, London;
Vincent McCormack and Joe O'Hara, *Enduring Inequality: Religious Discrimination in Employment in Northern Ireland* (1990); Liberty/NCCL, London;
Ian Linn, *Application Refused: Employment Vetting by the State* (1990); Civil Liberties Trust, London;
John Kremer and Pamela Montgomery (eds), *Women's Working Lives* (1993); EOC for NI and HMSO, Belfast;
Equal Opportunities Commission for Northern Ireland, *Casebook of Decisions on Sex Discrimination and Equal Pay* (looseleaf, 1990); EOC, Belfast;

Deborah McBride, *Family Law in Northern Ireland* (1991): ch.2 of *The Digest of Northern Ireland Law*; SLS Legal Publications, Belfast;
Ruth Lavery, *Children and the Law in Northern Ireland* (1988): ch.3 of *The Digest of Northern Ireland Law*; SLS Legal Publications, Belfast;
Children's Legal Centre, *Education Rights Handbook* (1987); Children's Legal Centre, London;
Ian Bynoe, Mike Oliver and Colin Barnes, *Equal Rights for Disabled People: The Case for a New Law* (1992); Institute for Public Policy Research, London;
Colin Barnes, *Disabled People in Britain and Discrimination: A Case for Anti-Discrimination Legislation* (1991); Hurst & Co, London;
Labour Relations Agency, *Encyclopaedia of Northern Ireland Labour Law and Practice* (3 vols, loosefleaf, 1983-90); LRA, Belfast;
Richard Steele, *Employment Law in Northern Ireland*: ch.11 of *The Digest of Northern Ireland Law*; SLS Legal Publications, Belfast;
Tom Hadden and David Trimble, *Northern Ireland Housing Law* (1986); SLS Legal Publications, Belfast;
Eileen Evason, *Social Security Benefits in Northern Ireland* (1992); SLS

Legal Publications, Belfast;
Rowland, *Child Poverty Action Group's Rights Guide to Non-Means-Tested Social Security Benefits* (15th ed, 1993); CPAG, London.

Table of Legislation

Table of Cases

(Page references to this book are at the end of each entry, in italics)

Index

Recent CAJ publications include:

Inquests and Disputed Killings in Northern Ireland. 1992 (£3.50)

The Casement Trials: A case study on the right to a fair trial in Northern Ireland. 1992 (£3.00)

Racism in Northern Ireland: The need for legislation to combat racial discrimination in Northern Ireland. 1992 (£3.00)

A Bill of Rights for Northern Ireland. 1993 (£2.00)

Killings by the Security Forces: An information pack for families. 1993